Kitto II

Mischief Island

Richard Gill

Bolotti

Kitto Katsu

This novel is entirely a work of fiction. The names, characters
and incidents portrayed in it are the work of the author's
imagination. Any resemblance to actual persons, living or
dead, events or localities is entirely coincidental.
Trademarked products are acknowledged and used fictitiously.
Warning: Graphic adult content.

Bolotti Press
An imprint of Bolotti Limited
This paperback edition 2024

1 3 5 7 9 8 6 4 2
First published in Great Britain by
Bolotti Press, an imprint of Bolotti Limited 2024
www.bolotti.co.uk

Richard Gill asserts the moral right to be identified
as the author of this work.
A catalogue record for this book is available from the British Library.

ISBN: 978-1-7397438-4-0

Printed by kdp.amazon.com

Contents

1 Wild is the wind

Freezing sleet pitted Thomas Bell's face. The wind chill bit into his joints as Viper clambered into view. His comrade struggled up the slope in the darkness and collapsed with exhaustion.

Bell gripped Viper's collar.

'Come on, we gotta get over the next ridge.'

'I'm so cold, I can't go on,' bleated Viper.

'But we're nearly at the Ukrainian trenches.'

'No, no more.'

'It'll get easier,' lied Bell.

'What about the minefield?'

'Yeah, there is that,' smiled Bell, grimly.

'You can forget it, then.'

Nursemaiding in the middle of a Russian winter; wiping snot from a whining kid's nose and zipping up his anorak.

'You've got the gall to tell me that?!'

'I die here.'

'You know what this means don't you?'

'I guess.'

Bell had Viper by the throat.

'Get up you bastard! If the Spetznaz and the FSB catch us, we'll be skinned alive!'

Elite Russian forces were particularly active in this eastern sector and were reputed to have tortured to death more than a hundred members of terrorist groups.

Escapees from a north Caucasus internment camp were a particular delicacy.

Foreign fighters even more so.

The GUR, the Ukrainian intelligence directorate, was keenly awaiting a special consignment. Bell and Viper were part of a unit which had been seconded with other UK special forces to assist Ukraine.

Viper seemed to have succumbed to early-onset frostnip by not wrapping up properly, a tingling numbness shutting down his vulnerable extremities.

'We have a delivery to fulfil and you say you're a bit cold?'

Ukrainian forces had fortuitously captured a Russian RTU 518-PSM self-protection jamming pod from a downed Russian Su-30 aircraft. The pods on the twin-engine, two-seater fighter forming part of the Khibiny-U electronic warfare suite, were in excellent condition. The RTU generates false emissions to mask the plane using Digital Radio Frequency Memory technology.

Bell and Viper's mission was to get this intel prize back to the Ukrainian defence ministry.

All the main circuit boards, including processor and memory chips had been stripped out before a Russian squad could beat the Ukrainians to it. The items in their rucksacks potentially held great intelligence value.

That was the background story, anyway.

The All Arms Commando Course exercise on Dartmoor was organised by the Commando Training School at Lympstone in Devon, on the estuary of the River Exe. Participants were identified only by their call signs. For the purposes of this intake it was snakes.

Bell, a qualified team leader, was aptly code-named Adder.

This final exercise was the climax of the course where you would be tested to your absolute limit.

Sure, Bell was cold himself but he had the stamina and he'd done this hike a couple of times before with the Parachute Regiment. You tend to become well acquainted with your pain and discomfort thresholds.

It was a shame to fail a promising recruit. It hadn't been too much further to the finishing line for fuck's sake!

If only his Commando aspirant had had the fortitude to keep going in the face of adversity. Dynamic strength and endurance were just part of a series of hurdles. Basic field-craft and a few press-ups just wasn't enough. Best not to be found wanting in the midst of real field operations.

That didn't necessarily mean that Viper, across all disciplines, hadn't earned enough qualifying points to be admitted into His Majesty's Secret Service. An operational officer also needed other attributes like emotional detachment, lateral thinking, improvisation and analytical skills.

Hey, can you keep a secret?

I can.

Bell wrenched Viper upright and handed him a pill.

'Here, take this. We'll soon be sheltered from the wind.'

A short rest plus the rush of amphetamine and chocolate had Viper back on his feet. Yeah, it was like spoon-feeding a toddler with stewed apple purée.

Bell knew that the abort-exit point would soon have them down on the valley floor. Minutes later they were over the ridge and yomping downhill with renewed vigour towards the treeline. They headed past a familiar granite tor which marked the route down to the village.

Bell swiped his barcode and hammered a button console which was discreetly strapped to a passing tree trunk.

Their unit status was transmitted to the Okehampton control centre as: 'Prematurely terminated'.

'I'm sorry about that,' griped Viper.

'Maybe next time, eh?'

'Have I failed the test?'

Bell ignored the question.

'I know a pub we can go to.'

A vision of the Swan pub in Lympstone immediately presented itself to Viper. Real ales and hearty pub grub at a traditional oak-beamed inn. Sink a couple of pints before a final night at the austere army barracks and an early train back to Exeter.

'I'm buying.'

'Not the Swan Inn,' laughed Bell.

It was snowing harder now but the wind had eased. They negotiated barbed wire fences and obscured ditches. A fast-running stream wended its way with them down the gradient. Bell caught sight of a faint light in the distance which grew stronger. The path led them right to the centre of the village which comprised terraces of sheep farmers' dwellings, a local shop and a pub called the Whittington Arms. It was a popular spot with summer hikers who tramped through with stout boots, laminated maps and orange cagoules.

Bell could detect the whiff of woodsmoke in the breeze as they cut down a narrow, stone-walled lane concealing a deep layer of mud under fresh snow.

Then, cottage back gardens, greenhouses and a steaming pig sty. The smell of warm pig-shit assaulted their nostrils which was curiously comforting. Finally, a deserted, dog-leg high street marked on the map as a B-road. No traffic at all at this time of night.

Bell opened the heavy pub door, much to the surprise of the dour publican who'd been looking forward to closing early.

No such luck buddy.

A couple of thirsty squaddies just walked in.

After removing their boots in the entrance vestibule, they were hit with a wall of warmth as the inner airlock welcomed them into an empty saloon lounge. Viper slumped down on the nearest banquette while Bell made for the bar.

After booking two rooms for the night and ordering a couple of pints of winter ale, Bell alternated his gaze between the laminated menu and the 'Specials' blackboard mounted on the wall. The publican continued to polish pint glasses with a tea towel while agonising choices were being made. They would be collected by an army truck in the morning, preferably as late as Bell could blag it with the CO.

The fillet burger with homemade chips and the crispy pancetta, spinach and ricotta bake caught his eye.

'We'll try the fillet burger,' announced Bell.

'Off,' came the instant reply.

'How about the pancetta?'

'Off.'

'What's on then?'

Chilli con carne came with rice and a poppadom, apparently. Disturbingly so. Each grain fluffy and separate, no doubt.

The pints of strong bitter went down easily as they settled into their blissfully snug refuge from the cold.

The flames of the log fire reflected off copper bed warmers mounted on the walls. Ceramic dishes and brass items adorned the wooden shelves alongside old bottles of Amontillado sherry and Jim Beam. There was still an ancient cigarette vending machine bolted to the wall, flanked by old photographs of village green cricket teams.

All shamelessly intended to engender a sense of relaxed bonhomie as gradual intoxication took effect.

Bell waited impatiently while the publican changed the barrel in the cellar. Their Vampire's Bite refills would have to wait a minute or two. Nothing much else to do around here in the meantime but listen to the wind howling down the chimney and read some of the droll notices pinned up behind the bar.

'Every hour is happy hour.'

'Whatever! - is a woman's way of saying screw you.'

'Nothing means 'something' and you need to be worried.'

Bell smiled at the assorted truisms as Mercedes-Benz HID Xenon headlights illuminated the pub car park.

At the moment Bell took charge of two freshly poured pints, the door burst open and two figures brushed past him, heading purposefully up to the far end of the bar.

A blur of puffa jackets, jeans, and sneakers trailing bubblegum-pink cabin luggage on castors. Both females wore ribbed cashmere hats embellished with fluffy pom-poms.

The publican was over to them like a shot.

They checked in, ordered food with drinks and disappeared upstairs. Bell was sure that he'd overheard the phrase: '...including breakfast.'

Bell was well settled with Viper and in need of a third pint by the time the girls made a reappearance.

The twenty-something duo were fully changed with their hair down. The reverent silence of a crypt was now replaced by intermittent bursts of girlish laughter.

Bell did the maths: Two become one; too many rooms booked, hopefully.

A second gin-and-tonic and glass of white wine were served as the girls ate. They seemed to be benefiting from out-of-character waiter service from Mister Stroppo barman.

'Do you see what I see?' whispered Viper.

'Down boy. At least wait until they've finished their chocolate mousse.'

'Mine's the blonde with big eyes and...'

'But I outrank you, don't I?' teased Bell.

'Ah!'

Viper looked momentarily crestfallen.

'Go on then.'

Viper was across the room like a honey badger freed from a steel trap. As the flamboyant army officer approached, blondie's Britney eyes blazed with excitement.

Bell could see the attraction.

A banal chat-up line had the brazen Romeo pressed up against the appetising pair only moments later.

Three's a crowd.

Blondie's sparring partner soon stood up and headed in Bell's direction. It wasn't eyes this time, but an alluring pout which indicated fiery defiance and indignation. Bell only had time to spoon one more mouthful of dessert before a mane of caramel-brown hair took a seat opposite him.

'Mmm, that looks yummy.'

'Gooseberry Fool.'

Mashed summer fruit folded into whipped cream, caster sugar, and vanilla essence. Bell offered a spoonful across the table.

'What's this? Intimate gestures even before we've been introduced?'

She leaned forward onto the mouthful of heaven and sucked it off. Bell is already in bed with her, feeling her quickening, hot breath against his face. A reciprocal presumption was hopefully causing a surge of sex hormones.

Damp combats not regimental dress, but men in uniform even so. That must account for some intrinsic attraction. You had to chuckle.

'You caught me on the hop, I'm Tom.'

'Been out rambling, have we?'

'Much more of this toxic brew and I will be.'

'Ah! Mr Droopy yakking drivel and falling asleep on me.'

'There's always a bluey,' laughed Bell defensively, enjoying the pre-coital skirmish.

'Your friend could have just as easily picked me. Are you telling me that I've got the one with the limp dick who's not up for playing at hide the penis? Runner-up Jenna here is actually your dessert but at least everyone's got chilli breath!'

'We both know that we'll be enjoying each other before the night is over,' soothed Bell.

'Whatever. You put it so sweetly.'

'I'm probing your defences.'

'Defences?! Probe all you like, I'm the leftovers, remember. Here on a plate so that you can totally drill me. That's what you want isn't it?'

Viper and Stacey were out of their seats. The your-room-or-mine question had been answered.

Bell stood up suddenly. Slower speed, more torque, that should cook it.

'Let's go upstairs and find out, shall we?'

***

The walls were as thin as rice paper. You didn't need to be a rocket scientist to realise that the couple next door were way ahead of them. Their bedhead broadcast metronome time as if to advertise a sense of urgency to less energetic hotel guests.

It was a crappy room but the cast iron radiator was piping hot and the mattress seemed firm enough. Not exactly a romantic love-nest but better than lying in a ditch with frostbite.

Bell set up some stuff from his rucksack on the table. After removing his Glock 18C pistol and its holster, he returned to Jenna who had remained standing in the centre of the room.

He slipped his arm around her waist and drew her close. She responded by pulling him closer still and moving in for the kill. The scent of her overwhelmed his senses as their lips met. Softly purred encouragement had replaced the playful indignation and caustic one-liners from earlier. Bell experienced no resistance as his fingers explored her crotchless pantyhose. The tantalising obstacle of a warm gusset blocked his advance in the same way that Jenna was getting nowhere with a heavy-duty combat zip.

The moment when she curtailed their delicious embrace was rapidly approaching. Her long-sleeved bodycon party-dress would be off in a flash, while he tore off the remains of his own clothing. Standard procedure; corsets, suspender belts and panties to be dealt with on an engage-at-will basis.

A breathless Jenna broke off as expected.

'Unzip me, will you?'

It took all of Bell's willpower to hesitate for a moment.

'Come on, I'm an easy peeler!'

'We can't get too comfortable.'

'What!?'

'We wait.'

***

Viper lay sated in a post-intercourse repose, drifting in and out of an hallucinatory twilight sleep. His disordered senses were playing tricks on him. One minute yomping across frozen wastes in high winds, the next performing between the thighs of a beautiful blonde. He awoke fully with a disorientated jolt and just about remembered how he'd got here. Stacey propped herself up on one elbow.

'Hello dreamy, where have you been?'

Viper found it hard to believe where he was. A surfeit of physical exhaustion, alcohol and energetic sex had robbed him of his ability to stay awake. The main culprit being the British Army. Hey, what about his admission tariff points?

What about them!

All that mattered was that he was in a warm bed with a hot woman and head-over-heels in love. When both tanks had been refilled, he resolved to try the reverse cowgirl position with this amazing babe: Apart from the titillating view, it was reputed to maximize anterior fornix friction. A spot of sexual variation which just had to be executed.

Stacey inched up closer so that she could whisper into his ear. At the same time she ran her fingers through his bristly high-and-tight military crewcut and stimulated one of his nipples.

Floating in heaven, but half awake.

'What do you do?' whispered Stacey.

'I'm an officer in the Royal Marines.'

'So, what were you doing out in the cold?'

'On an exercise, that's all.'

'Just running about?'

'We were out on tactical navigation endurance, no but really…'

Viper lowered his voice.

'…between you and me…we were on a secret mission to get some computer chips from a crashed Russian jet fighter back to base.'

'And then what?'

'We hand them over to experts in the Ukrainian Ministry of Defence.'

'But we're not in the Ukraine?'

'Exactly. These are top secret training simulations that are held in the UK.'

'So, back to square bashing after this, I guess.'

'No. I'm actually permanently transferring to the secret service.'

'Like James Bond, licence to kill?'

'Well, er, yeah.'

A few seconds later Bell and Jenna were standing next to the bed. The hotel door had almost been ripped from its hinges after Bell had torn off his earpiece.

'Hey, what is this?!' screamed Viper, bolt upright.

Stacey, completely naked, rose slowly off the bed and gave Jenna a high-five. Bell stepped forward.

'Game over, buddy.'

'What? You mean that this was all a set-up. The girls, the pub and the pick-up?'

'Yeah, a sticky honey-trap. We had to be sure about you.'

Viper called after Stacey.

'You bitch!'

She turned angrily in the doorway.

'Grow up little boy, I'm not your mom, okay? Don't make me call you a loser. All I have to say to you is: Gotcha!'

'But you...'

'I was just doing my job...'

'So these two girls...they work for…'

'Yes,' interrupted Bell.

'I was only…'

'You signed the Official Secrets Act, remember?'

Pleading puppy eyes looked up at Bell.

'But I'd already failed back out there in the snow, hadn't I?'

'I never said that,' smiled Bell.

'Is it all over?'

'It is now.'

***

Jenna's next mission, as with all her assignments, was classified.

Any clown with half a brain cell could have told you that. Their paths might cross again, but it may never happen.

All the more reason to treat every day as your last. No warning would be given as you took your last breath. They both knew better than to discuss MIX operations, especially while lying snugly in bed together.

Her head lay on his chest as she slept, while a snowstorm continued to rage outside. They had enjoyed each other's bodies for most of the night, just as Bell had promised.

It had been wonderful.

Only a few more hours before they must bid each other farewell.

Emotional detachment was a cruel discipline.

In the meantime, Viper would be in an army truck heading back to barracks on his own, nice and early. A dishonourable return to his regiment as a verified Military Intelligence applicant-reject awaited him.

2   Toxic shock

Wo Xi Tang was a senior scientist working on an advanced railgun project.

A railgun is a linear motor device that uses electromagnetic force to launch high velocity projectiles.

The fundamental principle is that it uses an electric current to create a magnetic field. This enables the machine to shoot darts made from conductive materials. The projectile doesn't contain explosives; its destructive capability is based solely upon speed, mass and kinetic energy.

Electricity fires the round, not nitrocellulose propellant which uses gas expansion.

Magnetism is a familiar concept, but electromagnets can do far more than simply stick to metallic objects. Rearranging the coloured letters on your refrigerator door is just the beginning.

The British and the US had agreed to share technical knowledge in order to deal with difficult scientific challenges which continued to thwart production roll-out. Problems that Wo was painfully well aware of, and which caused him extreme frustration.

A fieldable railgun had to be capable of multiple full-power shots while operating within accuracy and safety parameters. After you had resolved the heat and wear of the rails, the melting of equipment and projectile friction, you might have got somewhere. After that there was still projectile on-board electronic guidance and the gun's infrared signature to be considered.

Weapon minimum specification: Fire six rounds per minute with a rail life of three thousand rounds, meaning that you could be firing at the enemy non-stop for over eight hours.

In your dreams, baby.

The Chinese Central Military Commission wasn't going to be informed of a breakthrough anytime soon.

MIX knew that Wo was sharing his knowledge with the PLA in Beijing. How Wo had been given top-level security clearance at this Oxford university green-field site was anyone's guess. Maybe a Chinese billionaire's generous donation which had bank-rolled the whole complex had something to do with it.

Intelligence also indicated that Wo had a habit of running test firings on his own which was completely against regulations. An ideal scenario had therefore presented itself for Wo to succumb to an unfortunate anomaly in the electrical systems. The presence of high-energy components offered scope for a plausible mishap, as in touching the wrong thing which spontaneously turns you into a corn chip.

Today, Wo was preoccupied with orchestrating a marginal increase in the muzzle velocity. It meant an increase in power coursing through the warm, muscular cables which trailed across the floor.

Liquid metal? Maybe that was something worth considering. Challenges relating to projectile guidance were forced to the back of his mind. Plasma-tolerant, on-board electronics issues would have to wait.

Wo looked forward to the time when his work was featured on Chinese naval vessels, and he was lauded by the CCP for all his efforts. A recall back to China was on the cards, maybe a placement with one of the cyber, space or electronic warfare units. A switch to quantum cryptography was what he really had in mind, a neat jump sideways away from megajoule ballistics.

Meanwhile, he would run the railgun experiment again. The projectile was still way short of achieving a velocity of three kilometres per second. Time to try a risky increase in electric current to achieve greater kinetic energy.

Test status: Pre-firing checklist satisfactorily completed.

Coffee in hand, Wo took a moment to savour the serenity of the cathedral-like space of the ballistics long gallery. The stainless steel projectile would take a split second to hit the arresting point at the far end. The trajectory analysis could take hours.

Wo despondently headed towards the control cubicle.

To hell with it!

***

Thomas Bell turned a corner and entered the remote Oxford university campus site by way of a full-height security turnstile. After he had emerged from the millimetre wave scanner, he headed immediately for the locker room.

Restricted access credentials for this applied-physics department facility were on a par with that of a particle collider laboratory. US-UK know-how liaison was only possible because high-level security-clearance protocols had been implemented.

MIX field logistics had provided Bell with a false identity by backdoor-hacking the university computer system. While actively infiltrating using an authentication bypass, they had also taken the trouble to mess with the CCTV.

A swipe-card opened his locker cabinet and Bell retrieved a lapel badge, ID, white lab-coat and skin-colour latex gloves. He paid particular attention to his new spectacles. Not X-ray specs but bold-frame glasses which were discreetly fitted with a link to MIX, an integrated camera, a microphone and an earpiece.

Helpfully, there were a couple of text books relating to quantum computing to augment his egghead legend. Bell had been briefed in some of the basic quantum concepts, but any boffin who knew his stuff would peel away his flimsy veneer of knowledge in minutes.

Okay, enough cosplay alchemy.

In his eyewear, Bell looked super-intelligent, giving the impression that he was more likely to be unlocking the mysteries of the universe rather than snapping an assailant's neck like a breadstick.

The flaky storyline was that he was doing his PhD.

Interestingly, the Chinese billionaire who had financed the advanced applied physics laboratories that Bell was about to visit had mysteriously disappeared about a week ago. Early unconfirmed reports revealed that he had been abducted by security officers from the Four Seasons Hotel in Hong Kong. Rumours of corruption investigations and unwise regulatory criticism abounded while the charismatic CEO, famous for his open-necked white shirts and polished loafers, seemed to be missing or, as some observers might put it, 'out of contact'.

What was the investment bank president doing now?

Being re-educated?

Yeah, right.

Bell's polyamide boot-blade, hidden in his briefcase, had made it through the metal detector. Best to strap it to his ankle as usual. It was highly unlikely that the specialist commando knife would be needed for this job.

He belted up with a Taser and a cattle prod, both devices hidden beneath his starched technician coat. The cattle prod dealt with close-quarter tussles - short electrodes driven into the ribs or neck, whereas the Taser wires had a range of twenty feet.

These were non-lethal weapons which had been upgraded for life-taking combat use. No anti-felon ID tags to litter the floor - barcoded confetti shot at the same time which identifies the Taser user. Once the compressed nitrogen had fired tethered barbs into your skin and the electrical payload had been sent, you were toast.

Ventricular fibrillation with every hit!

Bell checked the time and headed for the Wan Li building.

Basement level.

Standing outside security door T107.

He swiped his card.

The discharge from high voltage capacitors could give you a nasty tingle, apparently.

Whatever Bell did next must look like an accident.

***

It had been no accident that Han Tu Won had lifted weights in the same gym as Dylan Evans.

Weightlifting to increase the strength and size of the muscles. General resistance training with fixed or free weights. Lose fat and gain muscle definition with a carefully controlled protein diet, mainly eggs, salmon, tuna, and lean beef.

Their relationship had developed amongst the barbells and the sweat into something more than eager chat about muscle-mass shakes and anabolic steroids. A surfeit of synthetic testosterone greasing the wheels of those with particular sexual proclivities.

It was no accident because Evans worked at GCHQ in Cheltenham as a codebreaker and had high level access to US and UK secrets. He had also been helping the US National Security Agency trace international money-laundering routes used by organised crime groups including Moscow-based mafia cells. He was part of a team of intelligence officers sent to penetrate US and UK hacking networks.

No accident because the Chinese Ministry of State Security had targeted Evans and had sent one of their best agents to turn him. Han had a variety of means at his disposal including blackmail, financial incentives and sexual entrapment.

It did not go well.

Han was directed to enter into a complex relationship with Evans, which enabled their mark to explore his confused sexuality, but at the same time make him vulnerable to foreign interference. Both of them greedily and desperately wanted something from each other in an unhealthy symbiotic interaction.

Their close physical association covered the whole gamut of mutual consumption, predominantly manifesting itself as a slave-master liaison played out at Evans's top floor flat in central London. Women's clothing, bondage, and exotic master-slave fetishes, with Han adopting the role of masterful dominant from the outset.

Six months of grooming and sophisticated psychological techniques had failed to turn Evans into a reliable double agent, despite a promising start.

Early classified data passed to PLA intelligence, which concerned signals intelligence, the Tempora programme and foreign power hacking operations, had been of limited interest.

Evans had, as an afterthought on one occasion, included some information in relation to the First Island Chain and a militarised base in the Spratly Island archipelago called Fiery Cross Reef, named after the British tea clipper which had run aground there in the year 1860. Despite opposition from Vietnam, the PRC had built a full airbase on it including hardened aircraft shelters and missile launchers.

Mischief in the South China Sea.

This information had whetted appetites in Beijing, even more so when Evans followed it up with details of a Philippines request, naming the PRC as respondent, for compulsory arbitration at the International Maritime Tribunal in The Hague. The issue centred on arguments over historical territorial waters, dubious claims, and ancient nautical maps.

Evans developed cold feet out of the blue, exactly at the moment when he was proving his worth.

Had something spooked him?

When Han challenged him, Evans clammed up and was dishing out the silent treatment. Evans had threatened to blow the whistle to his employers and have Han arrested on a charge of foreign espionage.

To Han's relief, an urgent instruction arrived from Beijing to terminate Evans without hesitation, mercy or discernment. It must be done in such a way to maximize British government embarrassment and to leave the Security Services with a puzzling riddle which was difficult to solve.

This adverse development could mean a recall back to Fujian province, something which definitely did not appeal.

Han had developed a taste for the delights of London as a natural by-product of regular assignations at his GCHQ mathematician's bolthole flat in Cambridge Street, Pimlico. Apart from carrying out other PLA missions within the greater London area, he had spare time on his hands to sample the degenerate and debauched Western lifestyle. Drunk on complete freedom, he was now fully acclimatised.

London's Chinatown. The thought of never again seeing Soho, Gerrard Street, Wardour Street nor Theatreland where he could push his weight around was abhorrent. People in the know were frightened of him. He was a Chinese assassin operating under the British intelligence radar and loving it.

Han had prudently saved his last casino chip.

Evans stood before him in a black latex bodysuit enjoying the exquisite feel of his shiny second skin.

Being a slave was not quite enough.

A craving to be an object with no human identity. A plaything to be used and abused that is grateful for any attention.

Han had denied Evans this transition…until now.

A human toy where bondage, isolation and pain were the default state. A poor wretch only to be brought out occasionally and then put away again.

A gimp.

A solo sex game gone wrong.

A body squeezed into a large sports bag.

Evans looked up into Han's eyes.

'I thought you loved me?'

'Bìng bù zhēn dì,' came the clinical reply as the zip was pulled tight and the padlock snapped shut.

The keys were in the bag.

Hypercapnia would set in quickly.

Carbon dioxide toxicity progressively causing: Mild narcosis, panic, unconsciousness, and death.

Han glanced back at the red holdall writhing in the bath and exited the bedroom ensuite, leaving the door ajar.

Lamentably, he was going to be late for work today.

Chores to do first.

Set the scene for a criminally mediated death which was suspicious and unexplained.

Female paraphernalia: Shoes, wigs, makeup, underwear, and leather boots. Items which, to Evans at least, encapsulated the very essence of femininity.

DNA, fingerprints, human hair, SIM cards, hard drives, digital video footage, and web history. The US State Department, FBI, British police and security services all at each other's throats over the public inquest.

Han took one last look at the front door and adjusted the thermostat with a latex-gloved hand.

No more seedy trysts giving pleasure to another man, artificially switching his sexual polarity for the sake of mother China.

Back to his day job as a lowly lab technician who checked meters and dials, and moved heavy equipment around.

No theoretical physics to worry about, only other PLA agents operating in the field whom someone needed to keep an eye on.

Taxi to London Paddington rail station.

Direct train to Oxford: fifty-five minutes.

First port of call: the Wan Li Building.

***

No sooner had Bell set foot into the long gallery firing range than warning sirens sounded.

These were complemented by overhead strobe-beacons and a decrementing stern warning.

'Take cover - test firing in one minute and fifty seconds…'

'Take cover - test firing in one minute and forty seconds…'

'Take cover - test firing in...'

Hmm, not the intruder alarm, then.

Bell sprinted in the direction of the control booth.

He was met outside by a familiar mugshot face offering him a pair of ear defenders. The quantum computing textbooks that Bell was holding were subjected to a big-eyed glance.

'Hurry! Get in!' the scientist screamed.

With the door slammed firmly shut, Bell was offered a seat while Wo Xi Tang jumped back in front of the main firing console. Bell's host seemed unconcerned that all the indicators had crept into the red, Wo simply raising his clenched fist with a yelp.

'High voltage capacitors at maximum!'

The fist came down on a red button at the same time as a loud bang outside shook their cosy hidey-hole and probably the whole building.

Bell's immediate inclination was to scream 'what the fuck was that!', but he knew very well what it was.

'Did it fire anything?' quizzed Bell.

Wo spun around in his chair.

'How did you get in?…what are you doing here?'

Wo was sweating.

Wet skin meant lower electrical resistance.

'This facility is restricted. I do not believe that you are on the access list. While we're at it, what is a qubit?' grilled Wo.

'I'm a PhD fresher. A qubit is a basic quantum computing information unit like a conventional binary digit. Multiple entangled states and all that,' smiled Bell.

Wo was curiously satisfied with the plausible humbug.

No time to dwell on it, though.

'It's over, Tang,' said Bell, softly.

Wo jolted as if he'd been struck by an electrical discharge of the same magnitude which Bell was about to administer with the cattle prod.

'Do I have a choice?'

'Not this time.'

Wo handed over his keys.

'Your quantum answer was impressive.'

A touching compliment but not enough to save his skin.

'Repeated parrot-fashion, I'm afraid,' laughed Bell.

It was regrettable to kill someone who knew so much. An enemy of the state, nonetheless.

Orders were orders.

Bell easily dragged Wo's scrawny, undernourished corpse out to the capacitor diagnostics display-board. He unlocked the steel mesh door right next to it which gave access to the entire capacitor bank. Only the likes of Nikola Tesla, the Serbian-American electrical engineer who pioneered alternating current back in the 1880s, could feel comfortable in a place like this.

Verdict: A bit of ill-advised and hurried meddling while on his own. Nobody would ever be sure how Wo had met his end.

Bell suddenly had the feeling that something had moved behind him.

Gantry crane hoist-chains swayed nearby in the still air.

Surely not caused by the test-firing blast-wave?

Han Tu Won knew that it was a definite recall back to Fujian province now that a PLA asset that he was responsible for had been murdered on his watch. He may as well go down fighting.

'That was easy, wasn't it!' shouted Han.

Bell spun around to see a muscular Chinese guy wielding a stainless steel monkey stick.

Although thirty feet away, the surprise aggressor was gliding forward slowly and deliberately towards him in some kind of ninja-shaolin stalking style. Bell guessed that the package came with formidable blocking and striking moves which were going to present a problem.

'Now, try me,' taunted Han, getting within range.

Whoever this Kung Fu chancer was, Bell could do without it. Getting out of here was overdue.

Bell squared up to the mystery assailant, opening his lab-coat and crouching down a little, like the Sundance Kid, while instantly drawing and firing his lethal combat Taser.

Toasted crisp or fried crouton?

Not fussy. So long as the outcome was a slab of freshly cooked meat.

Bell left both bodies lying next to each other and made for the exit.

3   King Concrete

Tuesday 05:30.

Colonel Zheng Wei stared at a plastic folder placed in the middle of a cluttered desk.

An early start in a shabby building located on the outskirts of the Chinese city of Shenzhen, in Guangdong province.

The smells of the nearby slum permeated the bleak office, as the State Security police officer thumbed its contents. Finally, he lifted a photograph of the person-of-interest currently under twenty-four-hour surveillance. The exhaustive file included several hair samples. How these had been obtained was undocumented.

That person was Gu Chang, the CEO of Dime Industries and the Everlong Property Group.

Gu was also making an early start on the top floor of the forty-storey Yitian Plaza Tower, swimming a few lengths in a heated pool while the sun rose.

Gu had been holed up there for two days while the finer details of a refinancing deal were thrashed out. Naturally, his office and private apartment occupied the top three floors. Not unreasonable if you were a billionaire who had commissioned, built and owned the most valuable piece of city real estate overlooking the Ng Tung river.

The Ministry of State Security in Beijing had despatched Zheng to this subordinate provincial office to keep an eye on things. Put another way: official blessing at the highest level to bust balls and crack heads open.

Gu was to be apprehended dead or alive.

Zheng looked more closely at the mugshot. Several of his comrade officers had observed that he had an uncanny resemblance to Gu. What was uncannier was that they were both born on the same day.

Zheng focused on the surveillance outcome.

Why hadn't the Shenzhen police stormed the Plaza building and arrested Gu already? and why was the senior officer absent in the middle of an operation?

Zheng was tasked with delivering results.

On cue, the police commissioner stormed into his office looking like a bag of crap. Zheng was aware that this guy had a penchant for opium dens, brothels and having affairs. The powerful stench of drugs, tobacco and fornication trumped the aroma rising from the open sewer in the alleyway right outside.

'Good morning, Qian,' smiled Zheng.

The commissioner was forced to take a seat opposite his own desk. Zheng wasn't budging because he easily outranked him.

Two scalding coffees arrived and Zheng held up Gu Chang's picture.

'So?' quizzed Zheng.

'Gu could be in there for days. We'll be waiting.'

'You do realise that he may have absconded already.'

'No way! We have the place surrounded!'

Zheng was unconvinced.

'Why…?'

'…haven't we raided the Plaza Tower already?'

'It had occurred to me,' came the icy response.

'In case you hadn't noticed, Gu has a Eurocopter EC120 sitting on the helipad up there.'

'So, we deploy a Z-10 attack helicopter with TY-90 air-to-air missiles.'

Qian had regained some of his composure but he still stank like a polecat – akin to the pungent, repellent stench produced by secretion glands on either side of its anus.

'What if they disable the high-speed lifts? It's forty floors!'

'We get some exercise!'

'But…'

'Daylight. It has to be done today. I'll book the Z-10 chopper.'

'How about 15:00 this afternoon?' suggested Qian, hoping for more time to sober up and prepare himself for a gruelling ascent in hot SWAT gear.

Zheng was more concerned with cutting the power for the whole building. The police assault unit would shut down the emergency generators as soon as they got in there.

'Nice try. 13:00 it is,' smirked Zheng.

Qian's puny attempt at holding sway had failed, but every cloud had a silver lining.

'I guess we'll be armed with the new QBZ191 assault rifle.'

'Whatever, but don't forget your flexi-cuffs.'

Qian punched the sky in his mind…he wasn't cuffing anybody.

Zheng concluded that they were all done.

'Any other business?'

'Er…'

'Let's go get him, then.'

'I think I need a shower, a shit, and a shave.'

'Oh, really? I hadn't noticed.'

***

Moles are overgrowths of skin cells called melanocytes, but the genetic factors involved in their development and inheritance propensity are not well understood.

No doubt about it, he had two small moles on the side of his face, just like Gu.

The evidence was mounting up.

Nothing for it but to get this thing checked out.

Discreetly, though.

Wearing plain clothes was a plus.

Zheng ensured that he wasn't being tailed and headed into the slum labyrinth. After snaking a series of lefts and rights he ended up down a dead-end alleyway in front of an unmarked door.

An unintelligible squawk on the intercom admitted him to a crowded waiting room full of women. Numbered post-it notes affixed to each left breast indicated orderly, sequential processing. After a flush of furtive female glances, it was eyes down again.

All of them except one had their heads bowed, deep in contemplative thought, knowing the awful procedure that they were about to undergo.

One beautiful girl, about eighteen years of age, with a ready smile and bright eyes, held his gaze as he ran the gauntlet.

Zheng presented his police badge to the receptionist at the far end. Moments later he was sitting opposite a doctor in a consulting room. Medical titles were dished out haphazardly in this meat processing plant, where knowledge of obstetrics was somewhat limited.

He obviously didn't need a termination, so what did he want?

Zheng explained and provided the necessary samples.

Express autosomal DNA profiling in exchange for not raiding and closing down an illegal abortion clinic.

Results normally took a week via a post office box.

Zheng's analysis would be ready in two hours.

***

Whichever bar or café he killed time in, he received guarded glances. It must be obvious that he was State Security police or an agent for some other shadowy government agency.

Now in his mid-thirties, he had given everything to claw his way up the armed forces hierarchy to better things. A stint in the PLA followed by the rest of his career in the Ministry of State Security. The MSS being the equivalent of the American CIA and FBI combined.

What had he got to show for it?

He had no family, no wife and no children - not that he knew of, anyway. Just a dwindling series of failed relationships. He didn't own anything of substance. He hadn't had any real fun or done much outside of work. The non-stop grindstone: investigations and perpetrators, keeping his nose clean and watching his back.

He instinctively knew that everything would change for him when the DNA results were revealed.

That girl! The stunning, alluring creature who had given him such a wonderful smile!

He had to see her again.

Zheng threw down a twenty yuan note and rushed back.

***

Xiong Yu had waited patiently in the queue for well over an hour. It was time to rise from her uncomfortable seat and be led down a long, narrow corridor.

A night of passion with an attractive young buck and a surfeit of alcohol had brought her to this. A crazy one-night stand with a fellow student.

The sticky acoustic gel was cold on her tummy, as a nurse traced the transducer probe back and forth. Presently, the elderly ultrasound machine displayed a black and white image on the screen.

It didn't mean that much to Yu, as she lay there passively obeying instructions. Although the equipment came with sonogram tools, the nurse retrieved her trusty pair of callipers. After repeated measurements of the crown-rump length, she turned to Yu with a grimaced smile.

'Fifteen weeks.'

Yu raced back through her mental calendar to that careless night without precautions or protection.

'Fifteen?'

'Look, you can see their hearts beating.'

Yu sat bolt upright in horror.

'Hearts!? You mean that…'

'Yes, you're carrying twins.'

***

Tuesday 10:50.

'It's your twin brother,' said the doctor, handing over the documentation.

Zheng lunged for his wallet.

An idea was beginning to crystallise in his mind.

The confluence of circumstance and serendipity.

A moment when the clouds parted and the sun shone down solely upon you and no other person: warm, bright and energizing.

'No, no, it's on the house,' winced the doctor, nervously.

Zheng had been excited to get back to the waiting room. The next person in line appeared to be number sixteen.

He felt distress that his sweet angel had already gone through, but consoled himself that she must be resting in a recuperation lounge. He guessed that meant an hour's daytime TV rather than the rigorous monitoring of post-operative shock, pain, and abnormal blood loss.

No problem, but he must catch her before she left.

Zheng placed a wad of yuan on the desk.

It was double the going rate.

The doctor looked astonished like it was part of a sophisticated sting that he'd fallen for.

'You offer an invaluable service,' smiled Zheng.

'It's our pleasure,' blurted the doctor, timidly.

'There is one other favour I need to ask…'

The doctor tensed visibly.

Dread creeping in. A fanged babadook was about to bite.

'One of the girls in the waiting room earlier…is she still here in recovery?'

'Ah!'

The doctor relaxed with a knowing smile.

Love in the fast lane: the sexual imperative.

Cruising all possible hunting grounds: cafés, bars, nightclubs, supermarkets, beaches, and…abortion clinics?

Instant attraction came with neither a stop sign nor a no-go zone.

Many of the girls were frequent visitors who didn't give abortion a second thought. Routinely dropping by for a quickie scrape was on a par with a manicure or a bikini wax. Another hook-up was normally the last thing on their minds.

'Number eight.'

'Hmm, we have a problem.'

'Like?'

'She cut short her pre-op exam and lapsed into a state of incoherent sobbing and wailing. Other girls tried to console her in the recuperation lounge, but there was no comforting her.'

'She said that she couldn't go through with it and that she was worthless and didn't deserve to live.'

'After a while she pulled herself together and took off.'

Number eight - a lucky number.

It was all that Zheng had to go on. He urgently needed to see whatever the clinic kept in the way of a personal record.

There was luck to be had yet.

'This is important, where does she live?'

'I'm unable to divulge that, I'm afraid.'

'This is a police matter,' came the agitated response.

A diatribe protesting the doctor-patient bond of trust, the legal and ethical duty regarding information disclosure, and the lack of patient consent followed.

Zheng leaned forward assertively.

'Remember that you're not a doctor, but a failed dentist who's winging it!'

The medical imposter looked back blankly knowing that he'd been well and truly skewered. They had a fat file on him.

Zheng was short of time and patience. The bonhomie and compliments from earlier had evaporated.

Seconds later, the self-styled obstetric practitioner had the muzzle of a semi-automatic pressed into his forehead.

'You were saying?'

***

Xiong Yu had a head start.

Twins! Her unborn children! Her little babies! Fifteen weeks!

She ran headlong back to her slum tower block and arrived at the front entrance in a flood of tears.

There was only one course of action.

She was focused and resolute.

Was thirty storeys high enough?

The building where she had been born awaited dynamite and the wrecking ball. This was her home, her life, and the cradle for her existence with extended family and friends, soon to be extinguished.

The only option was to take her own life.

Jump and it will all be over.

The pre-demolition teams had already started drilling to set charges and had severed the mains power cables. People were being forcibly evicted. Windows and utility connections were being smashed and vandalised so that no-one could return.

Yu started the excruciating trudge up the exposed stairwell, firstly to her family apartment on the eleventh floor and then onwards up to the roof.

When she had made it to the top, standing amongst the aircon units, aerials, and satellite dishes, she would be able to take in a final, distant view of the Ng Tung river.

***

Armed with general directions Zheng had made haste. He'd gone wrong a few times but had got there in the end. Now it was a matter of running up the staircase two steps at a time.

The door to Yu's flat was ajar.

He burst in and searched the place but it was deserted.

After being challenged by an explosives team and flashing his police badge, he had a hunch.

The roof!

Oh no! Was he too late?

Nineteen floors left to climb…

Eventually he burst out through some illegal washing lines.

She was standing right on the edge.

'Yu, it's Wei from the clinic!'

Yu turned slowly.

'Huh?'

A few more steps and he had his arms around her waist.

She turned fully to face him.

'You don't need to do it,' cooed Wei, wiping her tears away.

'I don't?'

'Let me take you away from all of this.'

'But you know…'

'Let's not worry about that.'

'Are you, by any chance, the goddess Bixia in disguise, the guardian of mothers and young children?'

'If I am, I'm offering you a new life and a fresh start.'

'And as a man?' she grinned, grasping his bicep.

'Then, I am the god Caishen bearing fruits and gold ingots!'

'Why have you saved me when you don't even know me?'

'Because you smiled at me and I am smitten.'

'Love at first sight?'

Their poignant embrace made him want her even more. She was lovelier than he dared to remember.

'If you'll have me, that is.'

'Even if they're not yours?'

'I will treat them as my own and we will be happy together.'

The number eight post-it note was miraculously still in place. How lucky is that?

A life of wealth, prosperity and good fortune.

***

Tuesday 12:40

The doors to Gu Chang's private lift chimed open.

Gu glanced in surprise at his lunchtime trolley standing there waiting to be wheeled out. He rose from his desk and walked over.

Twenty minutes early.

It may be nothing.

But nothing could be something.

He wheeled the trolley back to his desk and laid the takeaway meal out in a line while fighting the mouth-watering aroma.

It was a warning.

Two bottles of Zhujiang beer, spring rolls, chicken satay, chow mein, sweet and sour pork, egg fried rice…and deep fried seaweed, which he hated.

Gu tore open the seaweed oyster pail as the vibration of helicopter turboshaft engines passing low overhead shook the building. The five-bladed rotor and chin-mounted autocannon visible through the plate glass windows was unmistakeable. An armed police Z-10 helicopter loitering with intent in the airspace directly above him.

Someone had scrawled: '13:00' on the waxed-paperboard flap.

That someone was one of his private security agents who operated down at street level.

For his entire billionaire life he had prepared for this moment.

Known to the Chinese populace as 'runxue' or runology.

The art of running.

Bank accounts in Switzerland and the British Virgin Islands.

Property in London, New York and the south of France.

Other stable assets dotted around the world.

A foreign investment bank which had enabled him to obtain an equity line of credit.

It was imperative to avoid arrest and face certain conviction for corruption and sedition.

A series of planned steps equated to a life of freedom in the West.

The first being an escape unseen from Yitian Plaza Tower.

A short walk to a backstreet lockup garage.

Adoption of a disguise and a new identity before driving a modest vehicle out on to the riverside Binhai Boulevard, heading west.

A left turn at the main junction heading south into Hong Kong via the Shenzhen Bay Bridge, followed by a right, keeping south, towards Hong Kong airport through the Chek Lap Kok tunnel.

Parking up and switching to the Macau Bridge shuttle bus.

A thorough search by the police before crossing the Pearl River would reveal nothing.

In Macau, call in at a rented apartment and pick up fifty million dollars' worth of casino chips.

Visit the casino, play two hands of blackjack, cash in the chips, and head for the Macau port marina.

The superyacht the 'Beta Blanco' would be waiting.

Sleek and beautiful, all one hundred and sixty-five feet of her, registered in George Town, in the Cayman Islands.

It was all his!

Once out into the South China Sea the trans-Pacific voyage would be eastwards all the way to Hawaii for a brief stopover. A last leg up towards Vancouver would complete the trip.

For now, although the food was sitting there, he would have to go hungry.

There wasn't even time to break apart his chopsticks!

Seventeen minutes.

Gu made a phone call and ran a pre-set routine on the Yitian Plaza Tower master control console.

Lifts returned back to the thirty seventh floor and became immobilised.

External doors locked.

All power off.

Emergency generators disabled.

A male employee wearing an oversize EPG baseball cap had made it to the helipad to board the company Eurocopter. The bogus instruction to Gu's look-alike decoy was to meet and greet international financiers arriving at Hong Kong airport. The Eurocopter would head due south to Chek Lap Kok island, chased by the police Z-10 which might well shoot it down.

12:56 - four minutes remaining.

Gu walked briskly over to a Vermeer painting propped up on the sideboard and slipped it into its carrying case.

That's why they called him King Concrete.

Yeah, he wasn't the cement supremo for nothing.

All those ghost cities his companies had built.

Enough concrete to build a concealed elevator shaft which didn't feature on the official plans. Naturally, it was powered by its own generator. Once at ground level, getaway tunnels ran in several directions.

Gu located the switch and a secret panel opened.

Everlong Property was so overleveraged with debt that it was about to implode anyway. He'd got most of his wealth out of China.

He wasn't coming back.

There was no regret in kissing it all goodbye.

The Otis doors closed snugly behind him and he was gone.

***

Tuesday 13:03.

A shaped charge had blown the front doors of the Yitian Plaza Tower. Shards of glass lay thick underfoot as the police tramped around herding corporate employees into one of the ground floor conference rooms.

Gu could be hiding anywhere in the forty storey tower but Zheng guessed that he was long gone. It would be more than a flawed idea to reveal his newly discovered blood relationship with the elusive fugitive to his colleagues.

As expected, the elevators in the magnificent marble foyer were out of order. It meant that for a second time that day Zheng was sweating up concrete stairwells in a hurry.

Eventually the SWAT team got to the thirty seventh floor.

It was going to take another shaped charge to get past the robust security doors which gave access to the CEO's private quarters.

After blowing the stubborn airlock at their second attempt, they piled in at the double.

The three floors were deserted which meant that there was some serious explaining to do. That left a thorough search which so far was turning up very little.

After thumbing the offering on the glacial coffee table - art auction catalogues, Superyacht Global magazine and Fabergé quarterly bulletins, the CEO's desk was all that remained.

Zheng decided to plump his cheeks in Gu's executive chair and survey his twin brother's domain. He could get used to this! An oversize desk, panoramic views, Persian carpets, and a recently delivered Chinese takeaway.

Hey, the food was still warm and untouched.

The palatable smell was overpowering.

Zheng made a beeline for the sweet and sour pork with rice.

The Pearl River Brewery beer could wash it all down.

He had a gut feeling that there was a clue to Gu's whereabouts somewhere in this office.

Whoops, he dropped some noodles on to what looked like an expensive Pashmina-wool carpet, decorated with jasmine blossoms.

Better bend down and scrape the offending goo up.

Now on all fours, Zheng found a hundred-dollar casino chip under the desk which had been curiously camouflaged by the intricate hand-woven pattern.

Zheng ran an RFID reader over it.

The wave-form data displayed instantly on the screen.

It belonged to a casino in Macau, which is a special administrative region of the People's Republic of China, located in the western Pearl River Delta.

Macau had been leased to Portugal as a colony by the Ming dynasty in 1557, but handed back to China in 1999. Its gambling operation was known to be many times bigger than that of Las Vegas.

Whatever.

The casino in question was the Blue Dragon.

Casino tokens and superyachts.

I get it.

4 Blue Dragon

Thomas Bell rose from the four-poster bed and walked over to a scenic view framed by tall sash windows.

Another bed, another bedroom.

Brass door knobs, high ceilings and solid oak floorboards.

Low-lying mist hung over the extensive parkland, almost obscuring the Egyptian obelisk at the end of one of the gravelled walks. Beyond that were grazing fields and acres of woodland owned by the estate.

Judy's father had a magnificent place down here in Dorset.

The cast-iron radiator was stone cold and he quickly felt a chill against his naked thigh. Best to go back to bed and snooze, even though he was wide awake.

He crawled back in between the toasty sheets and stared up at the silk canopy in the half-light, enjoying the peaceful silence. It was early, but a tray of tea was soon to be left outside.

He glanced around the room and noted a white marble fireplace with a French clock on the mantelpiece, long drapes and other examples of eighteenth century furniture. All that was missing was an inlaid harpsichord and a matching stool so that insomniacs could tinkle the ivories in the middle of the night.

It was the antithesis of Judy's London riverside apartment.

Bell turned his attention to the back of her head, at rest on the pillow next to him. He inched closer and stroked her cheek.

'I'm still asleep,' she said, without warning.

Bell slid up and morphed into the contours of her deliciously warm body.

'I know you are.'

'Well, then.'

'Well, what?'

'Make yourself useful and go downstairs to keep dad company at the breakfast table.'

'Aw, you seem fully aroused,' cooed Bell, cheekily.

He breathed in the aroma of her, tracing his lips across her neck and tightening his forearm around her stomach.

She turned towards her tormentor.

'Okay bedbug, all you're getting is a kiss for breaking the spell. I'll be down in a little while.'

'This is one hell of a bed.'

'So, we'd better not bust it up with your antics!'

'Solid legs and florid features,' teased Bell.

'I hope that's not referring to me.'

'A quick smooch?'

'Come on, out you get. Chop, chop!'

'I thought this was the queen's bedchamber?' he persisted.

Judy slipped both arms around Bell's neck, drew him closer, kissed him, and then pushed him away.

'Yeah, and I'm the queen bitch.'

***

Bell filled his plate with a full English breakfast of sausages, bacon, grilled tomatoes, black pudding, and toast.

He replaced the lid on the last of the serving trays and took a seat opposite the master of the house.

Ryan Madden looked back at him from across the table. He had traces of strain in his eyes. He appeared to be curiously distracted.

Madden worked through his food mechanically, simply to fuel up and get away to his office on the floor above.

The girls would rather still be in bed.

How much money did her dad really need to be happy?

Olivia, her father's new love, sat next to him, picking at melon, half-dried figs and a croissant. She gripped a large coffee in both hands and dreamed of villas in hot, faraway places.

Spending Ryan's millions.

So long as she was sucking from the sweet end of the lollipop, she was a happy bunny.

Judy contented herself with porridge followed by an egg on toast laced with avocado strips.

Madden would issue a High Court writ today.

His stake in a Dutch telecoms outfit had gone tits-up. It was an open-and-shut case of misrepresentation and false accounting but the case would still end up in the Court of Appeal in London. The failed company's chief finance officer had since departed to undergo a series of treatments for stress and a suspected nervous breakdown.

Madden hoped it was in one of those clinics in Switzerland which removed your frontal lobe and administered electric shock treatment.

Unfortunately, the Madden empire had more odious investment problems to deal with, in the Far-East.

Casinos, gaming licences and syndicates.

Skimming, money laundering and VIP gaming.

No wonder he was a nervous man.

Bell finished off with a palate-cleansing cranberry yoghurt spooned out in seconds from a stylish glass pot. A final gulp of Earl Grey tea wound up the proceedings.

It was time to wrap up well and burn off some cholesterol.

A bit cold and damp for late September.

Tom and Judy held each other arm-in-arm as they emerged from the back of the house.

'So, is Olivia stepmother material, then?'

'More like stepmother materialistic!'

The gravel paths wove through immaculate lawns, bordered by towering Lebanon cedar trees, revered since biblical times for producing an essential oil similar to turpentine.

In no time they reached the pink granite obelisk which one of the de Nazelle family had brought back from the Egyptian island of Philae in 1821. Bell knelt down to peer at the inscription which had been commissioned by the priests of Isis in 124BC.

Baffling hieroglyphs and Greek characters, but it wasn't quite a match for the Rosetta Stone.

'Tom, I'm going back. You stay out and play if you want to.'

Their cold lips met.

'You need something warm inside you,' laughed Bell.

'You're funny, you know that.'

'Whaddya mean? Do I amuse you?'

'Yeah, yeah, wise guy.'

Judy broke their tight embrace, clasping her leather gloves together. He watched her lovely arse make its way back to the main building and disappear inside.

The expensive, silk underwear could come off later.

The scent of a woman…it was hard to resist.

As a willing fuck buddy she was truly beguiling.

If she sucked in the sack it would be a different matter.

A workable arrangement.

As a single child, the oppressive influence of her father had fucked her up, therefore Bell had assumed a pleasurable obligation to keep on unfucking her.

***

Bell was alone, not far from the ha-ha which physically separated the formal lawns from the grass pastures. Groups of sheep stared at him, their steaming breath rising lazily in the still air.

It was chilly alright, but not as bad as some of those hikes he'd done with the Special Boat Squadron across Dartmoor. He turned back and surveyed the large square building that was Kearton Lacey, slumbering in the mellow light. The Chilmark stone was lightly illuminated by hazy sunshine.

It was a large house of Italianate palazzo design topped with a six-sided cupola. It boasted stables, outhouses, and even an orangery. Inside, baroque friezes of fleur-de-lys, irises, lilies, fruits and lion heads adorned the walls and ceilings. The exquisite interior décor had survived several centuries of enjoyment by a long line of de Nazelle aristocrats whose family motto was 'Velle quod vult deus' - 'Desire that which God wills'.

Although long gone, their legacy lived on, now in the temporary care of a wealthy global financier.

Bell jumped across the earthwork in one leap and headed out into the open fields, tramping through coarse, sodden pasture. After negotiating a dense strip of woodland, he came upon the kitchen garden, lying fallow, and an estate cottage painted in the age-old maroon livery of the de Nazelles.

He proceeded up a long, open incline to a high ridge. Here he stood amongst dense heather groundcover and sporadic pine trees to be rewarded with a sweeping view down towards Poole and Studland Bay.

It conjured up thoughts of traditional English beach holidays with plastic buckets and spades, miniature paper flags, dripping ice-creams and gritty sand between your toes.

Armed with a childhood nostalgia fix, he headed back down into the valley to circumnavigate the lake.

The ground became increasingly squelchy up to the water's edge. Bulrushes stood motionless in the windless conditions, waiting for the slightest breeze to blow away the fluff of their ripened seed heads.

Dodo island dominated the lake with the ornate form of a Japanese pagoda summer-house at its centre which stole the show. Bell thought back to the time when he and Judy had eaten breakfast there together, rowing out from the boathouse armed with cooked food in insulated containers.

Summertime and your daddy is rich.

He smiled at the memory.

As he skirted back towards the main house, he stopped for a moment to enjoy the vista of thinning mist still hovering above the sweeping lawns.

The early autumn sun was now high enough to reflect off the upper windows. Ryan Madden would be hard at work, putting the final touches to his legal claim, while missing out on the sheer enchantment of the vast property that he owned.

He'd be sitting in his office behind a large desk, surrounded by computer screens, betting on commodities and Eurobonds, even though he had a team of people to do that.

Madden couldn't resist a deal or a flutter.

Bell knew that the old man had diverse business interests worldwide but he hoped that he hadn't got mixed up with some tricky people. The sort of people who'd have your balls roasting on barbecue skewers if it turned nasty. Achieving that necessitated slitting your scrotum open to disconnect your plums from their ancillary pipework - just a tad more invasive than a no-scalpel vasectomy. Ultimately, it didn't make a vas deferens.

Something glinted on the edge of the treeline.

It was slightly odd.

The unmistakeable phut of a sniper rifle broke the silence, followed by the shattering of glass on the first floor of the eastern elevation.

***

At that exact moment, Ryan Madden leaned across his desk to touch a bust of Kaiser Wilhelm the Second. Kaiser Bill had visited the place in 1907 just seven years before the outbreak of World War One.

Madden patted his good luck marble effigy as a high-velocity bullet had entered the room and passed through the airspace previously occupied by his head. It penetrated the wall opposite, narrowly missing a painting by Chagall.

Despite a reward, the $28 million artwork had never been found following a robbery. The art world assumed that the lost Chagall was most likely destroyed, along with the rest of some trash in a dumpster when, in fact, it had been passed on as winnings in a poker game.

Madden hit the deck, shaking and hyperventilating.

***

Bell dropped low and circled around to where he'd seen the twinkle of light most likely coming from a high-velocity rifle scope.

The spot where the assassin had taken aim so carefully was self-evident. He saw the tell-tale imprints in the soggy tree litter and a discarded 7.62mm shell case.

A camouflaged figure was making a run for it through the trees. The little runt was hotfooting it like hell with his firearm but Bell knew that he would be forced to avoid the lake to get back to the outer parkland wall. The figure turned and looked in Bell's direction before continuing to leg it.

The estate perimeter ran close to the main road at that point. Bell could head him off before he got there.

It made sense, but Bell was unarmed.

Bell doubled back over the croquet lawn and raced into the ornate Japanese garden, past tightly packed walls of bamboo, and burst back out into manicured woodland.

Just as he got his bearings, he caught sight of a shape pressed motionless against a tree.

Don't look now…he was staring down a gun barrel!

Bell hit the dirt as a bullet exploded into the silver birch that he was crouched next to.

The gunman wasted no time making a final dash for it.

He was getting away.

As Bell caught up he could see that one of the estate team had jumped the fleeing intruder.

It was not going well.

The estate guy had been clouted by the rifle butt and was now on the ground. The gunman had drawn a commando knife to inflict a series of stab wounds on the hapless park warden. The first strike went through the ribs just as Bell got there. A shout in Mandarin from the wall attempted to warn the gunman of Bell's presence.

It was too late.

Bell struck the gunman's head with a birch wood stake which sent him flying. The sheer force of Bell's expertly delivered blow would have killed most people.

Unfortunately, it wasn't enough to stop this combat-hardened operative from staggering the last few metres to the wall.

Bell took his time and loaded another cartridge into the carelessly discarded Remington M40A5 sniper rifle.

The ergonomic curve of the wooden stock felt smooth and comfortable. He was now at one with the killing machine.

Two bullets, fired in close succession, coming up.

The ninja guy would normally have been up the wire ladder in a jiffy, but today the fleeing chipmunk was struggling. Concussion and a bleed on the brain had kicked in.

As the gunman was being hauled up over the ridge, wire ladder and all, Bell blasted ninja guy in the upper back. The second bullet caught his accomplice in the shoulder.

Both operatives fell backwards in a gruesome embrace on to the top of a van roof with an almighty bang.

It was a shame that the gamekeeping guys hadn't laid out some illegal gin traps to catch poachers. Well-oiled mechanical traps from the Victorian era, which were the latter-day equivalent of Czech anti-personnel mines, could still give you a run for your money.

'Poacher dies in booby trap'.

Bell could visualise the headline in the local newspaper.

The M40A5 had paid its way but there was also a discarded Chinese semi-automatic. It was a model QSZ-92 produced by the People's Republic of China.

It would have been preferable to capture and interrogate at least one member of the sniper team.

Bell guessed that Madden knew the score anyway.

Unseen, a diesel engine kicked into life and someone with a single useable arm drove off at speed. It wasn't such a piece of cake as the intruders had anticipated. The failed operation had a definite oriental flavour.

Interesting.

Unfortunately, Bell hadn't managed to get a facial look at the gunman. A blood-soaked balaclava had seen to that.

Poor Braithwaite lay groaning and bleeding profusely from his abdomen.

The ambulance was on its way.

***

Ryan Madden inched the precious painting further away from the bullet hole in the plaster. It had been painted by Marc Chagall in the year 1916, oil on panel, in the cubist style.

Madden's complexion was mottled with the effects of either anger, shock or fear…or maybe all three, but he still managed to speak.

'Just missed it, thank God…,' he grimaced.

'…and my head, of course.'

A new pane of glass had already been puttied into place by the estate handyman. Madden's office was airtight again but his heightened anxiety couldn't be alleviated quite as easily.

An array of computers were hard at it carrying out international arbitrage trading operations along the opposing wall. This involved betting substantial sums of money on split-second opportunities where tiny differences in identical assets were recognised and acted upon by sophisticated software.

Madden took no notice as the screens ebbed and flowed in cascades of red and green characters. He simply eased back in his chair and stared across his desk at Bell.

There were a few stark truths to be mulled over.

'Macau is the only place in China where gambling is legal. The authorities filled in a stretch of swamp land between two islands to create the new Cotai district which is now home to the Venetian Macau, the world's biggest casino. Five other mega casinos are located nearby. Macau's gaming revenue is three times that of Las Vegas.'

Madden switched his train of thought without warning and leaned forward, as though to allow matters in Macau to simmer for a moment.

'For an accountant you do seem to be very, er…capable.'

Madden raised an eyebrow.

'I like to keep fit,' smiled Bell.

'It looks as if Braithwaite is going to pull through. He could be out of the ICU in a week's time. Internal bleeding and a cracked skull - I think you saved his life.'

'Anyone would have done the same.'

Bell knew that it wasn't Braithwaite's fault. A high-level security posture wasn't part of his job brief. Estate staff spent most of their time dealing with animal fodder and raising pheasant chicks. Neutralising Chinese assassins was a bit of a stretch.

'The two shots that you fired were quite remarkable.'

'I got lucky, that's all. They still managed to abscond leaving only tyre marks in the mud,' replied Bell, trying to downgrade his handiwork.

Bell knew perfectly well that he'd hit one of them in the shoulder and that he'd blown the other one clean away. The assassin's accomplice had done well to start the engine and take off with a bloodied stiff on board. The van hire company would certainly be lumbered with a messy steam-clean job.

'Hmm, remarkable, all the same.'

'The gun was bolt action, just like an air rifle. Quite simple really.'

Madden wasn't sure that he was buying this.

His daughter's escort seemed to evince a calm, pragmatic approach which only came with special training. But more than that, he was cool and clear-headed under fire.

The important thing was that he himself had evaded death.

For now.

'Money isn't everything, you know. It's at times like this that I realise I may have lost sight of that. Sleeping peacefully at night has its plus points.'

'Big hat, no cattle,' smiled Bell.

Madden spontaneously roared with laughter and hit the desk with his fist. The adage was borrowed from his own personal repertoire of pet financial expressions and phrases.

Time to get to the point.

'Someone wants to kill me for my controlling share in a casino in Macau. That someone being my co-investors.'

'I get it,' said Bell, grimly.

Madden scowled and raked his fingernails down his blotchy, unshaven face.

'Skimming, side-betting and money laundering.'

Madden spat the words out and provided a detailed explanation of the nefarious activities which had ended up threatening his life.

'All I have to do it sign my share across and I walk away. My signature on a share transfer document.'

'But that might not be the end of it.'

'What I'm trying to say is that it's solely on my head. I shall have to deal with it. Whoever's gunning for me has a long reach from another continent. Chances are they have been casing the joint for a period of time which includes detailed surveillance of all my known associates.'

Bell pointed at himself without saying anything.

'Yes, sorry about that,' smiled Madden, lamely.

Chinese facial recognition technology had a pervasive scope, even as far afield as rural Dorset in England.

'Which casino is it?'

'The Blue Dragon.'

5 Chips with everything

'You have a technical update at the Hsinchu Science Park tomorrow morning,' said Lambda.

'More specifically at the headquarters of TMFC, the Taiwan Microchip Fabrication Company Limited.'

Lambda was already out of his office chair, holding his putter.

'I myself will be playing golf on the old course at Sunningdale,' he grinned.

His boss lined up six new balls with the tip of his walnut-tan brogue and proceeded to take aim. The first ball headed off across the carpet into the jaws of the Putt-O-Matic which gobbled it straight up. The regurgitation was more of a bronchial-patient wheeze than a healthy cough.

Low battery.

The sluggish machine decided to hang on stubbornly to the second ball and withdraw its labour.

'Soddit! The bloody thing knew I was on fire!'

'You can play like a demon tomorrow, Sir,' consoled Bell.

'Dead right I will,' sighed Lambda, returning to his seat.

Sunningdale's heathland old course is arguably one of Britain's most aesthetically pleasing inland courses. It was expertly laid out in 1901 on the magical Surrey-Berkshire sand-belt, not far from Ascot. Gracefully lined with pine, birch, and oak trees, it was reputed to be a splendid place to play golf.

Apparently.

Maybe one day, Bell himself would have the time to be hacking his way out of possessive bunkers, while learning how to hit a golf ball consistently.

Back to business.

Lambda's spacious office, lavishly decorated in the Parisian boudoir style, seemed to have acquired a new console table decorated with bronze fittings of swans, lions, and climbing grape vines. Another Napoleonic-era item on loan from the Victoria & Albert Museum, no doubt.

Lambda's manner became celebratory and upbeat.

'Commendations have filtered down from upon high regarding the success of the Oxford operation.'

'The Americans are particularly pleased with the result. Crucially, the US-UK railgun knowledge sharing arrangement remains intact.'

'Rewiring a plug can be hazardous,' smirked Bell.

'That high voltage stuff gives me the willies.'

'How's the flak?'

'Two technicians electrocuted in an industrial accident has attracted little press attention. It's taken something more salacious to hit the mark.'

'You mean a cross-dressing spook with a penchant for asphyxiophilia?'

'The inquest will soon get underway in what the tabloids are calling the 'Spy in the bag' case. In fact, you could say that it's turning into a media frenzy.

'I think it's safe to say that if you hadn't had occasion to terminate the PLA agent, Han Tu Won, who was unknown to us at the time, the security services would have been none the wiser as to the fate of the GCHQ analyst, Dylan Evans.

'Legal council will be calling witnesses from the Security Services. The Foreign Secretary has therefore issued a Public Interest Immunity Certificate to avoid the disclosure of thorny details in open court session.'

'In the meantime, the police are trying to prove that an auto-erotic sex game is responsible rather than criminal intent.'

Bell conjured up the vision of an unsavoury boil-in-the-bag contest taking place in the tiny bathroom of a flat in Pimlico.

'A squad of naked police officers lining up to give it a go?'

'Yes, a pretty sight for some, I'm sure. Only we know the full story,' grinned Lambda.

'What about the unidentified sets of fingerprints found in Dylan's flat?'

'The boys in blue are thrashing around wildly, just like I will be tomorrow, searching for my ball in the heather.'

'A verdict of death by misadventure, then.'

'Mercifully, yes. In a nutshell, we won two prizes in the raffle. Allow me to laud you for a most fortuitous outcome.'

'Thank you, Sir.'

'Pity…you would have been perfect for a couple of other similar jobs involving harmful sino-subterfuge. I'm filling you in on these because they have an indirect bearing on your next assignment.

The first is in Veldhoven, in the Netherlands, this time involving silicon wafer photolithography.

'The second is at an international company headquartered in Cambridge whose primary business is the design of advanced RISC processors and system-on-a-chip infrastructures.

'In both cases, the foreign interference perpetrators have been quarantined, without their knowledge, until they can be liquidated in a suitable manner.'

Two wet jobs: Cauterizing canker sores, leaving no trace.

Lambda pushed two sheets of paper across the desk.

'The Dutch company is under strict export restrictions for its most advanced machinery. It is, however, currently authorised to make shipments to the US where the equipment is to be used in new microchip factories in Ohio and Arizona.

'The Cambridge outfit designs reduced-instruction-set chips which execute only a dedicated number of command types. These integrated circuits operate at a much higher speed, performing millions of instructions per second, or MIPS. One of the primary end users is the United States military. For example, the fly-by-wire interface on the USAF F-22 Raptor and F-35C fighter jets.

'The scary issue is the existence of a hidden backdoor not in software, but a malicious modification added to a logic microchip at design time. A cyber-attacker will have complete access to any system or device that contains the backdoored chip, be that a PC in a corporation, a laptop, a smartphone or an IoT device.

'Adulterated supply chains are of grave concern, since most chips are fabricated overseas by third parties.'

'You're saying that a squadron of F-35s could suddenly drop out of the sky for no apparent reason?' said Bell.

'Precisely. A state-sponsored cyber-warfare joker could shut down a supercarrier's nuclear reactor with one mouse click.'

'I get it.'

It all pointed to one thing and Lambda beat him to it.

'Chips with everything!'

Bell took the opportunity to offer his own take.

'…which includes cars, microwaves, tanning machines, and toasters, but not forgetting the Putt-O-Matic over there by the wall. Your novelty device could easily possess its own SIM card, microphone, camera and Wi-Fi circuitry. Spitting out golf balls might not be its main mission.'

Lambda blanched slightly, observing his golf accessory with renewed suspicion. He knew that all MIX offices were subjected to regular sweeps in the RF range from 10 Hertz all the way to 24 GHz, but Bell had made a valid point. Chances were that the bloody thing had more computing power than NASA's Apollo 11 lunar lander.

'Undercover PLA operatives are popping up everywhere,' said Lambda, after a sobering pause.

'Like the arcade game: 'Whack-a-mole',' observed Bell, drily.

'That's the business we're in: mole extermination. There's a lot of catching up to do.'

Lambda took a deep breath to elaborate at length on the main agenda item.

'Tensions in the South China Sea are rising. China contests sovereignty over the SCS with the Philippines and Vietnam. Over time, China has cleverly weaponised various reefs, islands, and atolls with airstrips and military installations.

'Its primary focus is the island of Taiwan, located one hundred miles off the Chinese coast. It is regarded as a breakaway province and China wants it back. As far as the CCP is concerned, Taiwan is an inalienable part of China under the One China principle, therefore reunification must be achieved, by force if necessary.

'In recent months there has been an escalation in naval exercises in the Taiwan strait, in conjunction with increased incursions by PLAAF jets into Taiwan's ADIZ, or air defence identification zone.

'China's coastguard now claims it has the legal authority to stop and inspect all shipping in the area around Taiwan. As you might expect, Taiwanese vessels have been instructed not to co-operate with attempts to board and inspect them.

'This board-at-will move is seen to be at odds with the freedom of navigation principle which is recognized in international maritime law.'

'What do the Americans have to say?'

'Not much. Violation of the Law of the Sea which deals with matters such as navigational rights, sea mineral claims, and coastal waters jurisdiction is bad for global trade. It's fundamental that the Taiwan strait remains navigable to all comers without obstruction or impediment.'

'The red line which could kick it all off,' said Bell.

'Exactly.'

A third sheet of paper was pushed across the desk.

Bell read the brief carefully and let out a low whistle.

Mission objective: Unthinkable.

Mission survivability probability: Nil.

Lambda was aware of the extreme risks that MIX agents had to take. All in a day's work.

'The CIA have asked for some special help with this one.'

'Mischief in the South China Sea,' said Bell.

It was plain to see that regular Chinese naval blockade drills, supported by large numbers of aircraft, could easily turn into the real thing.

Acclimatise then surprise.

Be out shopping in Taipei one day when a blizzard of PLA tactical missiles start to hit their long-awaited targets.

The geographical implications and the archival background were well documented.

Taiwan sits in the middle of the 'First Island Chain' which includes Japan to the north, running all the way down to the Philippines in the south. If China took Taiwan, it would be free to project its power out into the western Pacific, most likely threatening US bases on the islands of Okinawa, Guam, and even Hawaii.

Historically, the imperial Qing dynasty ceded Taiwan to the Japanese in the year 1895. The Japanese then ruled the island for fifty years until the end of the Second World War. In 1949, Chinese nationalists fled from the mainland and governed Taiwan for the next several decades. The present day sees Taiwan, aka The Republic of China (ROC), ruled by its own constitution and democratically-elected leaders.

Other than that, why is Taiwan so important?

The answer is that Taiwan dominates the global production of microchips. Over sixty-five percent of worldwide output is fabricated in Taiwanese foundries. The technology developed in Taiwan is so advanced that everyone else is at least ten years behind.

The balloon appeared to be ready to pop.

Most likely a large meteorological example with surveillance capabilities cleverly incorporated into its weather-monitoring payload. However, it was going to take more than an AIM-9X Sidewinder missile fired from an F-22 to defuse the situation.

'The Japanese say that the Taiwanese are their blood brothers. That is why Japan has changed its postwar constitution and are re-arming as fast as they can,' said Lambda.

A mugshot flyer was the last piece of A4 paper to travel across the desk.

Mission creep.

'Just a routine arrest at Amsterdam's Schiphol airport. Nothing out of the ordinary,' assured Lambda.

The murderous eyes of a venomous Naja-atra cobra scowled at the police camera. Stylish, clear-lensed glasses failed to mitigate the intelligent malevolence of an uncooperative felon.

'Nothing can mean something and I might need to be worried,' replied Bell.

'It needs a steadying hand.'

Lambda had been anticipating a burning question.

As the briefing was almost over, he decided to get in first.

'No, you're not flying to Taipei, business class or otherwise. No flight to Taiwan at all, in fact.'

Just as Bell had suspected.

The MIX virtual reality suite awaited him, not the VIP departure lounge at London Heathrow airport. All he had to do was go up to the ninth floor in the elevator and get changed.

***

Thomas Bell pulled on his avatar suit and waited for something to happen.

Presently, a figure approached him in the virtual world.

Doctor Ning Chan.

Dr Chan was tasked with showing Bell what all the fuss was about. She had been passionate about chemistry from a young age and held a PhD in this alchemy-of-matter discipline. Chan's speciality was in the field of reactive halogens, particularly fluoropolymer compounds and coatings. The fluorine queen held a demanding, senior-scientist role for her employer, the chip maker TMFC, but lamented that she didn't get out as much as she ought to. She wasn't going to meet anyone nice at this rate.

'Are you ready?'

'Of course,' said Bell.

'Welcome to Taiwan. Let's start with chemical element number fourteen, shall we? You'll find it at the top right of the periodic table of elements, sitting between aluminium and phosphorous.'

Chan conjured up her first dazzling display.

A 3D atomic structure representation of silicon revolved like a beachball in front of them. Fourteen of everything: protons, neutrons and electrons, a member of the metalloid family. She snapped her fingers and a blue-grey lump of silicon burst into view as the dynamic beachball faded away.

'Silicon is a hard, brittle crystalline solid,' said Chan, as she coasted into the rest of her erudite patter.

Silica, or silicon dioxide, is the second most ubiquitous material on earth. From the dunes of the Sahara to the beaches of the Mediterranean, it is what silicon chips are made of.

A pure silicon ingot with a perfect monocrystalline structure is the first requirement. The process begins by melting raw polysilicon in a furnace to a temperature of over 1,371 degrees Celsius to purge it of impurities. The liquefied silicon is then spun in one direction while a silicon seed is lowered in and spun the opposite way.

Once cooled, the silicon crystal emerges from the crucible which allows technicians to test its purity and molecular orientation. It's then sent for wire sawing where the ingot is cut into thin, circular wafers.

Dust is a central concern for all semiconductor production.

Cleanrooms are employed so that silicon wafers can have intricate circuit patterns photo-etched on to them. A single dust mote, smaller than a fragment of DNA, can destroy a chip.

As this was a virtual tour, there was no need to wear bunny suits which safeguarded fabrication against human-introduced airborne particulates.

Unlike in the real world, where even the type of shampoo you used could be important. A dry flake of dandruff was equivalent to a huge tarpaulin in microchip terms.

'I didn't know that you had scalp seborrheic dermatitis!'

'I don't!'

They entered the next clean-zone where an overhead monorail system transported individually-numbered pods. Each pod contained chip components and was controlled robotically. Once the atomically polished wafers of silicon had been prepared, they were ready for the next part of the process.

Microscopic circuits are printed on to the face of the wafer and built up in layers. The lithography is carried out using extreme ultraviolet which has an incredibly short wavelength. Each circuit can include billions of transistors. There is so little room for error that the etched layers must be lined up correctly to a tolerance of a couple of nanometres.

The photoresist process begins by coating a substrate with a light-sensitive organic material. A patterned mask is then applied to the surface to block light, so that only unmasked regions of the material will be exposed. A solvent, called a developer, is then applied to the surface. It dissolves away the light-exposed regions, leaving behind a coating where the mask was placed.

Singulation is the breaking up of the finished wafer into multiple semiconductor chips. Fluorine plasma is used to leach away the material in the dicing lanes between individual units. Once this process is complete, the chips are ready to be packaged and fitted to whichever device they will end up in.

'Dead simple, eh? Any questions?' smiled Chan, folding her arms with satisfaction.

But it wasn't that simple, it was gobsmackingly complex - the reason why TMFC was the global leader in its field and the jewel in the Taiwanese industrial crown.

'How small can chips get?'

She threw her head back and laughed. After the mane of dark hair had settled back into place, a mirthful eye-squinch preceded her reply.

'Hey, pal. That's not any question. That is the only question, and I don't know the answer!'

Bell was bowled over by her authentic patois.

'Spoken like a true Brit!'

'Like an artificially intelligent life form, you mean.'

'Are you?'

'My neural networks forbid me to say.'

Bell racked his brains for an AI-busting question.

'What are you doing after work?'

'Not sitting in a bar with you, unfortunately.'

'Nice idea. Next time perhaps.'

'We can get high instead.'

'High?'

Was this turning into a pharmaceutical encounter with a sentient robot which was hellbent on getting stoned? Or, was Doctor Ning Chan actually a fun-loving, flesh-and-blood tease who couldn't help but play a flirty little joke on him.

Chan came close and held out her hand.

'Come with me.'

A spherical plexiglass cockpit, vectoring exhausts and mosquito-like alloy skids came into view.

Bell got her clever gag.

Chan's playful sense of fun, AI or otherwise, was beginning to grow on him.

'This is a recent software plug-in called Baburu Jetto. It's supplied by our virtual reality fabricator in Tokyo,' said Chan.

'A two-seater bubble jet?'

'Although the power plant is notionally twin turbofans, we'll be getting around mostly in hyperspace mode.'

As this was VR, Bell correctly surmised that this meant hyper-jumps to preset locations, in three-dimensional space, at the speed of light.

'I presume that your android operating system is running on the latest version?'

'Yeah, an upgrade which includes a testosterone boost for an underutilised libido.'

Bell felt that he'd got out of his depth. Time for a straight question.

'Are you an artificial person?'

'Come to my office when we get back. I'll freshen up with a few squirts of WD40. The smell of a penetrating oil formula turns me on.'

'You'd better drive, then.' said Bell.

'Strap yourself in, partner. Let's go.'

With star-buckles snapped shut and feet locked in the stirrups, Chan engaged the electronics. The console displayed speed and their 3-D Cartesian coordinates, both as GUI and as numerical registers.

Chan eased the joystick and they ascended smoothly skyward through the roof of the building.

The sensations of movement and G-force generated by the aircraft seat took Bell by surprise. The real world was now a distant memory.

The craft hovered in a static position five hundred feet above TMFC's fabrication building number three. Chan set the bubble jet to rotate slowly clockwise on its axis for a full, panoramic rotation.

The Tougian river estuary was clearly visible down below, disgorging itself into the Taiwan strait. They soon turned to point at the northern-most tip of Taiwan, way beyond the boundaries of Hsinchu County.

'You can see the capital, Taipei, from here. Look there's the unmistakeable outline of the Taipei 101 building.'

After viewing the mountain ranges that ran down the island's spine, they were back to facing due west again.

'We need more height,' said Chan, her painted fingernails skittering over the controls.

An instantaneous hyper-jump later, the digital altimeter registered fifteen thousand feet and a vastly improved view.

Chan turned to Bell.

'You do realise that our VR universe is refreshed every millisecond, virtually on a real-time echo basis.'

Bell could see directly across the Taiwan strait with brilliant clarity to mainland China and the province of Fujian.

Chan explained the geography.

'There's the city of Quanzhou, and slightly to the north is Putian. As we turn to the south along the coastline we can see Hong Kong and Macau, and further south, Hainan island.'

'So, we're now hovering inside Taiwan's ADIZ, close to the median line?'

'Exactly. China regularly violates our Air Defence Identification Zone. There are the Penghu islands, by the way,' smiled Chan.

At that moment the bubble jet started to shake violently. It was followed by a Chinese J-20 fighter passing only one hundred feet away. A second set of shaking, more violent this time, followed it.

A flying wing cruised past right in front of them, at first Bell thought it was a USAF B-21 Raider but the markings indicated otherwise. It was a PLAAF H-20 strategic bomber. There was no definite fuselage to see, just a tailless bat-shape gliding elegantly by. Bell noted its gleaming surfaces which concealed pods, blister protrusions, vertical stabilisers, and serrated air intakes.

'We'd better get back,' said Chan, ashen-faced.

'Trouble?'

Dr Chan turned to Bell with a smile.

'Yes, and I had wanted so much to tell you about my dirty little secret.'

'What?'

Bell hadn't expected revelations about her sex life. Not until after a few drinks, anyway.

'Some other time, I'm afraid. I expect to see you again in the not too distant future…hostilities permitting.'

***

Bell was on his own again.

His avatar suit felt clammy and confining. It was time for a comfort break from sensory overload in the Far East.

Two new figures came into view.

One in a Taiwanese army uniform, the other in a sharp suit.

'Please come with us Mr Bell…'

'…we have something to show you.'

6 Rubyland

'So, you don't feel like talking?'

Tucker Cole said nothing. His whole life flashed in front of him. Cole knew that his cover had been blown and that he wasn't going to dodge this one in a hurry.

He'd made a mistake somewhere.

Gao Zi Xin studied Cole's baseball cap for a moment.

'What does the 'A' stand for?'

'Atlanta. It's an American baseball team based in the US state of Georgia.'

'I bet that you wish you were back there right now.'

'Yes.'

A clear vision of the Truist Park stadium, the home ballpark of the Atlanta Braves, flared in Cole's mind's eye. Sitting in the stand with a hotdog, gazing down at the Stars and Stripes draped across the field before the big game began.

'You often wear a stetson. There's a lot we know about you, Tucker.'

The venomous snake drew a cruel smile.

Cole adjusted his body in its bindings, slumped awkwardly in the chair opposite.

Not getting out of this fix any time soon.

The American's winning smile of perfect teeth cut no ice in this scenario: cosmetic orthodontia, veneers, and bleaching. Cole was amazed that Gao's hoodlums hadn't smashed his pearly whites in already. Implants torn brutally from their titanium anchor points to leave a mush of bloody, pink tissue.

Gao had a tempting proposal.

'The deal is this: Tell me something useful and you get to play one last game of chance in my casino before I send you on your way.'

Cole guessed that his host had chosen his words carefully.

The endgame, the final play, and the last roll of the dice meant that the jungle kingdom of Laos would become Cole's final resting place. Chopped into small pieces and left to float down the Mekong river.

'I have nothing to say.'

'Let me see if I can loosen your tongue.'

A jeroboam-sized ice-bucket, made of clear glass, was brought in and placed on Gao's desk.

No bottle of Laurent-Perrier Cuvée Rosé champagne, sadly.

'Your card-counting accomplice, I think,' laughed Gao.

The severed head of Cole's wingman and long-time associate Zack was immersed in a cocktail of clear embalming fluid and formaldehyde. Soulless eyes stared back at him through the viscous liquid. The cause of death was not forthcoming.

'Ugh!' gasped Cole, in horror.

'Oh, are you okay, Mr Undercover CIA Agent?'

'No, I'm not oh-fucking-kay, alright!'

'This seemed to be attached to his leg.'

Gao threw down a card-counting device.

'We normally let people off with a warning and the loss of a few fingers.'

The sight of blood and gore came with the territory as well as that of internal organs torn involuntarily from their owners. It seemed strange to Cole that, so far, they had left him entirely unscathed. He suppressed a tell-tale wince at the implications.

Although born in San Angelo, Texas, Cole had been educated at the Valley High School in Las Vegas. Once the final bell had sounded, it was time to wander the casino strip with his classmates and check out the endless slot machines. It wasn't long before he'd graduated to playing poker and blackjack, and had the gambling bug coursing through his veins.

He was a sports jock with a keen interest in baseball, in particular as a control pitcher. His academic achievement was limited to an uncanny prowess with numbers and probabilities.

A hopeful Cole attended a trial for the Atlanta Braves, but disappointingly he wasn't selected. His underdeveloped physique may have been the reason. Lamentably, no Major League Baseball career for him and all the rewards that came with it.

Hence, a clear-cut job choice.

Mother, I'd love to...

MILF rather than MLB - as much of it as you could handle.

Expensive lingerie torn off in a hurry, lying on the carpet by the side of a king-size bed in a casino resort suite. Staring up at the ceiling afterwards, as a painted talon ran through your chest hair while the other liver-spotted hand held a cigarette.

Despite a skinny build as a youth, too many meals in fine restaurants ensured that he'd put on the pounds by his late twenties. As a successful, party-animal gambler, who invariably wore an Atlanta baseball hat at the Poker table, everyone knew him as 'Mad Dog'. He was instantly recognisable wherever he went.

That was exactly what the CIA were looking for.

A loud-mouthed Texan with a big hat, hiding in plain sight.

His father's USAF overseas postings, especially in the Far East, added to Cole's provenance. He was instructed to gamble at the world's finest casino-laundromats at the expense of

Uncle Sam, while picking up regular winnings and valuable intelligence.

What was there not to like?

Sure, he and his team of card-counters had been banned from a couple of establishments, but that added to his credibility as a high-roller living on the edge. His controllers, based at CIA headquarters in Langley, Virginia, didn't seem to mind so long as the intel kept on coming.

Until his luck ran out.

The Las Vegas strip and Miami cruise ships was one thing, anarchic hotspots in Southeast Asia was another. Casinos in dangerous places, most notably in the golden triangle where Myanmar, Laos and Thailand meet. Lawless jungles ruled by drug warlords, miles away from civilisation, but where you could sit at a roulette table nursing your pile of chips.

For Gao Zi Xin this was his home turf.

Gao suspected that this guy worked for the CIA but he didn't necessarily have to prove it.

As head of a drug syndicate, with representation in South Korea, Japan and the Philippines, he was managing annual drug revenue of twenty billion dollars from the distribution of synthetics in many countries, including Australia and New Zealand.

Methamphetamine, heroin, opioids, and ketamine. Volume production taking place deep in the tropical rainforests of Myanmar.

Syndicate operations included shipping precursor chemicals across the Pacific to the west coast of South America. Chinese commercial fishing fleets operating a covert delivery service. Precursor reagents such as N-BOC-4-Piperidone - this substance, like others, features on the US chemical regulatory list #1 because it has a high potential for abuse by transnational gangs.

The processor crews on the ground received training in efficient preparation methods for synthesizing illicit fentanyl. The finished product to travel north through Mexico for onward smuggling into the United States.

Gao had more than enough spare cash to bankroll a Special Economic Zone on the banks of the Mekong river in Laos. The place was wired off with electrified fences and dog patrols. Gao's private militia policed every inch of the massive compound which majored in sleazy hotels, brothels, bars, and a private airstrip.

Thousands of Chinese gamblers flew in to place bets and party legally in this zone, the jewel in the crown being Gao's magnificent Emperor Nero casino. Taking a prompt from the drug kingpin's playbook, Gao maintained an extensive menagerie of exotic animals which included tigers, hippos and alligators.

The Laotian SEZ was authorised to deal with foreign exchange transactions. A well-oiled money laundering operation dedicated to rinsing all the narco-dollars which were sloshing around.

All possible methods were employed to circumvent formal banking systems. Diversification of his organisation's asset portfolio into alternative stores of value was *de rigueur*. As in property, rare metals, crypto, and diamonds.

But the list was incomplete.

By some sublime accident of geography and geology Myanmar produces ninety percent on the world's rubies, in addition to sapphires and jade.

Fortuitous happenstance in Gao's backyard.

Specifically, the legendary Valley of Rubies, which is to be found in northern Myanmar. Large blood-red rubies, with vivid saturated colour due to the trace presence of the element chromium, were a rare wonder of nature, highly valued and easily transportable.

Gao knew that Europol, the CIA, and UNODC - the United Nations Office on Drugs and Crime, were all after him. Tucker was the latest effort to infiltrate his operations.

It was therefore unfortunate that Gao had no option but to make an urgent visit to the port of Antwerp in Belgium. It was a mess which had got out of control, and could easily escalate into an all-out war with one of the Mexican drug factions. The Alacrán cartel had a reputation for a long memory and a taste for vengeance.

A second intermodal freight container had gone AWOL at the port - a sea can full of cocaine missing in a sea of sea cans.

Huge numbers of suspects had already been rounded up awaiting interrogation. It was now difficult to get an appointment for the dentist's chair, but the extensive soundproofing was doing its job.

Gao had been warned by the authorities in Beijing to resolve the issue which had potential to harm the PRC's geopolitical ambitions, or he would be terminated.

Gao's anonymity, his team of kickboxing bodyguards, and endless payoffs had protected him thus far. However, his Chinese sponsors would have little trouble neutralising a pesky insect which had been the cause of interference with their global game plan.

The thought of it sent a shiver down his spine.

While Gao agonised over his trip to Europe, Cole racked his brains for a suitable snippet of classified intel which would be minimally damaging but useful. Cole correctly sensed that Gao was ready to issue his ultimatum.

'Is it a deal or the champagne bucket?'

Cole had his answer primed.

'You will be arrested at the airport.'

Gao knew that Taiwan had no extradition arrangements with the rest of the world. Therefore, the first leg of his trip from Chiang Rai airport in northern Thailand to Taipei presented no apparent risk. It was the non-stop business class flight to Schiphol with Thai Airlines that posed the problem, if that was what Cole was referring to.

'Which airport?'

'Sent on my way, you said?'

'You have my word on it.'

Cole doubted that what he revealed next was going to save his skin. He was dead meat with only a solitary white casino chip left to play.

'Schiphol.'

Gao pondered the response carefully. It was a sobering revelation. The authorities seemed to have his full itinerary in their possession. What else did they have?

So, the CIA, police forces from ten countries, Interpol and the UNODC would be waiting for him in arrivals.

How touching.

An onward flight to Guantánamo Bay dressed in an orange jumpsuit and jangly chains, perhaps?

He would see about that.

His organisation could turn this to their advantage.

Yes, turn everything red…red as blood-red rubies.

***

Cole attempted to twist his head but it was bound firmly in place. He found himself cuffed at both ankles to a stainless steel chair which was bolted to the floor. There were also suspicious heavy-duty electrical cables attached to the armchair's frame. His bare feet had been clamped on to a cold metal plate which he knew for sure was for the purpose of electrical conductivity, aided and abetted by his cold sweat.

At least he was arms-and-hands-free.

The bullet-proof glass chamber was constructed like a squash court inside a bigger, pitch-black space. He correctly deduced that his current location was a basement, deep in the bowels of the Emperor Nero casino.

High-lumen spots lit him with brilliant clarity from all angles as if he was a fresh corpse laid out for dissection on a mortuary slab. It was an analogy which was not a million miles away from the reality of his predicament.

Although blinded by white light, Cole could just make out a tiered viewing gallery beyond the glass back wall. Dark shapes moved quickly to occupy the last remaining seats, each with its own computerised betting console.

A full house.

A betting event for a specialist clientele, many of whom had flown thousands of miles to be there.

Tired of the turn of a card?

Sick of the spin of a roulette wheel?

Repulsed by the roll of a dice?

Prepare for the pull of a trigger.

Genuine jeopardy for the jaded.

This was why Cole hadn't been eviscerated.

A polished hardwood box lay within reach.

Beretta, Heckler & Koch or Sig Sauer?

He just had to know, despite being told by the baton-toting referee not to move a muscle.

Cole stretched out to open the box.

He was instantly electrocuted with a low voltage dose.

The loudspeaker blared into life.

'Don't move!'

The referee entered, emptied the box contents and swiftly retreated.

On the table in front of Cole lay a gun holster which trailed a steel wire down to a floor-anchored D-shackle. There was also a screwdriver tool and cleaning rod which seemed to form an integral part of the ballistic gift set.

The loudspeaker barked again.

'…remove the gun from its holster and we can begin.'

Cole was disappointed.

Not exactly a modern semi-automatic with a polymer handgrip, more of an antique. The Russian-made M1895 revolver had its place in history but it wasn't necessarily the handgun to blow your brains out with. A glimpse of the lanyard ring was the dead giveaway.

Cole handled the firearm carefully knowing that one 7.62mm cartridge was already loaded. The M1895 rotary magazine comprised seven chambers. The double-action officers' issue example he held in his hand was in excellent condition.

Whatever.

Seven trigger-pulls and he would be set free.

Spinning the cylinder each time to reset the odds back to an eighty-six percent chance of survival.

A last game of chance, yet roulette was his least favourite.

Just as Gao had cryptically promised.

All bets placed.

But there was a way to spoil this parlour game and screw up their carefully laid accumulator bets.

Quick and painless was a better option than an excruciating transmutation into a hunk of electrically cooked meat.

Cole took a deep breath and put the gun to his temple.

The audience in the viewing gallery cheered.

Trigger-pull number one.

The gun mechanism delivered a robust thud into his skull which he followed immediately with a cylinder spin.

Keep going now, you're on a good ride.

Odds always at eighty-six percent.

Trigger-pull number two plus a spin.

Trigger-pull number three plus a spin.

Four to go.

Now for the shocking, showstopper surprise.

If anyone came looking for his body they would have to be quick. There were well founded reasons why the Mekong river catfish were outsized monsters.

He lifted the revolver for the last time.

Releasing the cylinder enabled a rotation of the single cartridge round to the firing position. A Russian-made bullet - hah! What a way to die.

With the tip of the barrel pressed into his temple he gave the startled audience the finger.

'Fuck you, you fucking arseholes!' screamed Cole.

It was a last act of defiance.

No repentance or regret.

Cruise ships were the best. It was the faint hum of the marine engines that did it. How many lobsters had he eaten? how many gala dinners? how many girls with stilettos tottering behind him as they giggled their way down hushed, carpeted corridors in the early hours?

Yeah, a helluva ride.

His index finger tightened on the trigger.

The M1895 mechanism engaged and ended it.

'Mad Dog' Cole Tucker CIA MIA.

Gao Zi Xin smiled to himself.

The toss of a coin or the flight of a bullet.

The Law of Probability.

Gao had read the outcome in Cole's eyes.

7   Innocent passage

Alex Gallen had joined the CIA to see the world and what had he seen? He'd seen the sea: The Gulf of Mexico, the Caribbean Sea, the Pacific, and now the South China Sea.

Reassignment to the realm of hotels and casinos could be better. No more water except getting tan babes wet on Supima cotton bed sheets: softer, tighter yarns against smooth, moisturised skin.

Picking up tail not parasites. Gallen suspected that his head would explode from a surfeit of pleasure and excess, unless a stray dumdum found its mark.

A chick on each arm in the high-speed elevator riding up the side of the building, making your way to a deluxe hotel suite.

The antithesis of mud, blood and choco-chip face paint.

He'd earned his spurs amongst the vats of gasoline and acid used to process coca leaves under plastic tarps in the South American jungles.

Yeah, like tramping through tidal mangrove swamps in Belize or Honduras hunting narco-submarines packed with bricks of cocaine. If a bullet didn't get you, the blood-sucking leeches and mosquitoes would.

Covert CIA operations.

Specifically, the SAC or Special Activities Center, a division of the CIA responsible for covert paramilitary operations. Seal Team Six training had given him a tactical edge.

The only highlight: attaching limpet mines while press-ganged submariners, welded inside a watery coffin for a transatlantic trip they would never make, screamed and hammered on the sub's hull. Then, radioing in coordinates so that a square kilometre of virgin rainforest gets vaporised by a 'daisy cutter' BLU-82 bomb which contains six tons of ammonium nitrate GSX slurry. Evac by chopper followed by a shockwave and a fireball rising above the jungle canopy.

Back to base for a hot shower, a cheeseburger and a beer.

He'd seen plenty of ceilings alright, the present one being only nine inches above his face as he lay on a top bunk in a sweaty cabin.

As far as the crew of the supercarrier USS Atlantis was concerned, he was simply a commissioned officer on a special assignment. A notional naval rank of lieutenant for a CIA field officer on the job.

US Carrier Strike Group Five plying its way in the open ocean and he was along for the ride.

Starting point: The Yokosuka naval base in Japan. Arrival point: The Subic Bay naval base in the Philippines via the Taiwan Strait.

CSG Five was presently deployed to the US Seventh Fleet comprising nine vessels in tight formation.

The USS Atlantis, hull number: CVN-83, was a Gerald R. Ford class supercarrier. Its escort included two Aegis class guided missile cruisers which were equipped with BGM-109 Tomahawk missiles. Also, a destroyer squadron numbering three vessels of the Arleigh Burke class whose primary role was anti-aircraft and anti-submarine warfare. To round it off were two Virginia class nuclear submarines named the Mississippi and the Tang, and a fast combat support ship supplying ammunition, oil, and logistical assistance.

At least it meant some extended shore leave once they got there, followed by a comfortable flight back to Washington.

But there was a mission to complete first.

A baby-sitting job.

His pager went off suddenly, one of the alarm sensors had triggered it. He grudgingly clawed his way to the bunk edge to lower himself down on to a cold floor, and instantly hit the deck.

***

Gallen stood alone in a far corner of the hangar deck.

Strict instructions had been issued for no-one to touch his little baby which was parked next to an EA-18G Growler. Like serious quarantine: cordoned off with yards of 'Do-not-cross' tape.

'Stick to it like glue' he had been instructed.

Not unreasonable in that each one cost the Pentagon one hundred and ten million dollars. That was the standard off-the-production-line cost for an F-35C stealth fighter jet.

He ducked under the tape and got up close.

This is my F-35C Lightning II.

There are others like it but this one is mine.

It has my name etched into its outer skin.

A fuselage coating which would normally be fibermat radar-absorbent material but which had been deliberately substituted with an ineffective dummy substance. Also switched were all major components of its advanced avionics system which might tempt others, incapable of their own technological advances, to blindly copy them: Logic chips, software systems, sensor fusion modules, the lot.

He had monitored the process in a secure hangar at Lockheed Martin Corporation's site in north Texas.

A Trojan horse operation.

'Hey, can we swap out a DAS unit?' hollered a maintenance technician from behind the line.

Gallen deduced that this was the guy who'd tripped the sensor earlier.

'No chance,' was the courteous reply.

The carrier group had already skirted the southernmost outpost of the Japanese Ryukyu archipelago, leaving Ishigaki island behind them. In thirty minutes they would pass the northern tip of Taiwan and head south.

***

Rear Admiral Dan Martinez held his bamboo cane up against a map displayed on a huge digital screen. He'd never got on with laser pointers. Best to confine that technology to target acquisition. He was not known for sugar-coating it and he had the full attention of the briefing room.

'Welcome to the US Navy show. I'm your game show host for today, so pay attention.'

The laughter died away quickly.

'The PLAN is watching our every move on the water, in the air and from space, even their commercial fishing fleet has been sent out to meet us. They have the unique privilege of knowing where we are, so we gotta stay frosty.'

The Rear Admiral braced the bamboo cane behind the back of his neck with both hands and leaned menacingly over the lectern.

'Okay, you dumb bastards, listen up. We ain't had no aircraft crunches on my watch...so far anyways.'

A detailed chart displaying the bathymetry and ocean currents of the Taiwan Strait hit the screen.

'So, when we get halfway down the west coast of Taiwan we're going to stage the mother of all fuck-ups when a V-22 Osprey crash lands on the deck in a fireball. I wanna see plenty of smoke and a convincing slide of an F-35C as she goes over the edge into forty metres of water. We're tight on space so we need to get as much airborne as we can muster.'

The bamboo cane whipped through the air.

'We have to fool the PRC that this is kosher, you got that?'

CSG Five was now making its turn to port to navigate south after crossing the shipping routes which ran from Keelung City out to the Matsu islands: innocent passage along the median line of the contested Taiwan strait.

Martinez glanced in Gallen's direction.

'Don't ask why we're doing this. It's classified. Just make sure that we deliver a plausible pyrotechnic spectacle. I hope that the Chinese fall for it.'

***

As the USS Atlantis approached the edge of the Chang-Yuen ridge, a V-22 Osprey was expertly crash-landed onto the flight deck which sent Gallen's plane over the edge and into the depths.

Target GPS coordinates for the crunch were at 24°25.4500' N by 119°10.2333' E.

The carrier had hit the spot.

The bridge dropped the speed down to five knots while the fire was being dealt with. The smoke machines were doing a great job sending dense plumes into the sky while asbestos suits and hoses weaved in all directions.

With the Chinese coast being only thirty-five nautical miles away, it was expected that the PLAN would have a UUV on the scene pretty quickly. All that remained was for the supercarrier to limp down to the Philippines while nursing superficial fire damage.

Amongst the chaos of a raging conflagration it was reported that an American XQ-58 Valkyrie unmanned combat aerial vehicle had decided to go AWOL in midflight. It had peeled off from F-22 escort duty and headed due south on its own. The news was quickly followed by an urgent communication from Creech Air Force Base in Nevada.

Creech had lost contact with another UAV launched from the Atlantis, which was controlled via satellite from the US mainland.

It was an X-47B, a tailless, blended-wing-body jet aircraft capable of semi-autonomous operation, with live ordnance aboard.

Two UAVs in the space of ten minutes?

Maybe in the Bermuda Triangle, but surely not here!

***

One hour earlier…

Creech USAF Base, Indiana Springs, Nevada is a command and control facility engaging in daily operations of remotely piloted aircraft systems which fly missions across the globe.

Hal DiMaggio emerged from a Dunkin' Donuts outlet in central Las Vegas with a bulging variety box and jumped into his Dodge Ram Laramie V8. Within minutes he'd joined US Highway 95, heading north to his place of work.

After rigorous security screening, he made his way to the Unmanned Aerial Vehicle Battlelab complex, psyched up for a flying shift as a ground-based sensor operator.

He slumped himself down with a coffee next to the pilot and logged into his own console.

Their X-47B delta-wing UAV was already taxiing into position on the deck of the USS Atlantis. In a few moments it would be connected to the electromagnetic catapult.

'Where are we off to? Mogadishu or Djibouti? I've developed an unhealthy yearning for the Horn of Africa!' laughed Hal, getting comfortable.

'The Taiwan Strait heading south to the Pearl of the East for us today. We gotta be on special alert,' replied his partner.

'Yeah?'

'Ever heard of the Hainan incident, back in 2001?'

'Er…kinda,' bluffed Hal, slitting his shiny box of fried dough treats - sticky joystick time!

Hal bit into a plain sugared donut and took a slug of coffee. He couldn't wait to catch sight of the glass citadels of Hong Kong shimmering on the horizon.

Twenty minutes later…

Heading south with the Chinese city of Jieyang off the starboard wing. Status: Speed - high subsonic Mach 0.7. Range - 2,100 nautical miles. Condition - green.

'Holy shit!' screamed the pilot.

Loss of contact with no warning.

The pilot threw his hands up in the air. Hal lobbed a half-eaten choccy donut into the bin and stared at a frozen screen. All sensory control including imaging, infrared and night-vision had vanished.

X-47B gone rogue, totally malfunctioned…or destroyed.

How did that happen?

What the fuck!

***

The controlling officer at Hainan PRC airbase watched from the tower as the US X-47B made a perfect landing, followed by a renegade wingman XQ-58 performing an equally exquisite touchdown on the runway centreline.

The Lingshui base is in a highly strategic location, being part of the Southern Theater Command, and within easy flying distance of the disputed islands in the South China Sea.

The island of Hainan is also home to a People's Liberation Army Navy submarine base, an underground facility capable of supporting nuclear ballistic missile submarines.

'Come home to mama,' he whispered under his breath, 'I permit my mouth to be able to rejoice!'

He burst open a chilled tin of Future Cola and downed half of it, punching the air with a shout.

'Victory to China!'

This is our backyard, after all.

What did you mothers expect from violating our airspace like that? Go take a long, hard look at the nine-dash line and stay away with your imperialist fleets!

We gotcha with this one.

A perfectly orchestrated operation of deception. Both US craft had lost control to ground-pilot clone teams operating from the Chinese Lingshui airbase, opposite numbers to those based in Nevada assigned to the 432nd Operations Group. A catastrophic loss of contact and disappearance off the radar.

The UAVs taxied off sweetly into a bomb-proof hangar and were gone.

What would they discover in the bomb bays?

Hopefully, what the decadent West termed 'Easter eggs':
Valuable prizes in the form of precision-guided ordnance that
required de-arming.

The Shenyang Aircraft Design Institute would be more than
pleased to reverse engineer the US Skyborg autonomous
aircraft teaming architecture.

Both hijacked aircraft delivered in perfect condition, unlike
useless pieces of meteorological balloon debris scooped up
from the seabed off the US coast of South Carolina!

Easter egg thoughts had triggered the munchies.

Hmm…where's the chocolate? I'm sure I've got some M&Ms
stashed away somewhere.

Ground pilot teams the world over are never more than an
arm's length away from junk food sustenance. Hal Dimaggio's
opposite number at Lingshui greedily tucked into a portion of
Dico's popcorn chicken and an egg fritter now that the flap was
over. It would be rude not to wash it all down with a lemon-
and-lime Juizee Pop and sit back in triumph.

An urgent classified signal came through from Beijing.

The F-35C lying underwater on the lip of the Chang-Yuen
Ridge is a decoy and a trap. Our cyber teams hacked Lockheed
Martin and all the other F-35C component suppliers ages ago.
We already have everything.

The US beaten at their own game!

What's next?

The lost province.

8   Schiphol skip

Thomas Bell had a bad feeling about this arrest. Nothing out of the ordinary, Lambda had said. He waited patiently, propped up against a pillar in Schiphol's arrivals concourse waiting for Cathay Pacific flight CX 421 from Hong Kong to land. His quarry had already made the connection from Taipei to HK as the first leg of his journey.

Taiwan has no extradition arrangements.

The Australian Justice Department had prepared the arrest warrant and under international jurisdiction protocols had added a swathe of additional charges. Gao would then be extradited back down under to face a long sentence for flooding Australia with heroin, ketamine and methamphetamine. A long stretch in the Goulburn Supermax, located south of Sydney, awaited.

The Dutch Ministry of Justice had been more than obliging.

Operation Kanga had taken years of dedicated work to get to this moment. Bell knew that the senior officers on the case would welcome any chance to be present for this important arrest. It was the biggest opportunity they had to get the elusive Gao Zi Xin behind bars.

Being here came with an element of risk.

The Dutch police were handling this caper; he was just along for the ride.

Mantra: Expect trouble; if it can go wrong it will.

Eternal truth: Nothing could be something.

The plane was landing in thirty minutes' time and people needed to be in position. At least the transport convoy comprising an armoured prison lorry, police cars and motorbike outriders had been coned off at the kerb ready for the transit to Amsterdam's Vught high security penitentiary.

Gao would spend a few nights in there before the flight back to Sydney.

Bell had noticed something strange going on in the distance.

One after another, at regular intervals, solidly built individuals were disappearing through an unmarked door, the sort of nondescript doorway that led into a cleaning-trolley store.

They were dressed in different brands of jeans but all wore the same soft-combat-boot footwear favoured by special forces worldwide. Urban or maritime styles in dark grey, flecked with camo styling.

Fit, capable grunts entering but no-one coming out.

Restricted door access at Schiphol, even for toilet rolls, was safeguarded by an ANSI Grade 1 deadbolt lock, so it could be legit.

Maybe it was a squad of the elite Special Security Missions Brigade tooling up just in case there was any trouble. The presence of a BSB counter-terrorism tactical unit would be most welcome at this juncture.

So, who were those guys?

Royal Netherlands BSB involvement hadn't been mentioned, just a routine custodial procedure they had said.

It might be nothing.

Yeah, right.

Why hadn't this section of the concourse been sealed off?

Where the fuck was everyone?

The officers who had attended the briefing at police headquarters seemed to be missing.

Bell was getting a queasy foreboding.

Wasn't Gao Zi Xin known for always travelling with a posse of kickboxing hitmen? Bell guessed that if that was true his bodyguards would be located close at hand in strategically selected plane seats and reassemble as a flash mob once they had cleared customs. If some local muscle was in on it as well, the prize exhibit could get clean away in a melee of jostling and gunshots.

What if Gao was aware of his imminent arrest?

What had prompted him to leave his jungle lair in Laos in the first place?

Bell decided to up sticks and go for a wander.

***

Gao Zi Xin reposed quietly in a private Embraer Legacy 500 jet as it flew north over Cologne. It was a delicious pleasure to know that nine police forces from around the world including the UNODC and Interpol would be waiting for him at Schiphol airport. What they considered to be a routine arrest was going to be anything but.

At a list price of around twenty million US dollars his luxury aircraft was nothing so flash as to attract unwanted attention.

One of his normal entourage wasn't on board; that person had picked the short straw to carry out babysitting duties.

Schiphol arrivals area would be turned into a lake of blood.

Piling up corpses was only part of the plan. His desire was to cut off the head of the serpent which was stalking him across the globe. Identify the senior case officers and kill them. Create the environment whereby others would be reluctant to follow in their footsteps, too scared to place their feet in uncomfortably warm shoes.

Get off my back or die.

The amusing thing was that his look-alike stand-in, armed with a Cambodian passport in his name, would be arrested in error. He, on the other hand, would be flying into the sleepy backwater of Antwerp Deurne Airport where his jet would taxi discreetly up to the apron. A convoy of black Audis and BMWs would be waiting.

A different country for fuck's sake!

Belgium not Holland.

Sadly, there would be no time to sample Flemish architectural masterpieces in Antwerp old-town like the Grote Markt, Rubens' house, and the Cathedral of Our Lady. Important drug trafficking business would be transacted in the clinical warehouse buildings which lay in close proximity to the container port.

The aircraft descended, ready to land, passing overhead of the Scheldt river and the Westerschelde estuary. He could see the cape-size ships tied up in neat lines. The Doel nuclear power plant became visible as the plane flew through the steaming output spewing from its massive cooling towers.

Landing: Ten minutes.

Turnaround: Refuel back up to thirteen thousand pounds of Jet-A1-type kerosene and be ready for immediate dust-off. Crew on standby to utilise open departure slots scheduled over the next twelve hours.

So much better not to be touching down in Dutch jurisdiction but rather the land of chocolate, horsemeat and diamonds. Not to mention thick-cut Belgian frites, a local culinary delicacy double-cooked in beef tallow for a soft middle and a crisp outside and doused with Andalouse mayo sauce.

After the main dealings were concluded it was a simple aerial hop from Antwerp to Biggin Hill airport, situated to the east of

London and well inside its M25 orbital motorway. Gao planned to travel into the City to see a firm of lawyers and deal with certain matters in relation to the British Virgin Islands. London happily had one of the laxest national identity and company registration regimes in the world.

After due diligence in the Square Mile, the itinerary back to the Far East included various stopovers, the first of which was Istanbul.

***

Bell spotted a group of eight police officers at a popular restaurant chain called Lekker which offered traditional Dutch cuisine. He approached the senior officer and showed his Interpol ID.

'I hate to ask this, does the code word Kanga mean anything to you?'

'Of course, won't you join us?'

'You know that flight CX 421 lands in twenty minutes.'

'We'll be out on the concourse in time, we're just waiting for the apple pie to arrive.'

'Apple pie? Don't you guys want to be in position well before that?'

'The plain clothes team is making the arrest. They have the warrant.'

The apple pie was delivered by two waitresses.

'So, where's the operation coordinator?'

'In the bar upstairs. It's happy hour at the moment.'

'Huh?'

'Are you sure you're not hungry? We've all enjoyed the pickled herring. Shame though, it makes me fart!'

Bell knew that the herring came drowned in a preserving fluid of vinegar, spices, and cider. It was normally served with a generous slop of diced onions. He also knew that if these guys didn't get focused and on station they could end their day in their own vat of embalming fluid.

'Okay, where are the SWAT team holed up? I haven't seen them around.'

Bell sensed that the senior officer was itching to pour cream on to his pie.

'They've been told to stand down as it's just a routine arrest. Relax…the detainee will be on a flight to Oz in a couple of days. Buckle up and bye-bye.'

'Stand down?!'

No special weapons and tactics backup, then.

Bell checked the time.

There had been no prior warning of this crazy laissez-faire approach.

Luckily, he had come well prepared.

***

Back against his pillar, Bell scanned the area frantically.

01:42

Still no sign of the arresting team.

The plane had landed and the baggage reclaim indicator was registering on the overhead screen.

Any moment now, Gao Zi Xin would emerge and be arrested.

Or would he?

The admission at the police briefing that they had no record of his fingerprints or his DNA had taken everyone by surprise. Mislaid somehow, database record corrupted or some other bullshit.

Yet, the API flight manifest had him listed.

All of a sudden, uniformed police and high-ranking officers from multiple jurisdictions appeared. For some, especially the ones wearing dumb ID lanyards, this was an exciting trip away from the office to experience some live action in the field, despite the danger. They were not to know that a hideous fate awaited them.

01:45

All other passengers had filtered out of the Customs hall and had gone on their way by now.

The last two travellers off the Boeing 777 finally emerged into the open. 888 would have been a better Chinese lucky number - the harbinger of great fortune, wealth and spiritual enlightenment rather than fraud, deception and death.

Gao Zi Xin and one of his personal bodyguards walked close together and came to a halt. Gao was dressed in grey business attire and silk tie, while his minder glowered in a loose-fitting shell suit.

Bell recognised Gao's intimidating escort from the grainy mugshots he'd seen. Known to the authorities only as Waiwai, a Cantonese nickname, he was a shadowy, hardened executioner for Gao's organisation. An authentic and seriously dangerous narco-corporation enforcer, seemingly on a child-minding errand this evening.

His speciality was grinding up human bodies mixed with rotting fish scraps into unidentifiable bait chum spiced with concentrated fish oil. The vomit-inducing, glutinous paste didn't last long once it had been dumped into remote tracts of jungle rivers.

Try running a DNA test on that.

Waiwai was also engaged to trim fingers off careless card counters with a torafugu cleaver. If you were really in trouble you'd be filleted and prepared as slices of sashimi. Despite his size, he could move like a ballerina and have both of your eyeballs skewered on a chopstick before you could blink.

It was Gao who didn't come across as the real deal. The face matched, but the venomous glare of a psychopath was missing. It occurred to Bell that he had the look of a hapless doppelganger who had undergone painful plastic surgery under duress.

Yeah, fingerprints and DNA – that would have been handy.

What was also absent was Gao's main bodyguard, schooled in the martial disciplines of Muay Thai and Krabi Krabong. If a kick didn't find its mark, you'd simply be run through with cold steel.

The smart money said this whole thing was a trap.

The bets were also on that the real Gao Zi Xin had concurrently flown into Europe with the remainder of his barbarous retinue.

What better than to kidnap or kill the senior police officers working on his case?

The cocksure investigators were all as good as dead.

They needed round-the-clock protection and not to be easily accessible while out and about.

Murdering witnesses was *de rigueur*; disposing of the entire prosecution team was one better.

The arresting officers stepped forward with the warrant and handcuffs in an effort to arrest the Gao-looky-likey stooge. On cue, combat operatives emerged en masse from the cleaning-trolley store to surround them.

Resistance was immediate and the uniformed officers were easily mown down in a hail of gunfire, their handguns being no match for a close-quarter, sub-machine gun onslaught.

A sea of blood, guts and death ensued.

The remaining personnel were rounded up, hooded, bound, gagged and frog-marched off in short order to the exit where their transport to hell waited for them.

Gao and Waiwai were ushered safely away, surrounded by a protective group of fighters.

The arresters had become the arrested.

The fire alarm had gone off and the emergency fire doors had closed. Other alarm bells had joined in. The noise was deafening.

A salvo of aerosol-anaesthetic grenades had been launched into the four corners of this sealed-off section of the concourse to neutralise any innocents unlucky enough to be caught up in this. Bell guessed that it was remifentanil, an opioid analgesic drug used as an adjunct to anaesthesia, suspended in the sedative agent halothane.

Bell had been quick enough to pull on his JSGPM combat respirator while dodging bullets and taking cover behind his pillar.

He was on his own.

Very soon he would be set upon.

Bell slipped the bulging sports bag off his shoulder.

Best to be well armed, can't be too careful. No advance notice was given that a hollowpoint round had your name on it and that you had taken your last breath.

Bell primed an M67B fragmentation grenade. He rolled the spheroidal device across the concourse floor and immediately bowled another.

Two explosions shook the building to its foundations.

His action elicited unwelcome attention which triggered a blizzard of automatic gunfire, shattering the pillar's marble cladding. Now curled up behind a bare concrete pile, he responded by lobbing a couple of M13 phosphorous canisters in the direction of the tragic bloodbath. Dense white smoke smothered the ongoing violence as wounded police officers were mercilessly dispatched with a bullet to the back of the head.

Bell had seen enough.

It was time to go.

Just a hundred-yard dash to a service stairwell descending to the subterranean car park.

He didn't want to be followed.

Bell shook a group of AIAs out of his goodie bag. They immediately initialised and sprung across the floor to take up defensive positions, automatically matching their body colour to the cream marble surface.

Eight eyes and bristly vibration sensors on alert.

Better watch your step.

A moment later, two BSB unit imposters, armed with Heckler and Koch HK416s and Glock 26 semi-automatics, emerged through the phosphorous pentoxide vapour. The clever bunnies had correctly identified Bell as a situation anomaly.

Bell was no match for them, armed with just a 9mm Sig Sauer pistol. A small mirror enabled Bell to see around the corner and monitor their vigilant approach.

Then a scream.

The first artificially intelligent arachnid jumped and gripped hold of the leading guy's calf.

Its miniature hydraulic joints clenched like a vice while its prey hollered. The tarantula-sized AIA sensed the pulsating flesh beneath its underbelly and injected a lethal dose of fast-acting Taipan snake venom.

In the meantime, another AIA had latched on to the thigh of the second unfortunate who sensed what was coming.

Body armour ain't gonna help you, buddy.

More screams of terror.

The spiderbot considered its options and decided to detonate itself in an unselfish act of self-destruction, blowing the poor grunts's leg clean off. A severed, bloody femur landed close by.

Bell's hairy-legged progeny didn't have him in their sights.

They knew that he was the mummy spider.

Let's get out of here, guys.

The remaining beasties required no prompting to jump back into his bag.

Bell made the dash and disappeared down the concrete steps to the valet parking level.

***

02:56

The exit barrier saw Bell's Mercedes-AMG E-Class Sedan cruising out on to the airport slip road and merging with a southbound lane of deserted motorway.

The convoy was five kilometres ahead of him.

The specially adapted MIX vehicle had all the necessary comms links and other tactical modifications.

All of a sudden he was hungry.

Damn! He should have wolfed down some apple pie earlier.

Happily, he remembered a bag of poffertjes he'd bought from a patisserie hours ago: small fluffy pancakes dusted with sugar. They would keep him going as he tailed the convoy south.

An MQ-9 Reaper had taken off from Spangdahlem Air Force Base in Trier, Germany, four hundred kilometres away. The unmanned aerial vehicle was relaying high definition images and video to the car's built-in screen consoles. Not only could the UAV track up to ten targets simultaneously, it could read a licence plate from two miles up.

Not so grim.

Its turboprop engines gave it a long loitering endurance and Hellfire missiles or Paveway II laser-guided bombs could be launched at will. The CIA, in conjunction with the DEA, had kindly obliged Bell's field requisition.

Just as well because no police helicopters were available.

The convoy was making sedate progress on the A4 motorway.

Bell could follow at his leisure in the Merc and be ready for the moment when they stopped to make a vehicle changeover.

So, where was the real Gao?

At what point was he going to get a look at snake-eyes in person?

Bell had at least been responsible for the death of five of Gao's foot soldiers. It wouldn't have been right that the transnational super-villain had got it all his own way. Unfortunately, at least six of the investigation team had been kidnapped to face torture and certain death.

He may not be able to save them.

Presently, the convoy turned off at junction 4 to arrive at the southern tip of the Westeinderplassen or West End Lakes. The vast area of inland water and wildlife sanctuary was sparsely populated but also hosted a large marina complex and a sprawling maze of boatyards and sheds on its banks.

The UAV ground control station reported the switch to Audis, BMWs and a Toyota Land Cruiser. A small contingent had broken away to leg it to a waiting helicopter.

Still dark…sunrise in two and a half hours.

Ultimate destination?

If not Rotterdam, the convoy would probably continue to head south on the A16, hopefully to wherever Gao was holed up. It was tempting to blow the chopper out of the sky, but better hold fire for now.

Bell's money was on Belgium.

What was on offer?

Finely-ground cocoa-bean chocolate, smoked horsemeat fillets and the port of Antwerp…and maybe some invasive dentistry.

The police had become aware of other wretched souls who had been snatched by drug gangs in recent weeks. According to the testimony of reliable informers: The abduction of bribed port managers, crane operators, and admin staff who were required to shed light on the unfortunate disappearance of several narcotic shipments.

The big players were blaming each other and wanted answers.

If your teeth ached or you thought that you had an abscess there was no need to worry…an appointment in the dentist's chair had already been made for you.

Plomo y acero.

Lead and steel instead of lidocaine and titanium.

Pliers not periodontal care.

Was it going to hurt?

You will curse your mother for bringing you into this world.

9   Gibbering gibbet

The hitman from the Alacrán drug cartel had enjoyed his business class meal. Other members of his team were dotted around the aircraft in economy, tearing at cellophane wrappers to release their unappetising contents.

A direct Lufthansa flight from Mexico City to Frankfurt.

MEX-FRA: Flight duration: 10 hours and 55 minutes.

Julio de la Concepcion Silvestre, a tall, slim individual, concealed a sinewy physique beneath his lightweight suit. His cold dark eyes missed nothing.

Julio Silvestre, also known as El Cartero, was a professional assassin who had joined the Mexican army as a teenager. He became a highly trained marksman and commando, taking part in black operations, having received specialist training at the Military School of the Americas in the United States.

Attributes: Fierce loyalty and merciless cunning.

He spent the latter part of his military career as a member of the army's elite Airborne Special Forces Group (GAFE), apprehending drug cartel members. Motto: '*Not even death can stop us. If death takes us by surprise, we welcome it*'.

Seeking higher rewards, he had switched sides and had ended up working for one particular drug lord as a paramilitary commander.

His boss, the narcotics kingpin, Don Salazar, had entrusted him with the execution of yet another odious job. In Europe, this time. An old world continent which had perfected the art of retribution and cruelty many centuries before Hernán Cortés had set foot on the Yucatán peninsula in 1519.

Landing in thirty minutes.

He always felt crabby after a long flight, especially when it might be your last.

The trek wasn't over yet.

A final leg into Belgium via Brussels, then things to do and people to kill in the port city of Antwerp.

Two missing containers of cocaine.

Unacceptable loss of product and compensation for inconvenience caused.

A debt to collect.

A transgression to be punished.

***

Bell parked the Merc and hauled his bulging sports bag out of the boot. After a bit of effort and a fortuitously placed inspection ladder, Bell found himself lying out of sight, flat on the roof of a meat processing factory which was located on the banks of the river Scheldt.

Kalkip Vlees BV was a turkey processing exporter who specialised in shipping prepared fowl products worldwide using refrigerated sea containers. It was part of the Kalkip group of companies which had gone tits-up only recently.

Operation Kanga was led by the Australian Federal Police and supported in different ways by multiple law enforcement agencies with interests in the case, including Canada and the US Drug Enforcement Agency.

It hadn't gone well or rather it had been a total fuck-up, and now a conspicuous motorcade of seven vehicles had given Bell the slip at the last hurdle.

The convoy had disappeared into a maze of covered rat runs which serviced a vast area of identical warehouse buildings.

MQ-9 tracking from twenty-five thousand feet, utilising the Reaper's synthetic-aperture radar, had gone out of the window.

The idle Kalkip plant seemed to be the most likely hideout but he could easily be mistaken.

No movement, vehicles or personnel.

Just a shrewd hunch.

Nothing tangible to report.

Although in a peripheral role, the US-UK liaison team had specifically made a MQ-9 available to augment the police helicopter surveillance which had been annoyingly absent.

The Netherlands boasted a nine-strong helicopter fleet of EC135s and AW139s but they were all in for routine maintenance at the same time. Probably a jobsworth in police administration, whose palm had been greased, had shunted the scheduling despite being in total contravention of the aerial surveillance SLA.

After the cross-border pursuit, the USAF ground control station in Trier undertook to keep its UAV circling overhead in a stable holding pattern.

There was nothing for it.

He would have to break in and take a look.

***

The peppery prickle of guano dust assaulted Gao Zi Xin's nostrils as he entered the deserted factory from the warehouse next door. Industrial heaters were whipping up a vortex of warm air which made matters worse. The stench was comparable to an unventilated indoor bird market on a hot day. A breathing apparatus was doubtless required to mitigate the chance of contracting histoplasmosis or even avian influenza.

What a shithole.

A fucking turkey factory!

The cartel delegates were due to arrive within the hour.

Waiwai supervised the preparations for the forthcoming meeting. A large square of carpet was rolled out over the concrete floor to give the place a hospitable touch.

Chairs, tables and snacks.

Bottled water, filter cigarettes and ashtrays.

Notepads, pencils and calculators.

Gym bags packed with US dollars and euros.

A whiteboard easel was inched into place.

Lines of fire and blind spots checked.

Firearms kept well out of sight.

All designed to conjure up the façade of a civilised corporate discussion.

Gao grabbed a seat for a minute and collected his thoughts. His ballistic body armour was a bit tight but he could live with it.

The arrest debacle was being broadcast on every single international news channel, focusing on the sheer scale of death and destruction at Schiphol's Terminal Three.

Five of his men down. Their corpses were regrettably going to assist the authorities with their enquiries.

Three blown away in two grenade blasts and two others taken down in an ingenious manner.

White phosphorous munitions deployed.

Clever.

A lone wolf had played him and was still out there.

Everyone had been paid off except the DSI, so was it a solitary counter-terrorism grunt who just happened to be in the vicinity? Simply bad luck that a Special Intervention Service agent had got involved? A major incident specialist who knew how to kick ass in a firefight. The choice of military ordnance put to deadly use said a lot.

It all pointed to the Dienst Speciale Interventies elite police unit...were it not for one crucial detail.

Gao studied the mechanical claw carefully and noted the life-like hairs, still coated in dried blood, protruding at regular intervals. It belonged to some kind of mechanical crab.

It screamed DARPA, the US Department of Defense responsible for the development of innovative military technologies.

That meant the CIA for sure, and probably the British MI6 who always got to try out any new kit.

Whatever.

Time to concentrate on the matter in hand.

He was going to be short-handed for this vexed face-off.

***

Bell began his traverse of the slanting roof panels. He could see an access hatch in the distance next to inspection grilles, a handrail, and some vertical exhaust flues.

Halfway there his MilChat communicator dinged.

'04-0010_DIR_xp_10:52'

Bell answered the USAF deployment instruction request with an order to stay overhead for another two hours. Wise not to be short of air-to-ground missile capability at the wrong moment. Response: The fuel status dictated that they could only give him another twenty minutes.

Hmm...nothing he could do about that.

He knew that the eye-in-the-sky was monitoring his every move and that they could probably read the label on the back of his pants.

As Bell got to the handrail, three cars drew up outside in the courtyard below. The vehicles were immediately surrounded. A group of people got out. One of the new arrivals looked strangely familiar. Bell focused his binoculars on one specific individual.

Hah! He'd recognise those snakeskin boots anywhere.

The lean, gaunt looks of a sicario from the Alacrán drug cartel were unmistakeable.

It was El Cartero, the postman.

He who always delivers.

It had been a close shave working alongside him in Ibiza. The last time Bell had seen Julio Silvestre was when they had lunched together at the Fenecia Prestige hotel in Santa Eulària des Riu, toasting their good fortune with Spanish brandies.

Well, I'll be damned, Julio, you crazy bastard!

The bastardo loco was up to something.

It could only mean big bucks and serious trouble.

Plata y plomo.

Money and death, but the guns weren't out yet.

The delegation was shepherded into the building in a politely respectful manner. Whatever the confab was about, it might not continue indefinitely in the same courteous fashion.

Gao had to be in there waiting.

There still might be a chance of making an arrest.

It was clear to Bell that the airport had been a decoy-trap and that the hostages, or what was left of them, may be on-site.

Better hurry up and find out.

The glazed hatch offered little resistance and a ladder led down to the uppermost floor level. Bell stealthily worked his way through partitioned spaces and extensive ductwork. An inactive conveyor system for hanging turkeys by their feet ran the full length of the building. Refrigeration units and pipework were everywhere. What really hit him was the smell.

Bird feathers and dust, a lot of it.

What else would you expect from a poultry processing facility?

The fine allergen particles caught the back of your throat and affected your eyes. Prolonged exposure to this environment would eventually see you suffering from asthma, allergic rhinitis and conjunctivitis.

Beware the involuntary sneeze or cough.

Voices could be heard echoing somewhere in the distance.

Bell inched his way along in the near darkness towards the source and searched for a concealed vantage point which would give him a clear aerial view of any ground-floor activity.

He found himself in the area where the fresh turkey carcasses were transformed into something that you could chuck into an oven: birds suspended on the conveyor hooks before having their throats cut.

Slaughtering first by electrical stunning and severing the jugular vein at the ventrolateral base of the bird's head. Then scalding, de-feathering, evisceration, and spray-washing. Stainless steel troughs lined the walls, most of them contaminated with mouldy, bloody goo.

Bell became aware of plaintive mewing and the creepy sound of persistent chafing, metal-on-metal, somewhere in the gloom.

His red-light LED torch drew him towards a human-shaped iron cage hanging from the turkey-conveyor track. There were dozens of occupied cages packed together, backing up the line.

The enclosures resembled gibbets, a confinement device which had been legally codified during the eighteenth century as a death sentence punishment.

If you were a convicted highwayman or a pirate you'd be suspended in one, close to the low-water mark of a tidal river, to die. Your decomposing flesh would gradually be washed away to leave a handful of sun-bleached bones as a testament to your former existence. The pestilential stench acted as a powerful warning to others. In modern times it functioned as a deterrent against getting caught up with organised crime syndicates, so it would seem.

A penlight beam, shone through the rusty slits, illuminated a gagged and bloodied human head. The shaking and whimpering stopped. A woman's eyes opened in terror, staring vacuously into Bell's dazzling, white torchlight.

There were no locks on these wicked coops; they were all spot-welded shut. She was bound tightly at the ankles and her wrists were trussed behind her back.

Bell reached in and gently tugged at the woman's duct-tape gag. Snot and blood continued to dribble from her wonky nose as she struggled to breathe. With difficulty, he eased the tape away from her mouth without tearing her delicate lip flesh. She was in bad enough shape already.

She gasped as the last bit of adhesive peel came free.

'Save me!' she spluttered.

Most of her front teeth were missing and her nose had been broken; it was a dreadful sight. Bell recognised her as one of the forensic accountants who had attended the police briefing and been present at the airport.

Everyone banged up in the line had been brutally tortured. A glance at the concrete floor revealed that it was awash with blood and urine.

It seemed to Bell that the interrogation phase had been concluded and that this barbaric method of incarceration, apart from being a space-saving hack, held some other sinister purpose.

He lamented that he could do nothing.

'Later,' whispered Bell.

But later might be too late.

Bell headed back to a vertical slit which cast a dagger of light along the floor, to take up a position of concealment in the darkness.

He unzipped his armament holdall and laid out his firearms of choice. The location offered a panoramic view which enabled him not only to see everything but to listen in to the proceedings taking place below.

The high-level discussion was already underway.

Silvestre and Gao, face to face.

The Mexican was speaking and Bell could see only the back of Gao's head.

What a shot that would be!

A bird in the hand.

The authorities would never forgive him.

Their foremost priority was a fruitful interrogation into the workings of Gao's transnational organisation, followed by a lifetime incarcerated in an Aussie supermax.

Best to keep his powder dry.

***

Silvestre was acutely aware that they had not been asked to surrender their firearms. He suspected that he and his five-strong team had been channelled through a concealed airport scanner without their knowledge. Evaluation of the metal they were packing gave their host an initial advantage.

When the bullets started to fly it would be six against seven. Waiwai's reputation for unalloyed violence preceded him and was one to keep an eye on. Meanwhile, it was time to ditch the small talk and make the first move.

Pawn to D6.

'CNN says that you've met your demise.'

'As you can see, the reports are exaggerated,' smiled Gao.

'The Dutch police have revealed the recovery of your body.'

'A body.'

'Ah.'

'A stray bullet got me.'

'Or a well-placed bullet?'

'It will buy me some time.'

'Enough time to cross my palm with silver?' grinned Silvestre.

Plata o plomo – silver or lead.

'Shipment number thirty-five was impounded by customs following a tip-off. Three tonnes. Okay, it's our loss.'

That was a whole lot of pure cocaine destined for incineration, not noses. A tonne: a non-SI unit equating to the mass of one thousand kilograms.

Rustic production: Hundreds of hectares of coca leaves yielding a tiny amount of cocaine-alkaloid paste per tonne of raw material. The stuff gets processed covertly onsite under black plastic tents while anti-narcotics Black Hawks, flying overhead, surveil the jungle below. Once you had a dry, yellowy-white block, the spent leaves, contaminated with the toxic conversion chemicals of gasoline, ammonia, and cement, are simply dumped into pristine rainforest streams.

'Exactamente. Ninety million euro.'

'Currency or crypto?'

'Bitcoin.'

Silvestre held his breath as the transaction was added to the blockchain. Half-way there.

Gao leaned forward and took a loose cigarette from the jade display dish. Silvestre stopped himself and dug out a fresh pack of Marlboros. The filter-tip freebies could easily be laced with potassium cyanide or a nerve agent.

'I prefer my own,' said Silvestre.

Now for the crux, the instrument of torture and misery.

'Shipment number thirty-nine was stolen by a rival gang,' said Gao.

'Six and a half tonnes,' exhaled Silvestre, soberly.

They both knew that the damage was one hundred and ninety million euro.

'We've interrogated everyone and we have all the answers. Only a small fraction of the original consignment has been recovered.'

Silvestre turned up his palms and grimaced.

'So, you're unable to pay us?'

'I want to be honest with you.'

'Si…bueno. What are you offering?'

'We pay you in instalments.'

'¿Más tarde? ¿Hoy no?'

'We need more time.'

There was no suggestion of any payment on account which needed to be at least one hundred million euro. Silvestre discerned what looked like sports bags full of cash, piled up against one of the nearby tables. They had to be the redundant shipment number thirty-five cash option which had been superseded by the use of Bitcoin.

'Although our respective organisations are partners, more time is something that you don't have, mi amigo.'

'Are you threatening me?'

'No, I'm preparing you.

'For what?'

Silvestre carefully retrieved a sheet of paper from his jacket pocket and pushed it across the table. Gao perused the typed schedule.

'Details of secret storage locations, incineration plants, and transit dates. The Belgian authorities have a backlog of twenty tonnes of cocaine to dispose of,' said Silvestre.

'You expect us to risk a crazy raid based upon this?'

'The intel was provided by an unimpeachable source within the douane seizure administration. It's on us.'

'Thanks, but things are too hot at the moment.'

Silvestre persevered with selling the idea.

'Minimal security and surprise: just walk in and snatch it! The stuff's stacked neatly on pallets, so what are you waiting for?'

Silvestre sensed that Gao was drowning in so much shit already that he would reject a totally viable plan to make everyone happy. It was a quirky proposal which had legs but was also designed to disrupt the flow of the meeting. An angry, irrational and unhinged negotiator was easier to deal with. Whatever happened, the Alacrán cartel wasn't going to leave empty-handed.

Gao smashed his fist into the table, stood up and snapped his fingers.

'Incineration? Just stroll in and get it, eh? Let me show you something.'

The turkey conveyor line behind them burst into life. The noisy trackway was on the move, bearings grinding and squealing as unladen hooks clacked past. Seconds later, the gibbet train came rattling into view, metal cages clanging and rubbing up against one another.

The procession came to a halt suddenly, the first six gibbets left of centre, swinging gently, were the police investigation team who had been abducted at the airport. A second group comprising seven persons, separated as a follow-up batch and occupying right of centre, were rival gang members and hapless port employees.

Gao took up position alongside a flamethrower unit which had been mounted on castors. It looked to be a German Flammenwerfer-35, nicknamed the 'skin-stealer', which could project a mixture of highly combustible gasoline and oil twenty metres away.

Waiwai stepped up and tore off the duct-tape gags but was puzzled by a lone woman's bare face.

The pitiful clamour of screaming, wailing, and pleading competed with the roar of air extractor units. Fierce updraughts of bird feathers and dust were soon to be followed by suffocating barbecue fumes.

'Hey, boss...'

'Later,' snapped Gao.

Waiwai contented himself with checking the readiness of his cattle bolt gun. A thumb-flick switched the device from 'Stun' to 'Kill'. How to operate: Simply press against a skull and pull the trigger. A pointed steel bolt penetrates the cranium, catastrophically damaging the cerebrum and part of the cerebellum. Tissues belonging to the vital centres of the brainstem and medulla are physically destroyed causing death.

A bemused Silvestre prepared himself for a theatrical form of intimidation. He didn't expect to be fazed by what he was about to witness. The endgame was fast approaching.

'Incineration, eh?' screamed Gao, shaking the weeping flamethrower nozzle defiantly.

Gao's blood was up.

Haemoglobin, plasma, and platelets, the lot.

He was on fire.

***

Bell hadn't been idle. He'd eavesdropped on everything that had been said at the negotiating table.

His military opera glasses were, by default, connected to a central ERS. The digital IDs of Gao's badass bodyguards had been uplifted to the Enemy Recognition Suite which had automatically distributed the intel to Bell's arachnid community.

Bell hoped that his hairy helpers had enjoyed their trip downstairs, randomly hanging on to the underside of the gibbets. By now they had jumped ship and taken up position awaiting instructions.

Yeah, let's even the odds up for Julio and his guys.

Once the bulk-cremation and brain-trauma carnage-fest was over, Gao returned to his seat as if nothing had happened. Waiwai certainly hadn't turned a hair as his boss clinically scorched each one of his hapless victims as a cruel execution warm-up.

With the extractor units switched off, the building had been returned to the eerie, sepulchral silence of a burial chamber.

The balloon was about to go up.

***

Silvestre marvelled at the return of his opposite number who seemed curiously invigorated. Gao's snake-like eyes stared at him with a new intensity. Irritation and irrational behaviour had been replaced with tranquillity and control.

'I need a drink. What's your poison?' said Gao, smoothly.

'Coffee…at this time of day.'

Silvestre promised himself a bucketful of tequila if he got out of here alive.

'Napalm is just as effective, you know. The smell of cooked meat always makes me thirsty.'

'Thirsty for what?'

The rehydration quip was ignored.

Gao took a moment to collect his thoughts.

A Pepsi and a bottle of cold-brew mocha were on their way.

'The new American president wants to intercept the shipments of fentanyl precursor chemicals flooding across the Pacific from China,' informed Gao.

'So?'

'Our information, also from an unimpeachable source, reveals that your organisation is prepared to accept lucrative compensation payments from the US government in exchange for destroying these shipments.'

Silvestre knew instantly that there had been a leak. The urge to stand up and make a cryptophone call was overpowering.

'What are you saying?'

'I'm saying it, aren't I?'

'That our business relationship is over?'

'Yes.'

Gao rolled his lips back inside his mouth till they almost disappeared.

A Muay Thai boxer appeared at the kitchen doorway in the distance, armed with the refreshments. Once beckoned by

Waiwai, the boxer-barman endeavoured to make his way across the expanse of bare concrete.

Silvestre saw the eyes of the snake widen.

***

Bell's vantage point enabled him to see that a pistol attached to the underside of the drinks tray was obscured by a waiter's cloth.

It was a split-second decision…

It had to end in a firefight anyway.

Bell's shot found its mark and the rookie bartender went down in an instant.

All hell let loose.

Silvestre rolled away into random table legs and drew his semi-automatic.

Gao's men were spraying the place with machine gun fire as Silvestre's team took cover as best as they could and managed to bring one of their opponents down. Unfortunately, two of them had bought it in the process.

Bell laid down suppressing fire from the balcony until the opposition worked out where it was coming from. He hightailed it all the way down the stairwell and launched a grenade the instant he emerged into open combat space. The grenade exploded close to three of Gao's men who were attempting to retrieve the money bags: one blown away and two wounded.

'Leave the fucking money!' screamed Gao.

Waiwai unleashed a wasted burst of M16 fire in Bell's general direction and switched to getting his boss out of the door. Gao, Waiwai and two survivors were escaping. Waiwai's farewell gesture was a DM51 fragmentation grenade, lobbed a fraction of a second before the outer door slammed shut. Two AIAs, working together like dung beetles, had enough time to grab hold of the grenade and roll with it behind a Komatsu forklift, thereby mitigating the explosive force.

By the time Bell shook off the effect of the blast and got after them, all he saw from the open doorway was the blur of an Audi and a superbike disappearing at speed down the alleyway.

Julio Silvestre was back on his feet nearby, unharmed, getting the first word in.

'Ah, mi amigo!'

'Bon dia, Julio.'

Lamentably, there was little time for pleasantries; the police were on their way.

';Tomás, nuestro salvador! You save us…but not all.'

';Vete ahora, rápido! Where are your vehicles?'

'In the next warehouse.'

'You'll have to hump your stiffs on pallet trucks.'

'You are forgetting something?'

'Uh?'

'The ninety million euro in cash.'

'Sure, grab it, but get moving!'

'We drink tequila later?'

'I'd rather die than miss it,' laughed Bell.

'Hey compañero, we sicarios welcome death if it rudely takes us, but you…you should not wish it.'

***

With the cartel team gone, the distant sound of police sirens became louder. Two police helicopters were now belatedly circling overhead.

After filing an Interpol Red Notice request, Bell switched to polishing his story. He doubted that the IRN and a plea to ground all flights leaving Belgium could be implemented fast enough. Gao was doubtless airborne already with Europe in the rear-view mirror.

The involvement of the Alacrán drug cartel could be conveniently omitted from the proceedings because they might be of assistance later on and needed to be kept onside.

There were at least fifteen bodies to catalogue, the cause of death for which was corroborated by a concrete floor awash with human remains: raw, sautéed or deep fried.

It was the gagging stench that got you.

Bird droppings, rotting offal, and incinerated human flesh.

Get me out of here! I need a drink.

***

After a hair-raising superbike dash, at times weaving down narrow, cobbled streets, Gao and Waiwai discarded the MV Agusta Brutale in the Deurne airport car park and ran into the terminal building. The hot machine was joined several minutes later by a black Audi which screeched to a halt right next to it.

The Embraer Legacy 500, with both jet engines warmed up and idling, had already received ATC startup and pushback clearance.

Gao raced up the plane steps and checked the time. A blanket police decree to ground all outgoing Belgian flights could come through at any moment.

Every second counted.

He pondered casting his surviving two team members adrift but he'd lost so many men already. Those steadfast guys didn't deserve it and he owed them for distinguishing themselves valiantly in mortal combat.

Loyalty bonus: Three extra minutes before chocks away.

Finally, two figures appeared on the apron and sprinted to the steps in time. With the door shut Gao took up position in the cockpit, perched nervously on the jump seat.

The tower granted permission to taxi and centre at runway-position 29. Agonising seconds passed as the Embraer completed the manoeuvre, perfectly lined up and waiting on the centreline.

Once the take-off roll had commenced, slamming on the anchors was out of the question.

Take-off compass bearing 293 degrees.

Gao gasped as the intercom squawked.

The pilot acknowledged the tower's authorisation.

'Cleared for take-off runway 29, B-KZX'

Flooring it on full power, the Honeywell turbofan engines accelerated the exquisitely beautiful Embraer into wind.

Gao exhaled completely as the plane left the tarmac. He was looking forward to breathing normally again, in all likelihood with an alcoholic drink in his hand. Seconds later they were crossing the E19 motorway and the Scheldt river basin.

Only after the starboard turn to head south-east towards Istanbul did Gao adopt a seat on the sumptuous, taupe-leather sofa.

Istanbul: three and a quarter hours' flight duration. He'd just have to crap himself every inch of the way.

Let's face it, fighter jets could appear at the wingtips without warning. He would permit himself to relax a little once they had left European airspace.

London and Panama would have to wait.

So, the CIA and MI6?

Yes, it had been an expensive close call.

The ungagged forensic accountant.

In his eagerness to fire up he'd rashly waved his observant lieutenant's concern aside.

Mistakes were unacceptable, especially his own.

A lone ranger had been up in the rafters watching the proceedings, fresh from his counter insurgency action at Schiphol airport. The ethereal stalker had adroitly tracked the fleeing abductors to pinpoint the turkey factory venue.

Yet, why had his skulking nemesis forfeited a chance to blow him away?

Gao shuddered at the thought.

There would be a next time.

The important thing was to get back to his compound in Laos and lick his wounds, but he was sinking in life-threatening, deep shit. No chance to sit back and chill; he was answerable to his intransigent and ruthless masters in Beijing.

Unfortunately.

10 El Mexicano gordo

B lood and skull fragments decorated the inside of an office window which overlooked the Gustav Mahlerlaan, in the prestigious Zuidas business district.

Venetian blinds were always a bitch to clean.

The senior law firm partner had been encouraged to write a short note in longhand which was required to occupy pride of place in the middle of his ornate, antique desk. He had also been taught how to press a pistol barrel up to roof of his mouth.

His fellow partners had suffered the same fate for disobeying cartel instructions.

Two well-dressed sicarios, carrying leather attaché cases, felt comfortable enough with their handiwork to take a hushed elevator ride back down to street level.

The plan was to meet the rest of the team, busy on another job, for an evening meal somewhere. It prompted one of them to speak.

'¿Ha reservado un restaurante?'

'Si, tacos, tequila y trasero.'

'¿Trasero?'

'Si, after food and drink we'll sate our appetites again. It's a short taxi ride.'

'¡Excelente! ¡Estoy hambriento!'

***

Amsterdam city centre, a short distance from the red light district. A night on the town.

126

Food, firewater and fornication.

Burritos, booze and a brothel called the Roze Ballon.

Prescribed R&R to blow away any residual combat stress.

Julio Silvestre, aka El Cartero, top dog assassin for the Mexican Alacrán drug cartel, made himself comfortable at the centre of a long table, back to the wall, eyes on the door.

The group of seven had taken over the restaurant, El Mexicano gordo, nestled in a side street in the Dammstraat quarter. The restaurateur hadn't really had a choice in the matter; other diners had been ushered out in a hurry. He was also obligated to become hard of hearing, develop poor eyesight and suffer from memory loss.

A wistful reminder of life back in Mexico City to kick the evening off, here in chilly northern Europe. Chilangos making fiesta duro – partying hard when away in foreign parts.

Tequila and beer arrived in abundance.

Crystal-clear agave tequila and bottles of Amstel.

Lime juice, salt and grapefruit soda on standby.

Silvestre spun the cap off the first bottle of Lunazul blanco, emptied it, and held his shot glass aloft.

Everyone else did the same.

'To those fallen in armed conflict.'

Seven glasses chimed together.

A sombre moment to remember compañeros who hadn't made it. Bodies left behind on the field of battle and others with life threatening wounds discreetly admitted to private hospitals, who may pull through.

If death takes us by surprise then we welcome it.

Everything in Mexico had to be strong to live.

The glasses thumped the table top and were immediately refilled. The laminated menus remained untouched while important toasts and acknowledgments were made.

Silvestre offered his shot glass for a second time and turned to Thomas Bell who was sitting to his left.

'To our English friend…mi ángel custodio. Why do you persist in saving me, Señor Bell?'

Six grinning faces leaned in and toasted Bell's good health.

Silvestre had explained to the other sicarios the background to their short working partnership: How a routine hit on the Balearic island of Ibiza had developed into a full-on bun fight.

Not only had the Englishman decapitated a hoodlum who was about to pump a hollowpoint round into his head, he'd rescued him from being vaporised into a crouton with only moments to spare. Silvestre shuddered at the recollection and mentally crossed his heart in appreciation.

Silvestre held up his left fist which revealed a black scorpion tattoo. Three bony fingers burst skyward in a shaking gesture.

'Antwerp was the third time!'

Everyone laughed at Silvestre's faux indignation and nodded in Bell's direction.

They had also been told that Bell worked for the British Secret Intelligence Service, MI6, and that his fortuitous contribution to Alacrán cartel affairs was held in high regard by El Padrino, Carlos Salazar. The British agent had an uncanny knack of being in the right place at the right time.

The eyes of the young sicario sitting opposite Bell blazed as he made a gang multi-finger salute, saying…

'¡Muy chido!'

'Ernesto says that you are so cool,' smiled Silvestre, 'He speaks in a dialect of Salvadoran Caliche.'

The impromptu translation service triggered a fiery exchange.

'¡Sos bayunco bicho!'

'¡No te entiendo! ¿Hablas espanol?' snapped Silvestre, in jest.

'¡Pura paja, hablo Caliche!'

'¡Pura vida!'

Ernesto held out his hands in mock submission, El Cartero was his section boss, after all.

There was an interesting story to be told over a beer.

According to Silvestre, Ernesto had led anything but a pure life. He'd been imprisoned in various young offender institutions from a young age. Nicknamed 'El Chango' he was a spider monkey scaling buildings, forging a successful career as a burglar until he was put away for a double murder. Bad behaviour in high security prisons led to being banged up in the new supermax penitentiary located in Tecoluca, San Vicente, El Salvador.

Traces of gang tattoos were visible below Ernesto's collar. MT17 affiliation.

Marabunta Trucha Seventeen.

Streetwise killers out to getcha.

Seventeen, a prime number which can only be consumed by itself or one. A snake devouring its own tail which represents the eternal cycle of destruction and rebirth. Ouroboros tats were de rigueur for gang members.

Ponte trucha - you betta pay attention!

Ernesto wasn't in the correctional facility for long. A truck full of military explosive parked illegally against the perimeter wall went off one night causing the biggest jailbreak in El Salvador's history. Twelve thousand shaven-headed convicts in white shorts and T-shirts running in all directions.

Ernesto fled northwest to the Honduras border rather than making the mistake of returning to the capital San Salvador, where most of the escapees were rounded up by army units.

Clever move.

He eventually arrived at a town called Choloma, close to the Honduras Caribbean coastline. There, he teamed up with a fellow MT17 gang member called José Gómez who was now sitting diagonally opposite Bell. Gómez had trained with the Salvadoran special forces and even the US Green Berets during a short military career. It was well known that MT17 were long-time allies of the Alacrán cartel.

The restaurant was filling with smoke.

No wonder José grinned across the table as he accepted one of Silvestre's cigarettes. As Silvestre prepared to conclude his rite of passage tale, he sat back and lit up himself, allowing Bell to get a word in.

'Angels, both of them. I'm glad that they're working for us!'

Silvestre paraphrased the sentiment into gang patois, which prompted appreciative mirth.

A stark truism was also uttered for Bell's benefit.

'Being murdered is a natural death south of the US border but at least you are bestowed an eternity to dwell upon your untimely demise.'

***

The food arrived in waves and Bell sensed the changing mood as bellies filled. He had enjoyed Julio's heartfelt, guardian-angel sobriquet which was a touching acknowledgment.

Terracotta dishes and bowls lay everywhere.

Pimientos de Padrón – Padron peppers.

Cocido gallego - Galician stew.

Churrasco - barbecued meat.

Burritos filled with lean ground beef and long-grain rice.

'Prison food, eh?' laughed Silvestre, tucking in.

Not quite like Mexico City, but close enough.

The pace of drinking slowed dramatically now that hearty sustenance monopolised the table.

While eating, it was time to enjoy your tequila with a swig of sangrita, on hand in a separate shot glass.

Sangrita - 'little blood' comprised orange, tomato and lime juices spiked with grenadine and hot Cholula sauce.

'We have to eat sometime, eh?' observed Silvestre, concluding his calorie intake with cheese and pico de gallo, served on bolillo bread.

Bell had already finished and sat there contentedly with a chilled Amstel, reliving the frenzied events of the day in graphic detail.

Just a routine arrest, they said.

Mucha sangre.

Yeah, right.

Silvestre lit another Delicados and turned to Bell, exhaling hard. It was time to discuss the price of corn.

What burning issue was on Silvestre's mind?

Shipping container sudoku?

New lines into Europe?

Narco submarines travelling across the Atlantic only to break up on the rocks when they made landfall in Portuguese waters?

The production and distribution of synthetics?

Silvestre worked for a narco-corporation, after all.

Where to start: a statement or a question?

'Any news of Pago?'

Bell had a stock answer ready regarding the whereabouts of the master criminal Ilya Pago, last seen in the Mediterranean heading west on board his superyacht.

'Nothing, Julio. The Valhalla was tracked to Gibraltar, then it hugged the north African coast past Tangier. After that it's anyone's guess. It may have sailed all the way south to Cape Town where it refuelled to traverse the Indian Ocean.'

'The Far East?'

'Perhaps…or he simply scuttled the Valhalla in the Gulf of Guinea: Ivory Coast, Benin, Gabon…take your pick…and did a runner into the jungle hinterland.'

'The cartel still wants his head.'

'If the service hears anything, you'll be the first to know.'

Bell still had Julio's business card. A realty front company with offices in Mexico City, Los Angeles and Miami.

'Salazar still leaves his dead nephew's Beretta, its grip inlaid with mother of pearl, out on his desk. Dario was so dear to him.'

An ill-fated drug deal negotiation had claimed the young candy man's life in the early stages of his career.

Narcotics was a risky business, not a pleasure cruise.

'And now we have another one that got away,' lamented Bell.

'Si, we're not doing very well are we?'

'Gao Zi Xin may have headed in the same direction. Vast archipelagos of remote islands offering a hospitable climate to lie low in.'

'No, I don't fall for that.'

'The Golden Triangle?'

'It has to be Laos. Gao is safe there in his fortified compound. He can hole up indefinitely under the protection of his armed militia. It's said that he has batteries of purloined Patriot surface-to-air missiles.'

'What? Discarded by the Americans in Afghanistan?'

'Si, transported down to the coast and shipped around to the Bay of Bengal. Muy fácil.'

If it was true, Gao had an aerial protective shield above his sprawling place on the banks of the Mekong river, courtesy of the American taxpayer. The MIM-104 Patriot's beam, created by its flat-phased array radar, was highly agile unlike a plain moving dish. It had the capability to detect small, fast-moving targets like ballistic missiles, stealth aircraft or even cruise missiles.

No airstrikes then!

'Any other hidey-holes?' said Bell.

'There is one but only if he had a compelling reason to be there.'

'The reason being?'

Silvestre rolled his eyes.

'Gao Zi Xin is not his own master.'

'You mean that he's a Beijing puppet?'

Bared teeth, revealing fine dental work, accompanied the answer.

'¡Exactamente!'

The restaurateur who had been hovering nervously with the bill moved forwards hesitantly.

Silvestre peeled off from a wad of two-hundred euro notes and settled the score with a smiley well-wish.

'Enjoy a long life, mi amigo.'

Plata o plomo – silver or lead.

Silencio o muerte – silence or death.

Silvestre's shot glass slammed into the table signalling that it was time to move on. The group was well fed and watered and champing at the bit to get to the Roze Ballon.

'We party tonight, yes?'

'One last drink with you and I'll be gone,' smiled Bell, lamely.

'¡Che, boludo! What is this? No chingar?'

'I stick to civilian targets.'

'No blonde, blue-eyed beauties from the Balkans?'

Bell knew that he'd been caught on the back foot as a pussyfooting lightweight, but he had an early flight to Switzerland in the morning.

A totally wet excuse but the affairs of state took precedence.

Swiss bank account and safety deposit box access-and-scrutiny orders needed to be conducted in a sober manner.

Best not to be drawn on what he had to do in Zürich.

There would be sufficient time to complete the work before racing back to the airport for a twelve-hour direct flight to Hong Kong with Cathay Pacific.

The alternative scenario was simply to go with the flow.

Bell knew how the latter half of the evening would pan out.

Crawling naked out of a hooker's boudoir at three in the morning on all fours, stoned and pissed, while a girl from Montenegro in high heels whipped your bare arse with a riding crop.

'No chingar tonight,' said Bell, fighting a noble rearguard action, 'Tengo mucha chamba!'

The lame plea that he had a lot of work to do didn't cut it.

Silvestre laughed out loud and hit the table.

'¡Un chupatintas! A pen pusher who can handle a gun! Come on let's have some fun, we are more than blood brothers now.'

The MT17 boys jumped in on the act.

They all wanted him along for the ride.

Bell was assailed with every valid reason why he should change his mind.

Tight girls from Eastern Europe.

Chicas calientes - hot girls.

Chicas offering company and intimate night entertainment.

It was midweek and they would have the run of the place.

It was an all-inclusive brothel. For a fixed fee you could fuck as much as you liked: FFM, FFFM, OWO, RO…

A buffet, all you could drink, a whirlpool, a sauna, nice bedrooms, and a minimum of fifteen working girls.

Bell wasn't convinced.

It was an early night for him.

They were more than at liberty to take their ciprofloxacin antibiotic pills and get their helmets out. Riding bareback while making the beast with two backs.

Good luck to them.

Okay, it was an all-you-can-fuck brothel and a great deal, but surely, your seed silos wouldn't refill fast enough.

You could only fire your gun so many times.

It sounded a bit like an all-you-can-eat seafood restaurant where you might get ejected from the backdoor amongst the dumpsters for cleaning them out of steamed shrimp. Lying face-down in a dark alleyway filled with rats to conclude a manic 'fruits de mare' evening.

Ernesto announced that everything below his waistline was on fire and that he was ready for all takers.

Bell delivered a clever riposte which triggered immediate hilarity and a high-five from Silvestre. Anyone else trying it might have found that their throat had been cut.

'¡Che, cuate! As long as it doesn't include your arsehole!'

***

The team emerged from the restaurant into the night air.

Silvestre led the way.

They located the Roze Ballon down a cobbled side street, arriving mob-handed.

Pink balloons, in neon, bubbled up and away on an animated signage display. Naturally, their booking was top of the list.

The bouncers on the door eyed up the latest motley crew. They could recognise immediately that they'd better be polite and respectful. These guys were packing and looked scarily capable.

The metal detector ceased to be a mandatory entry requirement.

The group rate for all contracted services was settled in advance with yet more two-hundred euro notes. Specialty and animal acts cost extra.

In the badlands of Mexico and Colombia cathouse payment could be made in high-grade silver ore, gold dust or nuggets…or cocaine. Other common rule variants were: no pissing in the cuspidors and no discharging of firearms in the rooms at the whores or at other patrons. Any discharge might come a few days later.

Silvestre and Bell were left standing together at the brothel bar after everyone else had disappeared upstairs.

A final sip of Amstel.

Two gorgeous beauties in thongs came up behind Silvestre and took an arm each, ready to escort him up to heaven.

A final buddy-buddy exchange took place before Bell headed for the door and disappeared into the night.

'Viajar bien. La ley del más fuerte, mi amigo.'

'La ley del más fuerte,' replied Bell.
'Adiós.'

11 Bottom feeder

Daniel Roxby had blagged an upgrade to business class with Turkish Airlines. His forthcoming eleven-hour night-flight from Istanbul to Hong Kong was going to be truly wonderful. So lavishly opulent that they would have to drag him off the aircraft, kicking and screaming.

Gourmet meals, a posh lounge, and a shower.

The TA top-tier flying category came with enough perks to make it feel like he was travelling in first.

SFU.

Suitable For Upgrade, as assessed by the check-in clerk.

Not by accident, though.

Roxby had selected the flight with the highest chance of success. He was a solo-passenger businessman, well-groomed and stylishly dressed in a well-cut, lightweight suit. Clean-shaven, suave haircut, silk tie, and expensive leather shoes from Foster & Son of Jermyn Street, London.

His manner was charm incarnate, laced with polite manners and well-spoken English. The cherry on the cake, if it was really needed, was his Star Alliance loyalty card presented with a winning smile.

SFU.

So Fuck You!

That sure fooled them didn't it?

Appearances can be deceptive.

The pretence and illusion of good lineage.

Roxby was stone cold broke and had spent the last ten days hiding in a cheap and awful hotel in a seedy quarter of Istanbul.

No airconditioning, bathing pools or cable TV.

More like allergic anaphylaxis, bed bugs and car horns.

He could handle it.

It was better than being banged up on a murder conviction.

His last dregs of US dollars had been enough to buy an economy airline ticket to a place where he might turn his finances around.

The sale proceeds of stolen jewellery went on an all-inclusive casino resort holiday in Hong Kong and Macau.

He had only four days to pull a rabbit out of the hat, otherwise he would be walking back to Europe in his bare feet.

It wasn't the first time that he'd been down on his luck. Vulnerable, naïve women were his area of expertise and the source of his transient, ill-gotten wealth, but gambling was the killer.

This time, he would cash in his chips when he was ahead...or simply put it all on red in a gesture of wanton bravado.

***

After his shower, Roxby sat comfortably in the premier-class departure lounge. He checked his travel documentation carefully.

A Gamer Tours International holiday itinerary resided in its shiny, cardboard folder. He traced his finger over the embossed GTI logo and down the front-sheet checklist:-

-Arrive at Hong Kong's Chek Lap Kok International Airport.

-Taxi to the five-star Ritz-Carlton hotel in Kowloon which occupies floors 102 to 118 at the top of the ICC skyscraper.

-GTI welcome meeting in the Lotus Suite.

-Cocktails and canapés.

-Dinner and a one-night stay.

-Morning: Luxury coach ride to the Pearl River ferry terminal.

-Arrive at Macau and check in at the Venetian Macau casino resort complex for a three-night visit.

-Daytimes: Optional guided historical tours of old Macau.

-Evening Two: Cocktails and dinner dance in the Taipa suite.

-Evening Three: Gala buffet or dinner at the Venetian Macau's acclaimed North restaurant offering a mix of Sichuan and northern Chinese cuisine; followed by a 'Disco Inferno' dance extravaganza in the nightclub.

Hmm, just can't stop…y'all gotta bop.

Okay, that was enough of GTI's travel plan.

Mooching through the old Portuguese quarter, led by a tour guide waving a muster stick, held little attraction: The ruins of St Paul's Cathedral, A-Ma Temple, Senado Square and Fortaleza do Monte.

Forget it.

What was of interest was finding his mark.

As an emissary of Beelzebub, he was already marked with the stigma diabolicum – the sign of the devil, ready to deliver fallen angel kisses on unsuspecting necks.

After the meal he would go completely rogue.

Who knows? He might have ensnared an assailable woman by then, dazzled by his flirtatious and entertaining charms.

There would, of course, be some serious gamblers amongst the tour group. He could card count with the best of them. Forget slots; poker or blackjack were his preference. However, roulette still had the power to draw you in for an insane flutter: Watching the spinning ball with everything placed on the black hole of Stygian oblivion.

Having stayed regularly at the MGM Bellagio in Las Vegas, Macau was going to be an enlightening experience.

The Ritz-Carlton Hotel boasted a swanky cocktail bar with spectacular views over the Hong Kong skyline. Armed with a complementary drink, this was his opportunity to get on it.

Target acquisition: A high value female responsive to the allure of a debonair lothario, like the fodder routinely found on cruise ships and dating websites.

Relieve them of their knickers and their money.

Looking for a Romeo to sweep you off your feet?

No problem.

How about a pink dolly bird with candy floss for brains, perky breasts, and a tiny waist?

He chuckled to himself.

No, that was not what he was looking for.

The delicious hush of the lounge made for a congenial sanctuary from the hurly-burly. He marvelled at his new Cypriot passport obtained using falsified credentials.

David Charles Rockwell.

Other passports, military identity cards and biometric residence permits were stored in a safety deposit box in a London bank vault.

Rockwood, Rockley, Rockliffe...

Who shall we be today?

A love rat on the run.

A phantom hiding in plain sight seeking his next victim.

A killer with a dark history and even darker secrets.

A callous sponger and a leech.

A bottom feeder: a marine creature that lives on the seabed and feeds by scavenging. A mean catfish with whiskery barbels probing the depths in search of an easy meal.

Roxby shuddered at his close shave in London's Harley Street where his medical scams had operated from private rented consulting rooms.

He had progressed through a series of spurious medical disciplines to turn a buck: botox, lip fillers, colonic irrigation and liposuction. Expensive medical equipment and an attractive nurse who marshalled the waiting room provided a credible veneer to his cowboy operation.

His medical knowledge was limited to the contents of the Reader's Digest Home Emergency Medical Guide. No need to worry about the Hippocratic Oath or the wellbeing of your patient.

His plausible website and clever search engine optimisation trawled in a steady stream of unsuspecting guinea pigs who were mostly sent on their way in a damaged state.

Mr David Roxborough FRCS, sex therapist.

A perfect opportunity to meet susceptible women that he could manipulate, sleep with, and fleece.

It hadn't been the first time that a patient had died from septicaemia. Ambulances had delivered others who were suffering from the initial stages of sepsis and immune system suppression to hospital A&E departments where emergency treatment was administered – not always successfully.

This time, angry relatives, on his case, had reported a crime of manslaughter, backed up by the grim findings of a coroner.

Police broke the door down as Roxby escaped via a gated rear courtyard into an overgrown alleyway.

The thirty second rule.

The art of going on the run.

He had left the country on the next flight and been forced to hide somewhere until his money ran out.

Although his medical scams were on hold, he was still at the top of his game and held all the cards. A stolen prescription pad and packs of clean hypodermic syringes always came in handy.

Sure, he'd left a trail of bodies, the last couple he'd buried in the Epping forest. Strangulation, suffocation and poisoning being the gamut of contributing elements of his victims' demise.

Mercy killing when he'd finished with each of them – first a dose of GHB, the date rape drug, followed by the cruel, merciless coup de grace from a psychopathic charlatan.

No regret or remorse.

A textbook narcissist with a personality disorder.

An inflated sense of his own importance, attention craving and no empathy.

Charming, convincing and vain.

Catch me if you can.

Roxby's phone rang suddenly – a WhatsApp call.

On a whim, he had decided to unblock her calls.

Once you'd got them onside and they had taken the bait it was difficult to shake them off.

It was always the same.

'Hello, baby,' cooed Roxby.

The weeping and sobbing dissipated a little.

'I…I love you, David.'

'I know.'

'Y…you…you've stolen my heart and taken all my money!'

Yeah, he had emptied her bank accounts. She had even taken out multiple loans and maxed out on her credit cards.

Stupid, clingy bitch.

It was a struggle to suppress a snickering fit.

'Now, now, honey…it was all for us, remember?'

He was tired of this already.

'I'm going to kill myself.'

That was a gloriously positive thing to hear. He hoped that she would leave a pitiful suicide note. What could he say to tip her over the edge?

Hoisted forcibly over the handrail.

Yes, if they had been on that luxury cruise she had always been carping on about, he would have enticed her into a romantic midnight stroll down to the stern of the ship and dumped her over the side into the moonlit propeller wash.

The thought of it made him smile.

'You won't ever see me again.'

***

Jana Cazenove's alarm had gone off but she'd immediately hit the snooze button. Despite getting up in the early hours to have a pee and gulp down ibuprofen and paracetamol tablets with a pint of tap water, she had a hangover.

A bad one.

An occipital headache throbbed in the back of her head.

She jolted her neck a couple of times, akin to a rudimentary form of damage assessment.

Ah, it hurts!

That wasn't all.

She felt a grizzling churn in her stomach.

Snooze period over, the alarm went off again.

She should have packed days ago…so, okay, got it done last night instead, but no. Now she had to pack in a frenzy this morning.

London Heathrow T3 for a Cathay Pacific flight to Hong Kong.

What had she been thinking of?

Red wine, brandy and port on an empty stomach.

Sorry liver!

Could it get any worse?

Yes, she'd overslept.

Horror of horrors, she had to be on that plane.

Urgent: Rehydration and more pills…we can beat this.

She staggered downstairs to the kitchen and hooked an electrolyte-rich sports drink out of the fridge door. She followed it with an orange juice chaser which may have been a bad idea.

Shit! The pain relief blister packs were back in the ensuite.

After a few minutes lying panting on top of the bed clothes, she knew what was coming.

Please don't let it be happening at both ends.

With her hair up in a scrunchie, she knelt down on a folded shower mat, lifted the toilet seat and gripped the sides of the glazed bowl.

Time to beseech the porcelain god of purgation.

There was no need to put her fingers down her throat; the first retch was operating on autopilot and needed no encouragement.

It was the second stomach contraction which surprised her.

Stronger and with much greater volume.

A blurry vision from last night of peeling king prawns came to mind. Twisting heads off decapod crustaceans and cleaning out their intestinal tracts.

Ugh!

Better have a quick shower before packing.

***

Two identical Samsonites lay open on her bedroom floor. The LBD, basic footwear, and lingerie were all in. The stilettoes and Louboutin high heels followed.

Lingerie had been a stresser.

The top half: A selection of unlined bras to create a more natural-looking silhouette. There was no time to spend agonising over her ideal breast shape. Well, as long as you understood the performance variation between high-apex cups and balconettes – what the hell. T-shirt bras…just chuck 'em in.

The bottom half: Granny pants still had their place but she was a die-hard La Perla fan. Intimissimi's Italian styling of luxe lace-trimmed and silk satin offerings came a close second. Lob a multi-pack of love-heart pants in there for good measure.

Biodegradable knicks made of fibres spun from wood pulp? Not this time.

It was alright for men - any old supermarket six-pack or Calvin Kleins would do. As far as nails were concerned, menfolk had no idea what us gals had to put up with. An overdue manicure was the only pre-trip essential that she had sensibly dealt with.

In flight: Sneakers, loose slacks, a T-shirt and a cashmere jumper should see her through.

But that was only part of the story.

She had her PJs stashed in her hand luggage. They were soon to become acquainted with a reserved seat in business class. A seat strategically located in row eleven, well away from the galleys, toilets and bassinets. That was the major drawcard: A luxurious bio-enclosure which stretched out into a cocooned, fully-flat bed. Bliss equated to twelve hours lying in a deep stupor while wearing noise-cancelling earbuds.

She was still struggling.

Now she knew how a corpse must feel.

Both Sammys were locked and by the front door.

A Berocca Immuno effervescent tablet swirled comfortingly in the glass of water as she waited. It supposedly had nutrients like selenium which supported your immune system.

The taxi would arrive soon.

It was twenty-five minutes westbound down the M4 motorway from her detached house in Chiswick, West London.

Living in this part of town was perfect for LHR.

In the meantime, she had stuffed all the important gear into her Bottega textured-leather tote bag: Money, passport, GTI travel itinerary and some fresh panties sealed in a plastic freezer bag: Bikini and boy-shorts styles, as you do.

Baubles on display: Cartier love bracelet, diamond stud earrings and a platinum-blue-sapphire ring.

All set but still feeling like shit.

Jana, dear, this has been a warning.

A clear incentive to stop binge drinking; recalibrate life modus operandi to get super-fit and super-toned.

ARLD - alcohol related liver disease: A red alert.

Cut out the bender boozeroos before it's too late.

Abstinence.

It said in that magazine that as your liver heals, positive health effects can be felt throughout your whole body: Increased energy, enhanced mental clarity, improved digestion, and better skin health.

Let's keep off the juice for two weeks and check it out.

Yuk! Alcoholic fatty liver disease.

No more sex, cocaine and alcohol. Just sex, I guess.

Hmm…what a shame.

Carnal union with younger, athletic guys from now on, then.

Yeah, she needed to stay alive because she'd end up squandering her lucky breaks:-

- A favourable divorce settlement.

- A successful online cosmetics and skincare business.

- A recent £9.7million lottery win.

It was a shame that the jackpot hadn't pipped over the ten-million pound mark, but she wasn't complaining.

She hadn't dared tell any of her friends.

What do you do with all that money?

At the very least, install a lap pool with the six winning lottery numbers incorporated into the pool-bottom tile design. Well, it seemed funny at the time.

It was fair to say that, despite her good fortune, you never know what is around the corner. A single, no-going-back moment when your luck changes and you lose everything.

Her only shortfall was an ideal lover. Someone with whom she could share her life and confide all her hopes and fears.

Someone to sweep her off her feet.

A Mercedes-Benz Viano MPV taxi pulled up.

The pink Sammys were on board in a trice.

Her hair was still damp and her stomach seemed to be on the move again. Come on, girl, cross your legs and clench your buttocks until we get inside the terminal building.

There had been enough time to apply a light foundation, mascara and some lippy. Keep the dark glasses handy and, dare I say it, my dear, we're looking quite convincing.

No vomiting in the taxi for God's sake!

***

Jana wheeled briskly into terminal three and navigated to check-in zone C. Minutes later, it was up the escalator to fast track security for business class.

Finally, the Cathay Pacific lounge.

The smell of the noodle bar had the adverse effect of setting her stomach off again. The abdominal discomfort and nausea indicators were all in the red. A gurgling knot of gastrointestinal queasiness signalled that she'd hit the PNR for chucking up again.

Noodles, steamed bao dumplings and dim sum were kind of seriously off the menu. The nap room, adjacent to the main lounging area, would have to wait.

The Ladies restroom.

Wall-to-wall marble composite and a landscape mirror.

End stall…trap six…door locked…seat up.

A couple of full-on retches finally produced something.

Was that green bile? Bile reflux, even?

Puking on empty.

Ugh, I'll never drink again!

She dreamed of the moment when, all snuggled up in her pyjamas, the Airbus or Boeing or whatever it was hurtled down the runway and lifted off.

She also yearned to be romantically entwined with a new love, cuddling up together on the stern of a luxury cruise liner, gazing wistfully at a full moon, then into each other's eyes.

12 Who let the cougar out?

Daniel Roxby sat on his own in the Ritz-Carlton Lotus lounge nursing an insipid cocktail.

There were too many men on this tour for his liking but he was the best dressed. No matter, it still meant that he was Johnny-no-mates imbibing gawkily through a floating layer of diced fruits.

Hey, hadn't they heard of straws?

Problem: He was not in the company of an attractive woman -something which had to be rectified pronto.

The tour-group compère took to the stage and commanded instant attention. Death by PowerPoint, starting with Hong Kong's top attractions.

After this tiresome briefing was over, the group would head up to the one hundred and eighteenth floor, which hosted the spectacular Ozone rooftop bar, to mix and mingle. With luck, it would result in a dizzying new liaison nurtured by a blend of alcohol and breath taking city views.

Steady on, nothing to work on yet.

Target acquisition status: inactive.

Best to ditch the cocktail at the first opportunity and order a proper drink.

Slides came and went…

The hour-long Macau ferry ride departs from the terminal near the IFC Towers in the Shun Tak Centre, on Hong Kong Island. On a good day it offers an open-air, breezy ride across the Pearl River Delta rather than taking a bus via the bridge.

Their hotel, the Venetian Macau, was a gigantic resort complex with an overriding theme of Venice. A must-see for tourists and one of the most well-known places in Macau.

Got it: Pristine, turquoise-blue canals and replica fourteenth century Italian architecture rubbing shoulders with fast food outlets and shopping malls.

As the VM was the second largest casino in the world you could jettison the stats about how many luxury suites, restaurants, gaming tables and slot machines it had.

If you shut your eyes for a moment, you could just about imagine that you were in Venice for real, standing in the middle of the bustling Piazza San Marco.

All you needed to know was that you'd be adding inches to your waistline, lose your shirt at poker and take a phony ride in a gondola.

As soon as the gondoliere navigates the corner of the reproduction San Luca canal, he embarrassingly breaks into a cheesy rendition of 'O Sole Mio'. No sunshine or icecream, though, you'd need to run outside for that.

Other casino hotels on the strip which were worthy of a gawp: the Grand Lisboa, the Wynn Palace, the MGM Cotai, and the Blue Dragon. The incessant assault of noise, bright lights and people in these glitzy temples-of-chance would ultimately engender terminal casino-fatigue.

The only antidote was to drag a kill back to a hotel room for some quality time between the sheets.

The compère spent a moment or two plugging upgrades for the Paiza Club which was for premium guests who wanted access to private gaming rooms.

Er, no thanks.

Getting to the casinos was easy, apparently, with most operating a membership card system which rewarded you with bonus play-points.

Free buses line up at both ferry terminals, and pretty women representing their hotels and casinos dispense coupons and information. Be warned! You can easily get lost in the biggest casinos - dining, shopping and seeing the shows; their labyrinth-by-design floor layouts see to that. To keep you gambling for longer a retail aroma of cucumber, sweet melon, rose, and green apple is vaporised into the ventilation ducts.

What chance an ace-high straight of TJQKA? He needed a poker hand like that to win a huge pile of chips.

To be fair, hot gambling tips and table etiquette were to be revealed after the break. Soberingly, it had to be borne in mind at all times that Macau was a Chinese special administrative region where you had to behave yourself.

A late arrival wearing diamond stud earrings discreetly took a seat. He noted that her figure-hugging LBD may be receiving assistance from some high-end shapewear.

Love it.

Control knickers were harder to get off which was a real turn-on. Maybe it was the open gusset, where you had to fumble with an elastic panel which did it. The curves of a woman's body never lost their attraction, especially on a fresh piece of meat.

The newbie made herself comfortable, focusing on the remaining blur of slides while sipping her complementary drink.

He prayed for the fifteen-minute interval when the lights would come back up.

His invocation was answered a few moments later.

The cougar was getting up to go to the bar.

Quick, after her before some other chancer gets in there.

He slid up behind her undetected, like a puff adder.

His prey was ordering a gin-and-tonic, unaware that an odourless, camouflaged predator tasted her perfume with its sensitive olfactory glands.

Chanel No. 5?

The essence of femininity; the scent of a woman.

Leaning over her shoulder, he noted her room number before the key card disappeared inside her Saint Laurent calfskin wallet.

As an unscrupulous seducer of women, what was his legend to be this time?

Tinker, tailor, soldier, spook,
Pilot, policeman, surgeon, cook.

A Michelin-star chef seemed wholly inappropriate; he couldn't really poach an egg and he didn't know the difference between a risotto and a rissole.

An arsehole, no problem.

More than to be expected if you were a callous bottom feeder scavenging the seabed. A blood-sucking leech with the anticoagulant hirudin in its salivary glands and a phial of the drug gamma hydroxybutyrate in its pocket.

Perhaps an airline pilot? Flight plans, tricky cross-wind landings and fly-by-wire system checks.

Countless hours spent on flight simulator software was enough to blag it. He knew the difference between an aileron and a flap and could splat a Learjet down on any Caribbean island runway.

Yeah, and an MI6 field operative as backup.

A two-tier cover.

Overt and covert.

Settled: airline captain, and when the going gets tough escalate to a Secret Intelligence Service agent on a mission.

Perfect!

Chat-up line?

'Well, here I am. What are your other two wishes?'

'You're so beautiful that you made me forget my pickup line.'

'Is it hot in here or is it just you?'

'You can't sit at the bar on your own.'

A voluptuous body turned to face him.

'What's your game?' said Roxby, smoothly.

A clever line, delivered with an assured smile.

'Watching my back, and your game is?'

He stole a glance at her blue sapphire ring and her Cartier love bracelet which was unmistakeably white gold, set with four high-carat stones.

The icing on the cake, with her long blonde hair up, were those diamond ear studs, refracting and dispersing colour and pure white light in a glorious, scintillating display of fire and brilliance.

'Admiring yours.'

'Hah!'

A second sassy line was rewarded with a cougar smirk, but no handshake.

'Hi, I'm David...David Rockwell, pleased to meet you.'

'So, what do you do, David?'

'I fly Airbus A330s, mainly.'

'Cruising on autopilot with your feet up?'

'Not all the time. I like nothing better than lining up on a tiny landing strip below me.'

Before Roxby could embroider his spiel with tales of the world's most challenging airports, another late arrival entered the lounge.

They both watched a fit, urbane guy in his mid-twenties slide effortlessly into a vacant Chester-back banquette. A waiter was there in seconds, taking an order.

The pixie dust had been spilt; the magic moment had passed.

The hand holding the gin-and-tonic placed it back down on the bar. Magenta-nailed fingers released their grip of the glass and morphed into a mock semi-automatic, pointing at Roxby's sternum.

A steely smile passed her lips.

'I'm Jana, thanks for the chat. See you later, maybe.'

Roxby pushed his soggy cocktail away in disgust and ordered his own GNT. Gifted and talented? Come on Danny boy, you're slipping.

He watched as Jana's shapely arse weaved its way through the tables, homing in on its target.

***

A long sleep on the plane had put Jana back on top of her game, followed by an hour's getting ready in her deluxe Ritz-Carlton room. Sixty minutes of preparation which included lining her stomach with houmus on rye bread, and yogurt laced with fresh berries and nuts.

Go easy this time.

She was never going to look any better than this.

Pumped up, sharp and in focus.

She'd even had time to answer a couple of emails.

David's pitch had been funny and smart, delivered in a magnetic and charismatic manner. A player accustomed to breaking many hearts, no doubt.

An opportunistic libertine, probably.

An odious narcissist, possibly.

A smooth criminal and hot felon, most definitely.

But attractive all the same.

The allure was hard to resist under normal circumstances.

He could almost be her ideal man and soulmate.

Jana knew that she was so choosy.

I want someone who is trustworthy, sweet and kind.

A landing strip?

There was no groomed rectangle running down to the upper edge of her vulva to be seen. No pubic hair trimmed and coiffed into a neat, narrow strip.

Instead, a perfectly smooth mons pubis - waxed and sheeny.

Blow me?

Cheeky bastard!

Her jewellery had blown him away, though.

Disturbingly so.

She had spotted something better, a commodity that she really desired. A horny piece of merchandise that was up for grabs: the cool fella who had taken her seat.

The second half was about to begin.

There was nothing in her way.

I am on top, as is my preference, and I am completely empowered. I can do anything and have it all.

Jana made her way back to her original seat and peered downwards at the person now occupying it.

Chat-up line? Easy-peasy!

'What's your game?'

A fit young man stood up politely.

A chivalrous start.

'Game? Can I help you?'

Standing in her high heels his eyes were on a level with hers.

'Thank you for keeping my seat warm.'

'Ah, forgive me but I didn't notice anything. Maybe your bum isn't as hot as you think,' came the roguish answer.

Jana threw her head back and howled with laughter which got dagger looks from Roxby, still propped up at the bar on his lonesome.

'I guess I deserved that! It was a cheap come-on, but I'd like to think that my butt is still hot. Let's sit together so I can hear about yours.'

Jana plumped herself cosily down without asking.

'Well...'

'You don't need to tell me, I can guess,' said Jana.

'Who's your friend?'

'Just a PUA barfly down on his luck...'

'He looks it.'

'Say, I think I owe you a drink.'

She snapped her fingers and a waiter appeared.

Jana's arched eyebrow posed the question.

'Surprise me.'

'I'm Jana Cazenove, by the way.'

Her right hand presented itself as the lights went down for the second half. She was in no hurry for him to let go of it.

'Thomas Bell. I'm enchanted to meet you.'

She inwardly breathed a sigh of relief. Being given a bum's rush in the middle of the Lotus lounge would have been embarrassing to say the least.

Time to dig a little, straight out of the gate. When one has so little time one needs to get a move on.

'So, I take it that you're on your own like me?'

On your own sounded less intrusive than *single*.

'Not any more,' smiled Bell.

The GNTs arrived and they chimed their glasses together.

This had all the hallmarks of a home run.

'I reckon you think I suck at flirting and that I'm winging it.'

'Don't worry, you'll soon have me crawling on all fours.'

Jana took the liberty to grip his hand again. Hers had already been kissed in an unexpectedly gallant gesture.

Keep going next time and kiss me all over.

'Let's see how much fun we can have, shall we? By the way, I'm not normally like this. It's just that I'm riding high and really enjoying myself.'

'No law against it, but don't let your bravado run away with you on the tables.'

Wow! I really like this guy, someone to watch over me.

'You can see that I don't get myself into trouble!'

An escort-you-back-to-your-room offer later on?

She hoped so.

Any nightcap ruse which got two entwined bodies into a waiting bed-chamber would do.

That was what all her expensive lingerie was for. Hot breath pressed up against her hotel room door, the fumble for the digital key that, when swiped, registered an unequivocal green light.

He's younger than me, but what the hell.

Frenzied disrobing: buttons and zips behave!

Don't worry about the La Perla gusset.

Hurry up and do what you need to do to me.

Wet, wet, wet.

No more teasing.

Squeeze the life out of me with that ripped body of yours while I spread mine out for you.

Open your heart, I'll make you fuck me.

The vision of her long fingernails dug into his naked buttocks flashed into her mind.

***

Bell sipped yet another gin-and-tonic as he surveyed the Ozone bar's panoramic view of the Hong Kong skyline.

A serendipitous clinch was the perfect extra cover.

It enhanced his authenticity as an innocent punter hanging off the arm of a gregarious sugar-mummy. Hidden in plain sight in exchange for companionship and sexual intimacy.

Chinese tour guides weren't always what they seemed.

Although charming and polite, they were also trained to look out for lone-wolf spies and saboteurs, assisted by the pervasive cloak of facial recognition which haunted every public space.

There was still a mission to complete.

He could feel the heat already.

He and Jana would consume each other at their leisure. A steamy tryst burned in a crucible at a high temperature.

When the time came: A sudden tactical exfiltration from the theatre of operations, never to be seen again.

No goodbyes, regret or remorse.

A broken heart in a heartbeat, leaving only fractured memories of a whirlwind liaison in the Far East with a stranger.

That was the discipline.

In the meantime, Bell was more than happy to listen to Jana revealing her life story. Another drink, big eyes, dazzling diamond ear studs, and endless laughter.

The university years.

The marriage.

The divorce and the financial settlement whereby she ended up with a lifetime income and a large detached house in Chiswick.

The meteoric rise of her online skincare business.

Global sales at stores like Fenwick and Saks Fifth Avenue.

Expensive serums, creams, and foaming cleansers used by celebrities and recommended by Internet influencers.

Skin killers: sun damage, smoking, stress.

Skin saviours: SPFs, retinoids, vitamin A derivatives, balms and oils.

Hydration milks and moisturisers were the top sellers.

He learned that anti-ageing potions were a scam and totally ineffective. She had assembled a team of talented biochemists and dermatologists to create a product range which claimed to reduce pigmentation and wrinkle depth while thickening, plumping and firming the skin.

The high-priced stuff flew off the shelf and there was more to come. She was on a roll and unstoppable.

Her beauty advice to Bell was that men should be doing all this stuff as well. Think: broad-spectrum UV protection. Although males had thicker skin, they should be taking meticulous care of it.

Bell knew that it was going to take everything to save his skin later on.

'I'll stop there. I'm glad you didn't get me started on collagen supplements! Don't do a runner on me, will you!'

Jana scooped up her bag and headed off to the Ladies.

He enjoyed listening to her life-story gush; she came across as intelligent, discerning, and demanding. To say that Jana was a lonely MILF cougar would be too harsh. She wasn't a slut or desperate, like hanging out in bars and going home with any random man left over at the end of the night.

She was attractive and confident. His new-found escort simply wanted to have fun, offering sexual expertise, and open to new experiences.

Beyond botox and balms, butt plugs and BDSM beckoned.

What exactly she knew or had to offer he was about to discover. As soon as she returned from the Ladies, he expected her to cut to the chase and get down to business.

The long walk down a hushed corridor, late at night.

Moist lips pressed together in a hotel room doorway.

The crush of perspiration and Chanel No. 5 as a fumbled key card induction-loop engages and allows two bodies to spill over the threshold.

Pristine Egyptian cotton sheets at the ready.

The final part of her story explained her dalliance with drugs and where she was right now:

Until she had split with her investment-banker-supremo husband, Jana had been used to shuttling between London, Monaco, and Geneva.

A glitzy lifestyle pharmaceutically sustained by a cocktail of sleeping tablets and Xanax - a short-acting benzodiazepine prescribed to treat people with anxiety disorders. Not to mention occasional snorts of cocaine, mainly at dinner parties in Hampstead, Mayfair or Knightsbridge.

She had nearly become a Monaco citizen.

Jana was racing against time to burn the candle at both ends. A reveller hell-bent on getting as much life in as possible before the screaming banshee of menopause swooped down to spoil it. She was braced ready for courses of HRT rocket fuel and testosterone…prescribed privately, naturally.

***

Jana leaned over the marble washbasin in an empty Ladies and admired herself in the supersize vanity mirror. She spent a moment or two checking all angles, especially her hair. Canapé debris: nil…teeth: perfect.

Still looking fantastic, girl.

Punching above our weight.

Isn't he lovely?

So, who are they calling an arrogant plastic witch and a cougar now?

Eat your hearts out you jealous bitches!

Jana retrieved a lipstick from her bag.

Iced magenta: neutral pale pink with a rimy glow.

Mmm…lustrous and creamy.

A satisfying frosty shimmer.

She pressed her lips together, admiring her reflection.

Better not leave lover boy for too long.

A final pout and a flare of the nostrils and she was gone.

Jana emerged from the restroom, weaving lithely back through the swanky bar melee to return to her seat.

It was mostly men in this heaving bullpen with barely a single choice specimen on offer.

She had her bull and he was in prime condition. A high libido and an eagerness to mount were the basic requirements.

Was it hot in here or was she in oestrus?

A lick or a sniff around her vulva-perineal region would settle that. A pre-menopausal hump, please.

Jana leaned forward with a kittenish smile. She couldn't stop mentally undressing him.

'You've heard all about me, so what about you?'

'International finance and stuff, I get by.'

'You're not only here for the gambling, are you?'

'Let's say that I've some unfinished business to attend to.'

'Hmm, that doesn't sound like laptop and briefcase stuff to me. I like a man who can handle himself.'

'You're not here just to play slots.'

'Sure I like to get laid, so what of it?'

'You want someone to play with your slot.'

'Bullseye! My slithery slitty clitty.'

'Your admission leaves little room for strategic ambiguity,' laughed Bell.

He'd got her started now.

'Look, I don't want someone who's chomping blueys down to get a hard-on! Give me a ripped flat stomach, a sag-free scrotum and a male who can juggle a set of balls without dropping them, you get me?'

'I got it. Yours or mine?'

'Ladies privilege, I like to stay close to my toothbrush.'

Her blisterpack of Doxygra lay on the bedside table. She should get a chance to gulp a pinky down.

Bell stood up.

'Let's get to it then. After you.'

'You'll find that I'm not wearing big pants underneath this cocktail dress.'

'Is there anything else you need to tell me?

'I'm off to Thailand after this trip, are you able to come?'

That was a coded instruction, dear lover.

***

Bell turned to glimpse the golden hair fanned out on the pillow. Britney eyes watched him standing next to the king-size bed, getting his kit off.

She really had let her hair down.

He nursed his naked abdominal muscles pensively. There was something in there which still twinged occasionally; a recent combat injury where the muscle fibres were still regenerating, no doubt.

Laughing boy David had left the bar before them. He had studied their snogging and groping through a crack in his door only eight rooms away down the corridor. The voyeur-stalker had an unhealthy aura about him which Bell had recognised from the outset. David had managed to identify Jana's room number somehow and he was going to be troublesome. That was why Bell had attached a microscopic tracking device to their stalker's jacket as he brushed past at the bar.

David was actually standing outside Jana's door right now, most probably with his ear pressed against it.

Jana was getting impatient and had something to say.

A glistening vulva awaited.

'I can't put my finger on it, but aren't you in a hurry like me?'

Bell pulled his trousers off and a wad of Swiss banknotes landed on the floor.

'Hey, you don't have to pay before you've tasted the merchandise!'

13 Baijiu binge

B aijiu is a popular drink in China.
It's the country's national tipple which outsells the likes
of gin, vodka, rum and even whisky.

Baijiu is distilled from a variety of grains, including rice, corn,
wheat and sorghum, but it is categorised by its aroma, not what
it is made from.

The convoy of coaches carrying groups of Chinese nuclear
and missile scientists commenced its fifty-five-kilometre
journey across the Hong Kong–Zhuhai–Macau bridge to the
former Portuguese colony.

A corporate-style jolly had been authorised for the technical
teams who had worked their fingers to the bone to hit their
PLA armament development targets.

The nuclear fission contingent were known to be gung-ho
party animals once their cage door had been unlocked.

This compared with the patient and dogged fusion teams
who still hadn't quite managed to harness the process by which
two light atomic nuclei combine to form a single heavier one
while releasing colossal amounts of clean energy.

The pursuers of the Holy Grail of renewable power were
more likely to become despondent and morose after a few
drinks, rather than monopolising the dance floor and dragging
hookers back up to their rooms.

Whatever. At least it was five days away from the grindstone
and a welcome change of scenery.

The official instruction had been not to open the presentation
boxes of 110-proof baijiu until the delegates had arrived at their

casino resort hotel. However, the allure and custom of ritualistic, hard liquor baijiu drinking, which offered floral, spicy and fruity flavours, proved to be too much for many of the delegates on the scenic coach ride.

It wasn't long before the alcohol was flowing freely. After all, they didn't get the chance to let their hair down that often. The baijiu binge wasn't the only free gift; a pile of casino chips was waiting for each invitee which was an integral part of their all-inclusive jamboree.

Their radiation badges and workloads had been left behind at remote laboratory locations where there was little entertainment except particle accelerators, rocket thrusters and decaying nuclear isotopes to play with. Some of them hadn't had sex for over a year…with another human being, anyway.

This was going to be like a school trip where every possible manifestation of enjoyment could be explored. They were all wearing college-style blazers with their particular discipline logo embroidered on the breast pocket.

Of course, the real nerd element had brought hieroglyphic text books with them. Hookers, cocaine, drinking and gambling were not really for them. What floated their boat was the province of subatomic particles rather than up-and-down on a hotel bed with something that they'd managed to charm into their room. The discovery of a strange new type of quark was their form of ecstasy.

There were set lunches, speeches, and talks which required obligatory attendance, but for the rest of the time it was a quest to see how much trouble you could get yourself into.

Someone from the Shenyan Institute for nuclear fission was going to give an after-dinner lecture, as well as senior Rocket Force guys running a series of mini-seminars. Attendees would just have to sit through these on the basis that an arsenal of technical know-how was fundamental to the hegemony of Zhongguo - the central kingdom which is China.

After the bender came to an end with a bad hangover, a hole in your nose-septum cartilage and the clap, you'd know that you'd nailed it. Maybe you hadn't even had time or given a thought to changing your underwear.

The white chalk dust which explained particle physics equations on a blackboard had been replaced by a line of coke on a whore's bare buttocks for too short a time.

The convention was hosted at the Wynn Casino hotel complex located in the central district of the northern peninsula section of Macau. It was conveniently situated close to the Nam Van lake and the Portuguese old town, but only a few of them would get to be aware of that. Fewer still would notice that the police headquarters for Macau SAR was, not by accident, located only a few streets away.

***

Colonel Zheng Wei, a shrewd operator, had been authorised to pursue the billionaire businessman, Gu Chang, to Macau following the botched arrest attempt at the Yitian Plaza Tower, in the city of Shenzhen.

Gu had somehow escaped from the fortieth floor of the building, right under their noses. How this had come about remained a mystery. Although a general all-points bulletin and BOLO instruction had been issued, all indications were that their fugitive had headed for Macau. This was corroborated by CCTV footage of a number of suspects matching Gu's description boarding the bridge shuttle bus.

Since that sighting the trail had gone cold and several police teams were working around the clock to flush him out in the world-renowned casino hotspot.

Unfortunately, one of those teams was headed up by none other than police commissioner Qian who was hell-bent on rectifying his earlier mistakes by being the officer making the crucial arrest.

Zheng knew that if that was allowed to happen Qian wouldn't be too bothered whether Gu was apprehended dead or alive. This concern was borne out by the fact that trigger-happy Qian had gunned down an entire floor of harmless employees during the Yitian Plaza Tower assault operation.

Zheng also suspected that Qian was holding a grudge against him for undermining his authority and would do anything in his power to discredit an interfering MSS agent. That anything could involve a stray bullet that blows away part of his skull.

The imperative was to find Gu first.

It was of passing interest that a large delegation of top armament scientists had descended on Macau for a five-day conference.

Yeah, a symposium shindig which was code-speak for an unbridled piss-up.

A thought had occurred to him as a trained investigator.

What if there was an assassin in their midst who had been despatched by a foreign power to liquidate them en masse?

Had this unnatural concentration of some of the best brains to be found in China been a sensible idea? Individuals whose insights and knowledge into WMD was irreplaceable. It seemed to him that the arrangement hadn't been well risk-assessed and that it was a dangerously dumb idea.

Who had authorised this folly?

They were all clearly identifiable from their matching blazers while packed tightly together at group events in the Wynn casino conference halls. Mass eating arrangements and entire corridors of rooms had been block-booked in close proximity, no doubt.

Zheng could visualise the carnage that might be visited upon the hapless boffins.

Perhaps he was imagining things and getting too creative.

His ability to place himself inside the minds of China's sworn enemies was getting the better of him.

Nah, surely nothing could possibly happen.

He was overthinking it.

Forget it…he had enough police business to be concerned with already, never mind a potential new wife who was carrying two unborn children.

There were several tough challenges to overcome before he found himself relaxing in a superyacht stateroom.

Come on, get a grip!

***

While other officers were staking out casinos and making other enquiries, Zheng had taken the trouble to visit the Macau marina complex.

He was standing on the quayside right now.

There were only three ocean-going yachts resting at their moorings but each of them looked to be a likely candidate.

The Nordia, the Caligula and the Beta Blanco.

Zheng studied their sleek lines and multiple decks with awe while crew members occasionally appeared on deck.

The cool breeze blowing off the Pearl River estuary focused his mind as waves lapped the tetrapod blocks protecting the sea wall.

If he was right about Gu's getaway plan, it could be any one of those wondrous beauties. Or none at all if they managed to arrest their elusive billionaire in time.

Even with China's full surveillance apparatus at his disposal, the police had been unable to locate his twin brother, Gu.

There was nothing for it but to visit the Macau Security Police headquarters which was located in the Edifício Conforseg, Praceta de 1 de Outubro, close to the old town.

Chinese National Day, a holiday on October 1st to mark the formation of the People's Republic of China, had been celebrated only a couple of days ago. Therefore, the mood at the HQ should be cooperative and helpful; compliant enough to accede to his request for some expert resource.

Xiong Yu, his newfound love, was waiting patiently in a hotel room with strict instructions to stay put...or so he hoped.

He hadn't told her that the plan was to do a runner.

Just a new life.

Zheng decided that he'd better hurry straight back and explain everything. The implausible and absurd truth might still spook her.

***

Xiong Yu had never set foot in a hotel before.

As far a she was concerned her new boyfriend, who seemed to be a police troubleshooter, had taken her along on a routine arrest excursion. This was because her apartment block had been demolished just hours after he had saved her on the roof.

She needed shelter, especially in her condition. The whirlwind events had happened so quickly that it was only now, sitting on her own, that she was able to rationalise her situation.

The future was a bit vague, hopefully moving into his place under his kind care and protection.

It was exciting but a little bit frightening.

She resolved to commit to her new circumstances with all her being. As the wife of Colonel Zheng Wei, a senior security officer, with two young children, she could see her life mapped out before her. A happy and secure future for the four of them.

It was the fresh start that she had signed up for.

She had never expected to visit Macau.

Her eyes had been opened, what a place!

It was an opportunity to get to know each other as lovers while they still had time.

But there was a nagging doubt.

In the back of her mind lurked the troubling notion that this guy made a regular thing of picking up girls in abortion clinics and that she was one in a long line of predecessors.

The high-profile arrest warrant could be some sort of sophisticated scam, yet he hadn't laid a lustful finger upon her.

What was his hustle?

Was he really a policeman?

Her instructions were simply to sit still without a cellphone until Wei, if that really was his first name, returned. Don't leave the room; don't answer the door; don't speak to anyone.

Yu suspected that if there was any weird elaboration of the fantasy-world scenario which she had already accepted, that would kill it.

A tap on the door interrupted her fretful contemplation.

Their embrace was short-lived.

Wei got the first word in.

'Thanks for being patient but I've got to go out again.'

'Again?'

Wei had read Yu's mind.

'I'm sorry that we can't go out for dinner.'

'So, I stay here and call room service?' smiled Yu.

'I regret that I have to visit police headquarters.'

'The manhunt?'

'It's more than that.'

Yu sensed that a bombshell was about to explode.

'The fugitive is a property billionaire who is my identical twin brother. He's escaping tonight on a superyacht and we're going with him.'

'We're leaving China?'

'Yes.'

'But he's now in custody, isn't he?'

Wei grimaced painfully.

'No. I've not met him yet and we can't find him. He doesn't even know that I exist.'

Hmm…just nod and go along with this.

She had heard enough.

'Okay.'

Yu wrestled to conceal the doubting look in her eyes.

'Please believe me. A new life for us, we can do this.'

'Okay.'

Wei held her close again, managing a weak smile and a kiss.

'Wait for me and I will return for you. Be ready, my love.'

Maybe not.

We're all done here.

Come on babies, what's the quickest way back to Hong Kong?

***

Colonel Zheng requisitioned an incident room with the flash of his ID. What he feared was a sudden recall instruction from Beijing. The clock was counting down.

He settled in for an intensive session in the Edifício Conforseg – the PSPF security headquarters.

He felt that he was tantalisingly close to tying all the strands together.

The endgame: Cruising out into the South China Sea on a superyacht. Heading for the Bashi channel and emerging into the vast Pacific Ocean with a scheduled stopover in Hawaii. Most importantly, Yu would be with him.

It all hinged on his twin brother.

If Gu Chang was in Macau, the blanket of all-pervasive facial recognition should have flushed him out by now; he definitely hadn't been spotted in the Blue Dragon. Gu had to be inside the confines of the region of Macau somewhere.

Time to put surveillance technology to the test.

A young guy called Yuze walked in and introduced himself: A trained hacker, cyber expert and systems analyst.

Yuze knew his deep web from his dark web.

His computer equipment was wheeled in on trolleys. Yuze was well accustomed to hot-desking around the various police operation rooms when there was a flap on.

Now fully set up, he stared across the table at Zheng.

Yuze looked to be as sharp as a nail; if anyone could root out a billionaire on the run, this techie could.

'All we have to go on is a hundred-dollar casino chip and a photograph,' lamented Zheng.

'Okay.'

'Let's start with how to dupe facial recognition.'

'Not gait analysis?' quizzed Yuze.

'Huh?'

'The analysis of human locomotion, like FR.'

'Yeah?'

'A person's gait can be digitized using high-resolution sensors and cameras to map any individual's unique walking style.'

'Er…maybe later…let's just stay with FR, shall we?'

'Occlusion or confusion?'

'Any kind of faking it, I guess,'

'A balaclava leaves the most important facial features exposed – the eyes, the mouth, the nose – rendering the concealment ploy ineffective. A deep learning framework, trained on fourteen key facial points, has been found to accurately identify partially-occluded faces most of the time: It can peel away glasses, fake facial hair, and even latex-nose prosthetics.

'Are there any effective FR counter-measures?'

'My money's on a PSIP.'

'What's that?'

'A Personal Surveillance Identity Prosthetic is a 3D scan of someone's entire face which can include imaginative digital alterations. It's a mask made from a pigmented, hard resin using a photo-realistic rendering of every facial feature, such as skin tone, texture, moles, scars and hair.'

'So, like an ice hockey mask on steroids?' laughed Zheng.

'Infrared interference has also been known to confuse sensor interpretation.'

Zheng puffed his cheeks up as he digested the info-overload. It was dead right that they covered all the bases. At least Yuze was well versed in all this stuff.

After a cigarette and a coffee they got back to it again.

'Say, Yuze, that was a jaw-dropper. How about superyachts?'

'Shoot.'

'I've identified three suspect boats moored up at the Club Maritimo Nautico.'

'So, what about them?'

'I want to know if you can link them to any of the following organisations: Dime Industries and the Everlong Property Group.'

'You mean like ownership, recent movements and collateral agreements for maritime mortgages?'

'Whatever you can trawl up for the Nordia, the Caligula and the Beta Blanco.'

'I'm on it.'

'It's already getting dark. Shall we say one hour tops on this and then we break again for a bite to eat?'

Yuze's expression was cool and non-committal.

'Don't worry, we'll need a rest and I'm buying,' laughed Zheng, jovially.

Zheng's cheery demeanour masked a man getting close to a nervous breakdown. Even when he found his brother he had to ask him, maybe plead with him, whether he could come on board with his pregnant girlfriend. What would happen if it was a 'No'?

It all seemed to be hopeless and, in the harsh light of day, a totally nonsensical idea.

***

Yuze and Zheng scraped their plastic seats together in the strip-lighted police canteen. It was just a week after the Chinese National Day celebrations. Petty crime dipped at this time of year and the force was having a pleasant time of it.

They worked their way through some shitty noodles, a couple of mantou-steamed buns, and a soft drink. The depleted canteen vending-machine was limited to candy rolls wrapped in edible rice paper.

Zheng hoped that his darling Yu was occupying her time watching TV and eating hastily purchased supermarket snacks. He agonised that Yu could easily pull the plug and head back to Hong Kong, giving up on him and his crazy scheme. Leaving her with a loaded semi-automatic may not have been a good idea.

Leave China? It was madness!

'I recognise your accent,' said Zheng, casually.

'I was born in Xi'an, the capital of Shaanxi Province.'

'Got it. The starting point of the Silk Road and not that far from Beijing.'

'Sorry...I haven't found anything.'

'Hmm, everything cloaked in secrecy, as I had suspected.'

'Yeah, overseas companies with shares held by nominees. Yacht registrations in George Town in Grand Cayman, and Valletta in Malta.'

Zheng became wistful and morose all of a sudden. His brother might not even be in Macau at all.

'You're a bright young man. Make sure that you enjoy life.'

'You mean that my human essence is draining away unnoticed while I'm working too hard?'

'That's it,' smiled Zheng, ruefully.

'Do you have a family?'

'I have a beautiful wife and young twins.'

Zheng enjoyed embroidering the truth a little.

'I envy you, I still have to find someone.'

'When you do it will be wonderful. My soulmate is as dizzyingly alluring as the first day I set eyes upon her.'

'The harbourmaster's office issued a final mooring fee invoice today…for the Beta Blanco,' said Yuze, casually.

'What?!'

'…and it was fully refuelled today.'

'Why didn't you say?'

'You were explaining the joys of life to me!'

Zheng was overcome by a surge of new energy.

'The casino token! Let's get a better look at it.'

***

Zheng was pressed up alongside Yuze as they got to work with fresh vitality, both staring at his dual-screen setup.

The RFID reader's radio transmission activated the tag which caused it to respond with data.

'I'm importing all the information from this token,' said Yuze.

Every field, every character.

According to the website, the Blue Dragon membership card comes in five flavours: Opal, Emerald, Sapphire, Ruby and Diamond.

'I have identified the unique serial number of the token: <STX>09002D4EA2CBFE36<ETX>.'

'It's coded in hexadecimal, of course; this one is sixteen digits. Casino chips are totally worthless tokens until the serial numbers are validated and added to the database inventory. The rest is process automation, both in the cashier's cage and in the table game racks on the casino floor.'

Simple.

'Wait a minute, you accessed the harbourmaster system, didn't you?' said Zheng.

'Yes.'

'...so could you...?'

'No problem. It's a general condition of operating a business in Macau. Watch this.'

Yuze suddenly had administrative access to the Blue Dragon casino operations software.

'I'm looking for a table which stores token-inventory. Look, I've found it – our token is logged as not being in stock.'

'So?'

'It must be out there, issued to someone.'

'Who?'

'I'm searching for entries in the tokens-issued table.'

A single line populated the screen grid.

'How does that help?'

'We have identified the membership card number it was issued to, so therefore we can retrieve the player name.'

Zheng could hardly contain himself.

Fingers skated over the keyboard.

'In the name of 'Ji Yinan'.'

Zheng slammed his fist into the desk.

Yuze continued.

'It's a low-grade Opal card - a basic 'you-can-play' bit of plastic given to everyone who walks in through the door. Issued five weeks ago and hasn't been used since.'

Shit! Another dead-end.

Zheng stared at the 'O' capital letter in one of the table columns.

'Let me look at the database schema again,' said Yuze.

Time for another cigarette.

Zheng grimaced as Yuze approached the coffee machine in the corridor.

'I've found something!'

'Huh?'

'The card has been upgraded to Ruby, a quantum leap over Emerald and Sapphire from Opal.'

'What?'

'Only Diamond is higher – for international high-rollers and issued solely by personal invitation.'

Ruby membership benefits: Super-reward points, free chips, gourmet meals, and five-star accommodation. Crucially, no betting limit, no cash-in ceiling, and non-existent ID verification.

They raced back to the office.

'Look at this, four hundred and ninety-nine chips were issued in the same denomination, the remainder with smaller values.'

Zheng calculated this to be worth around fifty thousand US dollars which was hardly billionaire-on-the-run territory. Whoever this dude was, it wasn't the person they were looking for.

Yuze clocked Zheng doing the math and arranged for a lavender-rimmed casino token to pop up in the centre of his screen.

Token value: One hundred thousand US dollars.

Zheng did the math again with his mouth open.

Fifty million USD total.

'When was this card last swiped?'

'Nine minutes ago.'

'He's in the casino now?!'

'Just won two hundred dollars on red.'

'Playing using an alias?'

'Exactly.'

Zheng had to get to Gu Chang fast. He must have tricked FR somehow. What was needed was a diversion on the casino floor.

'Can you control the roulette wheel from here?'

'Yeah, but slots is easier.'

'Go on…'

'How about random machine jackpots?'

Zheng visualised the chaos that would cause…drawing unnecessary attention away from a face-faking individual placing small bets for the sake of appearances.

'Which roulette table?'

'Table four.'

Unlucky number…the omen of doom.

Zheng ran out of the door and jumped into an unmarked police car. Minutes later he was on the Ponte da Amizade elevated highway, heading south.

Hey, can't this clapped-out clunker go any faster?!

***

Earlier in the day…

Gu Chang, the CEO of Dime Industries and the Everlong Property Group, surveyed the sparse apartment lounge.

This place had been bought by one of his subsidiary companies some time ago, in careful preparation.

A safe house and a refuge.

He was busy perfecting his disguise as a sick old man.

Decrepit.

A limp and a stick…a limp dick and a tic.

Twitchy, listless and languid.

Garbled speech.

Dated, ill-fitting clothing.

Gu tried on the baseball cap. It used an array of tiny infrared LEDs wired to the inside of the brim-visor to project dots of light on to the wearer's face.

These dots were invisible to the human eye but confused the facial recognition algorithms to render a human face unidentifiable.

The device could not only hide the wearer's identity.

The array of dots could make facial recognition sensors think that the target was someone else altogether, a person who was already stored in a central databank repository.

He was in two minds about this chancy excursion.

The Blue Dragon.

A specialist travel agency had supplied the casino tour package which included chips, all paid for by his company in Chinese yuan. A clever stratagem to convert mega value legitimately into US currency.

Play a few tables and exchange your bag of tokens – all fifty million dollars of it…or play safe and forget the idea because there was a warrant out for your arrest.

The cautious option:-

Ditch the Dragon and the fifty million.

Get a taxi to a seamy, harbour watering-hole.

Buy a drink and head out the back past beer crates into the darkness, only to emerge furtively on to the quayside lined with mooring bollards and tethering ropes. Walk a few hundred metres to the gangplank of a superyacht and give the order to cast off.

Blissfully watch the lights of the Pearl River Delta disappear into the distance.

The reckless option:-

Ride the Dragon, grab the money then get the taxi.
Come on, one last roll of the dice won't hurt.
Funny that…a single hundred-dollar chip was missing.

***

A little while later…

Gu Chang swiped his Ruby membership card and headed for the aisles of slots. The Loony Monkey and Inca Gold one-armed bandit machines acted as good company while he got comfortable with his surroundings.

As far as he could see he wasn't under human surveillance, but he was no expert.

Blackjack and roulette beckoned.

Just a few hands and a series of spins of the roulette wheel. After some tortuous and stressful minutes standing at the cashier's cage he could be on his way. His huge exchange of tokens would necessitate supervisor verification, unfortunately.

Blackjack was a washout, simply placing a series of modest bets for appearances sake. Roulette meant that he didn't have to think so hard; on his third spin he won two hundred dollars on red. This could actually be fun!

At the far end of a line of illuminated fluted pillars some kind of commotion seemed to have kicked off down one of the slots aisles. A couple of floor-walkers ran past him, heading in that direction.

Best not to hang around too long.

14 Pillow talk

'What now, Tommo?'
The heartfelt term of endearment felt warm and natural.

Bell stood directly behind Jana as she savoured the panoramic view of the Cotai district from her hotel room window.

It had been a busy, bustling morning to get here.

A slick check-out from the Ritz-Carlton in Kowloon plus a coach transfer, followed by the Pearl River ferry, another coach ride and a Venetian Macau check-in; not to mention the various security hurdles.

A quick stroll through the casino was followed by a welcome and mandatory drink in the bar.

It was nearly midday already.

Jana's pink Samsonites lay burst open in the corner of the bedroom. She slipped out of her skirt and threw off her top in a deliberately provocative manner.

She snuck up close and gripped Bell's hardening crotch.

'You'll have to tear the rest of it off yourself.'

'I tell you what now.'

'Yeah?'

'A quickie, a post-coital nap, and a taxi up to the old town for a late lunch.'

'A stopwatch speed-bonk?! Not being brought to the boil in an achingly slow manner? I was expecting you to thoroughly squeegee my bits again. What is this?'

'An act which is cold and devoid of feeling; a mechanical and robotic experience leaving you pleasured but only partly satisfied,' he teased.

'Is this some kind of foreplay I don't know about?'

'If you like.'

Her new lover held her gaze and allowed the moment to float in silence. He was every inch an assertive alpha male who was comfortable in his own self-worth, accustomed to steering interactions and seeking no validation.

'Okay.'

'How about the lunch?'

'Eat me instead.'

'Daytime fornication always seems dirtier.'

'The promise of proper sex later, is that it? A girl can only take so little.'

'If you're up for it.'

She suddenly felt that she was overstepping the mark.

'Sorry to be a bossy bitch, but you had me worried. I thought that maybe you needed a *pre*-coital nap. But I can't talk - I'm sure that jet lag, late nights, and alcohol are catching up with me.'

Not to mention the hot sex.

So combustible that she had no problem taking up arson.

'You're on top form, Jana.'

'You know I like to be on top.'

'A reverse cowgirl, this time?'

Permission to explore and stimulate her deep vaginal erogenous zones had been previously granted. Please continue to roam at will.

'So, are you going to get your cock out or not?...and no wiping it on my curtains.'

She pulled the bed covers back in one movement and slid into position.

A pair of Calvin Kleins hit the carpet and Bell followed her.

'Tomolito dear, how do you want me?'

All men make love in different ways, directing the progress of the sexual choreography in accordance with their deep-rooted desires and erotic fantasies. The awkward repositioning of limbs and torsos at intervals, urgent whispered commands, and frantic roll-offs to locate a tube of lubricant would never make great TV, but everybody knows that.

As long as the basic playbook was up there with dusted, cocoa-bean bonbons.

Gimme chocolate!

How would the cream-filled confection be delivered this time?

'Turn over.'

A couple of pillows were plumped beneath her stomach in short order. The hors d'oeuvre was ready to be served.

'Don't rush.'

A quickie didn't need to be that quick.

***

Wednesday, 3rd October, 23:10.

Location: The Incident Room, West Wing, The White House, Washington DC.

'They're on the move, something is happening.'

'All bases in their eastern theatre of operations are buzzing with battle-ready activity, and that includes civil defence muster points and air raid shelters,' replied the Secretary of State, responding to the declaration made by the US President, James Donald Smith.

Satellite surveillance had monitored the sudden build-up.

The Secretary of Defense, holding a position of command and authority over the military which is second only to that of the president, was itching to say something, but he would have to wait his turn.

'As President of the United States, this is my Cuban Missile Crisis moment. It's popped up sooner during my term of office than I would have liked. My duty is to step up to the plate. The buck stops here.'

The three of them weren't sitting around the table on their own. Also present were the Chairman of the Joint Chiefs of Staff, the Director of National Intelligence, the Director of the Central Intelligence Agency, the National Security Advisor and several senior aides.

The Secretary of Defense picked his moment.

'The naval blockade of Taiwan is a regular occurrence; the vessels always disperse after a few days. Chinese National Day was just over a week ago, I believe it's just bluster and sabre rattling. The US seventh fleet is on standby.'

The President voiced an immediate response.

'Well, I don't like it. If anything is likely to kick off, we need to get in first. What other important dates or anniversaries are coming up in South East Asia?'

The Director of the CIA had the answer.

'It's National Day in Taiwan on the tenth.'

'They wouldn't, would they?' said the President.

'Someone in the Zhongnanhai may have a wicked sense of humour,' replied the wily foreign intelligence veteran.

Everyone in the room knew that the Zhongnanhai compound in Beijing, located in a former imperial garden, housed the leadership of the CCP and the State Council. It was the equivalent of the Kremlin or the White House.

'Seriously?'

'It would be historically poetic to snuff out the ROC on its National Day. The sea state in the Taiwan strait tends to be at its best in early October,' continued the Director.

It was time for the Director of National Intelligence to chip in.

'As we tighten our grip along the First Island Chain, China's window of opportunity to mount a full-scale invasion in the South China Sea closes, but the lure of unfettered access to the Pacific may be too much to forfeit…and worth a terrible price.'

'Everyone in this room has to voice an opinion,' declared the President, 'The foundation of war is economics. We have been overtaken as the biggest kid on the block by a bigger kid who'll steal all our lunch money. How does the song go? - '*It's now or never…tomorrow will be too late*'.'

The jocular remark from the POTUS raised the mood of the room. It kind of proved that he was the right man for the job, shouldering ultimate responsibility at a time like this.

The Chairman of the Joint Chiefs of Staff leaned forward and raised his hand.

'We're still at the top of our game militarily and we have a track record of combat experience going all the way back to the Korean war. Having said that, we'll be fighting in the Chinese backyard where we have long supply lines to the islands of Okinawa and Guam. In addition, there's the logistical challenge of co-ordinating effectively with our regional allies: Japan, South Korea, the Philippines and Australia.'

'What you're saying is that we should lance the boil?' paraphrased the President.

'Yes, having compressed and maintained pressure on the pus-filled furuncle, simply rupture and drain it. Flush with sterile saline solution and sew it up.'

'Thank you for that incisive assessment, Bob. I didn't know that you were a physician!'

'I dropped out of medical school to join the US Marine Corps. Sucking out the core of a boil is analogous to an offensive military operation, as I see it,' came the reply.

It was the National Security Advisor's turn to speak. All eyes became fixed upon him.

'It would also be wise to consider the Chinese viewpoint. They regard Taiwan as a lost province which belongs to China. It is unfortunate that the Qing dynasty signed it across by treaty to the Japanese in 1895 and that the Chinese nationalists fled there in 1949 when the PRC was created. The PRC missed a chance to grab it back early on, for example, during the Korean and Vietnam wars when the US was overstretched. Taiwan supplies ninety percent of the world's advanced logic chips, the importance of which cannot be overstated.'

'So, are they preparing for war?' said the President.

'The answer may lie with certain peripheral details like the wholesale dumping of US Treasury bonds to insulate the yuan, and a nationwide scramble for blood donations,' replied the NSA.

The President had a conciliatory point to make.

'The USA rebuilt Europe after World War Two with the Marshall plan and triumphed with the Berlin airlift in 1948.

'I guess that certain people would see Hawaii, New Mexico, Arizona, and Alaska as stolen treasures, and they might have a point. Just as the Chinese might have a much stronger argument with regard to Taiwan.'

James D Smith took a quiet moment to consider his position while everyone else around the long table sat in silence with their own thoughts.

I'm James Donald Smith: sworn in as Republican president at the age of forty-three, with over three hundred days in office under my belt.

I have a majority in Congress and the Senate, an extreme MAGA lawyer appointed as Attorney General, and the Supreme Court of Justice in my pocket.

I'm capable, energetic, and brandish a clear agenda.

The American public love me for it because they have given me the mandate to turn everything around, put everything right, and Make America Great Again:

-USA energy – drill, baby, drill.

-Drug dealers – an automatic death penalty.

-Fentanyl – destroy the precursor pushers killing USA youth.

-The wall – a tightly sealed southern border.

-Defence – a next-generation missile defence shield.

-China – take on the Asian giant hornet and win.

The President had one last question, primarily directed at the Director of the CIA:

'Do we have anyone on the ground in China?'

'Not at present, but British Military Intelligence have an operation underway, something which will do more than tickle the dragon's tail. Our Japanese allies are also toying with a couple of undercover initiatives.'

'Dark ops: Play dirty – I like that. Please keep me informed.'

'Yes, Mr President.'

'We have a unanimous decision, then.'

***

Gao Zi Xin was back in northern Laos, safely ensconced in his secure compound. He took a tour of his Emperor Nero casino. It was not as busy as he would have liked. The reason for the low footfall was rooted in new travel restrictions recently imposed in mainland China.

Private time to lick his wounds and consider his position which had been interrupted by an unwelcome visit.

He had displeased his masters in Beijing which had resulted in some unwanted PRC security personnel arriving at his private airstrip only an hour or two earlier.

The subject of precursor shipments, no doubt.

It was the price he had to pay for state patronage.

They had ordered him to fly to Taipei within the next eight hours and stay there until further notice. The classified blueprint which outlined an internal insurrection against the Democratic Progressive Party government in Taiwan had been collecting dust. Gao had assumed that it would never happen.

He was wrong.

An obligation to get his butt over there and await instructions in a nearly derelict building, located between an eco-hotel and a dental surgery in downtown Taipei.

The three-strong team from the PRC Ministry of Security had been provided with a meal and a pile of free casino chips. Gao knew that basic freebies wouldn't be enough to initiate any kind of dereliction of duty.

The team leader revelled in the delivery of an admonition monologue, uttered with a priggish grin.

'Your Patriot defence systems won't save you – you will be obliterated by a Dongfeng DF-15 rocket aimed at your charming riverside residence.'

'You are to carry out your orders as stipulated or we will forcefully take you back to Beijing for re-education. A full frontal lobotomy will leave you out of sorts for a week or two. Electric shock treatment and organ removal will also be part of your rehabilitation therapy.'

'In a word, we turned a blind eye…now we're calling it in.'

Gao stoically took the reprimand with half-closed eyelids and a neutral smile.

You don't speak to me like that.

No one was going to get anywhere near his prefrontal cortex.

Gao selected his words carefully.

'Before I send you on your way, please allow me to thank you for your visit. Fly well and goodbye.'

The verbal charm disguised the subterfuge of a pit viper. Only Gao's unsettling, venomous glare might give the game away.

The delegation would fly back to Beijing in a few hours' time aboard their Russian-built YAK-40 VIP jet.

That meant overflying swathes of impenetrable jungle as their flight took them into Vietnamese airspace heading north-east for Hanoi. The YAK-40 was a trijet which had been specially designed for poorly equipped airports with short unpaved runways, while being capable of operating in challenging weather.

Onboard ingress was via a rear-entry stairway. The captain, co-pilot, an engineer and two PRC security personnel had been instructed to safeguard the plane around the clock.

It boiled down to gaining access to an inspection panel on the underside of one of the wings. That or a routine diagnostics check of either of the turbofan engines. The armed security guards had been the hardest to prise away, standing doggedly to attention for hours on the smooth concrete in full battle dress.

Food, casino chips, alcohol, a comfortable bed and a shower, a lounge with movies, drugs and mild threats had all failed to shift them. A dose of Polonium 210-laced sushi would take too long.

Gao's aeronautical engineers needed twenty minutes to install an explosive device which would blow a wing off in mid-flight. With what was about to be unleashed off the coast of Fujian province, a missing Yakovlev jet would be the last thing that Beijing would be worried about.

Time to send in the sorority-squad ball-busters.

Candy, Kara and Tiffany.

Daddy's little darlings.

Three of his top girls.

They could suck a golf ball through a hosepipe faster than an elasticated thong hitting the deck.

Hey, hadn't Candy trained as a psychologist before going on the game?

***

A team of airplane cleaners armed with vacuum equipment on trolleys made their way across the hangar towards the YAK-40 Trijet.

Two hard-nut sentinels in camo-combats, standing guard by the plane's rear staircase, eyed up the three female cabin-cleansing operatives as they approached.

Workwear: Overalls, trainers, latex gloves, and scrub caps.

'Hi boys, we're here to empty some tanks,' said Candy.

'Yeah, we're going to get really dirty,' said Kara.

'Squeezing into all those tight cracks with a flexible hose makes us horny,' grinned Tiffany.

'Back off, this is a restricted area,' came the senior officer's deadpan response.

'Come on boys, give us some slack, it's hard enough being bent over with our butts in the air,' said Candy, taking charge.

'You're not cleaners at all, are you?'

'Let me give you a clap. Like the flavoured condoms we get our clients to use, we come pre-lubricated. So, what are you two, a couple of asexual robots?'

'Horny chicks aren't your thing, I guess,' added Kara.

Candy had the last word.

'Come on girls, let's leave these eunuchs to each other. We'll just have to lick each other out instead.'

The blue touch paper had been lit.

'Wait a minute!'

'What have you got, big boy?'

'Can we do all three of you?'

***

Daniel Roxby was incandescent with rage.

He'd paid off the hooker with counterfeit US dollars of North Korean origin. They were of startling quality. He fixed himself a drink and ordered another girl for an hour's time.

What did he know so far?

The lovebirds seemed to be inseparable. The best that he could hope for was her young buck upstart getting bored with the bitch. However, that didn't look likely so he'd need to get him out of the way by some other method.

He was running out of time so it needed to be done tomorrow at the latest so he could benefit from a fortuitous rebound.

If only that cheeky young puppy hadn't made a late appearance at the welcome meeting. It was the same kind of bad luck that he'd had on the tables; now he was even more desperate.

He had tailed lover boy to the hotel foyer.

Somehow he'd been given the slip.

Injure or kill him. Hey, why not alert the authorities about a suspicious person? Get him detained, perhaps plant some Pyongyang hundred-dollar bill fakes on him…that could work.

It would be evident at the Taipa suite cocktail party and dinner dance tonight whether they were still an item or not. There was an outside chance that he might have got bored of her already.

Roxby couldn't stop visualising her jewellery. It was a well-founded barometer of her underlying wealth. Sure, he'd looked her up on the web and found her listed at the UK Companies House registry.

A prize worth fighting for – she had already proved to be on the hunt for a new partner. This one was worth considerably more than some of the other poor wretches he'd swindled and caused to end their miserable lives. He was sure that exhortations or persuasion to commit suicide were triable offences under the UK Suicide Act of 1961, but he hadn't been rumbled yet!

Mistreating and humiliating women always gave him so much pleasure. Breaking their spirit early on in the process was key. He never tired of overpowering and subjugating them with his superior strength and sadistic nature.

Skewering the lovely Jana could solve all his problems.

Was he prepared to kill to achieve his objectives?

Huh! Like wringing a cat's neck – he wouldn't give it a second thought.

***

Jana's strawberry-blonde hair lay fanned out on the pillow.

She awoke with a jolt.

'Where am I?'

'We overslept.'

'What?!'

'We'll do the restaurant tomorrow.'

'There's something I haven't told you…I was dreaming about it.'

Bell inched closer and ran his index finger over her bottom lip. Her tongue darted out for a split second.

'A confession?'

'Er, yeah, but don't study me too closely! I'll go and clean my teeth first.'

Bell watched her bare arse disappear into the ensuite. The sight of her voluptuous naked body gave him an instant hard-on. Later tonight, Jana's desirable form, which he had completely explored, would be concealed beneath a long, black satin dress. Right now, he couldn't get enough of it.

Seconds later, he stood astride her as she sat on the toilet seat with a snatch of loo paper at the ready.

Bell leaned down and fingered her moist vulva.

'I can still taste you…and I'm about to pee,' smiled Jana, as Bell stole a sticky, gummy kiss off her.

'I know.'

'Here goes.'

A jet of urine bathed his right hand which he retracted after a final squirt. He licked the warm lady liquid from his fingers and wiped the aromatic essence across his stubble.

He savoured her potent scent for a moment: female gland fluids, metabolites, enzymes, and urea. Therein, the fluid held residual traces of the processes of recent arousal and orgasm. Unfettered sexual consumption - eat, penetrate and drink your partner, driven to form union with a woman by a craving, testosterone-powered lust.

Jana was left holding his cock.

'My wee turns you on?'

'Everything about you girls turns us guys on. Our sex drive has some of our number screwing blow-up plastic dolls and engaging in bizarre kinks and fetishes. The size of your labia doesn't bother us, by the way, so why is labiaplasty considered to be a desirable cosmetic option? All that matters is that your underwear hits the deck. We love you the way God made you. It's what it means to be a bloke, I guess.'

'Men!'

'Let's get something to eat.'

'A bit more cuddling first, though.'

'Proper sex later.'

'On a promise…it's a deal.'

'I'll call room service.'

'Knickers back on for now, then.'

***

Bell sat upright in bed nursing a mineral water, braced for her imminent revelation. He hoped that this wasn't going to be anything medical.

Jana lay with her head on the pillow.

'I recently won nearly ten million pounds in the National Lottery.'

'So?'

'So, that's a lot of money, isn't it?

'What are you saying?'

'I'm alone and I have no one to share it with.'

It was ironic that someone who didn't need the money had won a life-changing prize. Maybe that was how Lady Luck dished out her favours. Bell surmised that, including her cosmetic business, she must be worth somewhere north of twenty five million.

'Beware dating apps and rom-cons, Jana. What's to say that I'm not a chancer, down on his luck, who will empty your bank account?'

'A lonely MILF cougar picked you up, remember?'

'Maybe I'm a bad-boy squeeze who will end up controlling you in a toxic relationship? You don't really know me.'

'You're upsetting me now.'

'The thing is Jana, I won't see anything bad happen to you on my watch. I think you know what I'm talking about.'

'Yes.'

'There will be other predators.'

'I'll be careful.'

Bell grimaced.

'That may not be good enough and I won't always be here to protect you.'

'What do you do…really?'

'International finance and stuff. The City. Mergers and acquisitions. See how smoothly that rolls off the tongue? It could be total bullshit.'

Murders and executions, more like.

'I get it.'

'Go on, quiz me about something else.'

'What's your body count?'

He'd walked clumsily into that one.

'Hah!'

'Gotcha!'

A crimson fingernail was pointing at him.

Body count: a number which indicated the size of an army of previous liaisons. A metric which could serve to haunt the other partner and sour a relationship with deep-rooted resentment. A cumulative total best left undisclosed.

Also classified: the existence of a second list.

An assassin's rough tally of mostly nameless cadavers racked up in the course of duty. A mortal statistic known only to himself and MIX.

'I do alright.'

Jana smiled at the cagey answer.

Bell was more than happy to let her expound her own back-story.

'I admit I've made some bad dating decisions in the past. My twenties were spent going out with unsuitable men.

'I sense that there's something real and genuine about you, Tom. I can't quite put my finger on it. I feel that I can discuss anything with you.

'We're having so much fun together. Younger guys have an inexhaustible athletic stamina, but they often need to be shown the finer points of a woman's body.

'My gateway young gun was the eighteen-year-old son of a girlfriend of mine. While tipsy on sangria, it started with a passionate snog behind a beachside restaurant in Ibiza. Before I knew it we were going at it doggy-style in the villa pool-house. Then there was Angelo, Piero and Davide.

'I was right back in my twenties again, but this time gulping down Doxygra and night-after Levonorgestrel pills.'

'Pinkies and ECPs?'

'You guys will never know what it's like to fear that you're pregnant after a one-night stand.'

'The Child Support Agency wanted-list is our bugbear.'

'I'm not looking forward to losing my passion for life. We're talking about the big 'M' and losing my looks. Night sweats, hot flushes, anxiety, and insomnia are an unattractive proposition. Shagging an elderly auntie could be deemed to be one of your bizarre man-kinks and fetishes.'

Bell cut in to soothe her anxiety.

'My suggestion is that you banish your worries about your ovaries and plummeting oestrogen levels and simply enjoy the moment.'

'You don't think that I'm a bunny-boiler in incontinence pants, then?'

'In designer shapewear, maybe,' smirked Bell.

'What?!'

'…and more like a botoxed-up baby snatcher.'

'You bastard!'

Bell laughed heartily as she slapped his arm.

'You'll have me calling you princess next.'

'Yeah, while on your knees!'

'Now it's my turn to confess.'

Jana's eyes widened in alarm.

'As soon as we've eaten, I'll be gone. I have some business to attend to.'

A bottom lip trembled.

'Will I be seeing you later?'

'You'll be on your own this evening...'

The look of disappointment intensified.

'Oh.'

'...for the most part...'

Jana's expression registered a flicker of hope as Bell sweetened the bitter pill; she'd passed the clingy-needy-test thus far.

'...the dancing goes on till late, doesn't it?'

'A tardy appearance to lead me in a slow dance?'

'I'll see.'

Bell knew that predator David would be in there like a rat down a sewer-pipe the moment Jana was on her own. A key test of her newly-tutored rom-con resilience.

Stage one of his mission beckoned.

15 Dragon's keeper

Bell surveyed the kit piled up on his unused bed.
A choice of weaponry.

A Heckler and Koch MP5SD, a Glock 19 semi-automatic pistol, a subcompact Glock 30S, a choice of grenades, C4 military explosive with timers and detonators. Not to mention spare magazines and ammunition, commando knives, garrottes and deadly poisons which could be administered in a variety of ways.

An ordnance delivery package courtesy of MIX field logistics who had, phantom-like, left the consignment of death and destruction in his pristine hotel room. More drops at other locations had been arranged.

The touchstone of what he had to do this evening was stealth and secrecy with an emphasis on sound-suppression…all until he flicked the ignition switch.

It was fortuitous that Jana had a predilection for staying close to her toothbrush. He had deliberately taken the trouble to move to a cheaper room which overlooked the back of the Venetian Macau complex – clearly, the wrong side of the building. A stairwell led out to mature ornamental gardens and a sleepy taxi rank rather than the exit of a bustling hotel foyer.

Bell studied the detailed layout of the Blue Dragon casino. It had a total of six floors, topped off by luxury penthouse quarters. The executive management placed a strong emphasis on augmented security. This translated to the presence of well-trained goons who were employed to deal not so much with lairy punters but with bodyguard and rival incursion duties.

Bell had his work cut out to bludgeon his way in there, neutralising everything that ever walked or crawled that got in his way.

Mission objective: Multi-faceted.

A shockwave distraction, a diversion of police resources...plus a scalp.

The outcome would be attributed by the authorities to a sudden flare-up in gangland warfare which would shake the calm of Macau to the core. More retributions and reprisals would spiral gambling syndicate conflict into a full-blown conflagration which was bad for business.

Bell smiled as he checked his velcro-enabled overalls.

So long as he ended up with a head on a stick.

***

Donato Gauci was the CEO of the Blue Dragon Group of companies. He had been ruthless in his rise to power having intimidated and strong-armed everyone else out of the way. He possessed a killer streak inherited through his Eastern Mediterranean bloodline. He had a penchant for hard liquor, fast women and ultra-violence.

Gauci's core motivations gave some indication of the origin of his nickname – 'Barbie'. Many attributed it to the fact that he was always seen with a different, superficially attractive but insipid young woman. Others were aware that it was because Gauci routinely tied victims down over a lit BBQ once the sirloin steaks and burgers had been cooked; he was even known to paste spicy marinade-sauce over their bodies as they screamed. The stench of burning human flesh smelled of power, Gauci was reported to have declared.

Bell guessed that Gauci's take on napalm was something similar. Having said that, Gauci also seemed to be blessed with a soft, cuddly side.

The intelligence indicated that the BDG supremo would be entertaining a young lady this evening whereby a specified period of three hours had been allocated when under no circumstances was he to be disturbed – no matter what. Anyone who did so would be next on the grill.

Connoisseur dining and intelligent, engaging conversation.

Bell imagined an intimate dinner for two in the penthouse suite, surrounded by fine furnishings with no expense spared in the wooing process. Fine wines and cocktails, romantic music and ambience, gourmet dishes sent up from the basement kitchens in a dumbwaiter lift, as the ebbs and flows of lovebird interaction took place.

First the dinner table, followed by civilised after-dinner liqueurs on sumptuous sofas as giant, indigo-glazed Chinese dragons watched over the courting couple. A loving and caring behavioural anomaly curiously resident within Gauci's complex personality profile. It had to be an accident of nature.

All the while, money poured in on the casino floors below.

As if that wasn't enough, greed and power had driven Gauci to extend the BDG reach across the globe with the launch of his Betto893 gambling website which majored in moreish E-bingo and compulsively addictive slots. The dark underbelly of it all was the tally of resistive unfortunates who'd been snuffed out, and the enemies that he had accumulated.

Whatever.

Gauci was revelling in the despotic governance of his fiefdom.

***

Bell had been dropped off by taxi a block away. In his overalls, Nike cap and carrying a heavy kit bag, he was an emergency plumber out on a job, if anyone asked.

What's in the holdall? Mind if I take a look? That's a lot of plumber's putty or marzipan you've got in there, Sir. Okay, nothing to worry about, but it does look suspiciously like RDX-based blocks of high explosive.

Yeah, I'm seriously sick of blocked toilet call-outs – next time, flush your pet caiman down the pan instead.

As he turned the corner, the temple of cupidity and grand larceny presented itself.

The Blue Dragon.

Powerful searchlight columns animated the night sky from its corners, and what was reputed to be the largest glitterball in the world revolved lazily on the roof, sending penetrating beams of high-lumen light out in all directions.

Bell's focus drifted to the illuminated top floor.

Up there, a middle-aged thug with no neck and a hairy back was sweet-talking the object of his desire.

The explosive charges he was going to set would blow the lid off this mother and take innocent family man Gauci with it.

Collateral damage?

A necessary evil committed without regret or remorse in the line of duty.

Bell crossed the street and headed for the staff car park at the rear of the casino complex.

Ripped velcro revealed a Blue Dragon floorwalker in full uniform including a tie-pin and name badge in the name of 'Jeffries'. An unmarked back door opened slowly after a series of frantic knocks and some gameshow-host grinning into the fisheye peephole.

One of Gauci's goons looked Bell up and down. European and American casino staff who had cut their teeth in Monaco and Las Vegas were not necessarily out of place.

'Whaddya want?'

'I've been sent round by the front desk.'

'Yeah?'

'There's a guy in the foyer who says he's from the International Gaming Commission.'

Bell inched closer.

'So?'

'Er…so, here's his IGC ID. He says that he must speak to a Mr Donato Gauci, chief executive officer of the BDG Group, as a matter of urgency.'

The goon drew a breath and relaxed a little. Bell's attire and plausible storyline had hit the mark.

'Show me.'

As the goon's eyes focused on a worthless piece of plastic, Bell pumped two 7.62 calibre rounds into him and pushed the body back into the hallway, slamming the door shut.

One down, four to go.

The narrow stairwell led all the way up to the penthouse.

Next stop, the guards' coffee room, two floors up.

Bell retrieved the guy's walkie-talkie and silently ascended the concrete steps, MP5SD submachine gun at the ready.

As he approached the landing, jovial laughter and chatter became evident, mostly drowning out the soundtrack of a porn flick which was reaching one of its climaxes.

Bell had the element of surprise as he set the MP5 trigger-group position to *Einzelfeuer* – semi-automatic, until the walkie-talkie squawked suddenly.

Bell kicked the door open prematurely and blew the three of them away in short order. Blood and sloppy noodle spray from aluminium trays spattered the walls and the floor. He left the double-penetration running on-screen as he headed up the final two flights to deal with goon number five - the gatekeeper sentinel on duty at the penthouse airlock.

As Bell turned the last corner, several handgun shots pocked and splintered the polished concrete walls from above. Nothing for it but to switch the MP5 to *Feuerstoß* – fully automatic and roast this guy. Hey, buddy, I'm going to blow your fucking head off!

A fresh corpse, stylishly bedecked in a short-sleeved shirt and dual shoulder holsters, crashed down the steps and came to halt at Bell's feet.

A final ascent and a 50-round magazine change.

Phase one completed.

It was time to slip through two airtight doors and see how far the mating ritual had progressed.

***

Bell stole furtively over the deep-pile carpets seeking out some form of life in the opulent space. The searchlight beams reflected eerie light over the walls as their motorised bases rotated in accordance with digital choreography. The mirrored glitterball dominated the aerial view through the skylight windows.

What Bell stumbled across wasn't exactly the classic union of a man and a woman *in flagrante delicto*, but something a little more sinister.

Bell detected a wounded, agonised mewing sound in the lower lounge area. As he got closer, undetected, it became apparent that a girl was bound, gagged and strapped inside some kind of restraint frame.

The distressed female appeared to have been lashed up in there against her will, under extreme duress.

As Bell got closer still, he could make out Gauci's furry back, glazed with a sheen of sweat, bobbing up and down rhythmically between the poor girl's thighs. She arched in severe discomfort, unable to scream because of a strap-on mouth gag.

Not quite the scene that Bell had imagined.

The soft thud of a silencer would have been simplicity itself. The easy plunge of a commando knife too prosaic.

This was a propitious moment to savour, as against the repugnant sight of hairy buttocks and a ball-sack.

Where were the gelding irons when you needed them?

A suitable form of restraint and punishment could be improvised until it was time to end Gauci's existence.

Neither of them was aware of Bell's presence…yet.

The girl's eyes remained closed as she winced in pain at Gauci's cruel dildo thrusts. Her mouth was so tightly muzzled that she was forced to breathe heavily through her nose.

Open your eyes, honey…it's not for much longer.

Gauci's deep, resonant grunts sounded like a wild boar mounting a sow. The coarse, bristly hair, evidently covering the entirety of Gauci's body, did not seem to be at all out of place.

The girl's eyes suddenly saw Bell and she flinched.

A blonde, blue-eyed beauty from the Balkans.

Bell acknowledged the recognition of his surprise presence with an index finger hush signal, followed by a slit-throat gesture.

She'd got the message.

Good girl.

Bobbing Barbie turned awkwardly, realising that something had happened. Bell was already upon him with his military-grade cattle-prod, driving the electrodes into the tormentor's meaty neck. The high-voltage discharge, set to a couple of clicks below the red 'Kill' zone, delivered its pulse, via conductive, sweaty skin and its subcutaneous dermal layer, to within a whisker of causing fatal cardiac dysrhythmia.

Gauci's body froze rigid, then collapsed in an unconscious heap on the floor.

Bell leaned forward and undid the naked girl's gag.

'Thank you. Can you untie me?' she gasped.

'Let's start with the arm restraints.'

'The vibrator and the love eggs first...if you don't mind.'

Bell gently eased the phallic sex toy out of her vagina and turned his attention to a loose cord hanging from her anus.

'Pull firmly but gently, no yanking!' came the girl's deadpan instruction.

Once the first egg had appeared, the others shot out in a flood of lubricant. Bell was rewarded with a beaming smile as he tackled the remaining bindings and nipple clamps.

'I can wipe you, if you like? You're bleeding.'

Bell's offer went unanswered.

'Have you killed the bastard?'

Bell eased the girl upright on to the floor.

'No.'

'Good.'

'You'll get your chance when I'm done. What's your name?'

'Aryna from Kyiv. A captive sex slave for over three years. You?'

'Tom. I flush away toxic human waste.'

'A hitman?…and you're British.'

'Okay, much as I'd be quite happy to stare at your exquisite body all evening, you need to get some clothes on and get out of here. I can help you.'

Gauci was starting to come round. Bell casually kicked him in the gut and cattle-prodded him again.

'Fully dressed and then what?' said Aryna.

Chances were that she was haemorrhaging internally from the brutal sexual abuse. She really needed medical attention. Uncontrolled blood loss was always a concern.

'Are you physically alright? Your hip joints… and other parts of you which were being abused?'

'As you can see, I'm bleeding down my legs. I'm sure that he's ruptured me all the way up to my cervix.'

Bell produced a carton of potent painkillers.

'I need to ask Gauci some questions before I kill him. Could you help me lash him up?'

'You're really an assassin?'

'Kinda,' laughed Bell.

They heaved the dead weight into position, trussed like a frozen chicken. Bell chucked a champagne bucket of watery slush over him as Aryna went off to clean herself up as best she could. There was more than a post-intercourse discharge to deal with, and she was fresh out of pantyliners.

Gauci jolted back into consciousness and immediately realised his predicament.

'Hey, bastardo!' croaked the gross glob of shit.

Yeah, try squeezing that around a U-bend.

Gauci's eyes blazed with vitriol while tugging at the taut nylon straps.

'It's not me you have to worry about,' smirked Bell.

'Who are you?' asked Gauci.

Bell ignored the question, but his own might give Gauci a clue as to his interrogator's provenance. Bell suspected that Gauci knew that he was a dead man whose last act of recalcitrance was to take his secrets to the grave. The velvet pouch containing high-carat, blood-red rubies that Bell had found on Gauci's desk had provided Bell with a line-of-inquiry starting point.

'You are a known associate of Gao Zi Xin and you have visited his casino in Laos, the Emperor Nero, several times. Where is he now?'

'Mur linfern!' spat Gauci, uttering what was most likely a Maltese expletive which conveyed acute displeasure.

'It is believed that you recently put out a contract to liquidate a former business associate in Dorset, England?'

'Go to hell!'

Bell turned to speak to Aryna.

'How angry are you?'

'Very.'

'Like, incandescent with rage?'

'Yes.'

Bell offered her his Glock 30S, loaded with .45 ACP rounds.

'Maybe you can get some answers for me.'

'Do you have a knife?'

Gauci sensed that something nasty was about to happen.

Bell stood up brandishing a razor-sharp, serrated dagger, and disappeared to make a phone call.

***

Aryna slipped into Bell's warm, ringside seat.

'I always got a kick out of dissections...and vivisections. I wanted to become a vet when I was a little girl, you know. Just don't fart in my face, Barbie boy.'

'This is going to hurt, like you hurt me.'

Aryna traced the blade tip along the underside of his scrotum.

'The autopsy report will categorise my amateur surgery as a revenge vasectomy. Okay with that, Barbs?'

RV: An act of wanton butchery of male genitalia by someone with little or no knowledge of human anatomy.

'I'll talk if you stop...just shoot me!' screamed Gauci.

She made a note of his panicky answers and strapped the gag tightly in place.

'Yes, I know we made a deal. How about that? I'm reneging on it. Now, not a peep from you while I get to work.'

'One last thing, Mr International-playboy-rapist. This is for every dick and dildo that has ever penetrated me against my will. Here goes, you hairy arsehole.'

She drove the knife in and thrust it upwards so that it emerged out the other side. Gauci bucked and writhed in his bindings as the procedure was carried out.

She sawed the blade up and down the full length of his flaccid shaft back up to the frenulum and the glans and split his member fully open along the length of the urethral canal.

His testicles dropped neatly out on their cords and she severed both with a couple of neat crossswipes. She split the spermatic cord, unwittingly performing a textbook orchiectomy in the process. In the end, it didn't make a vas deferens.

A Prince Albert piercing gone wrong, blood everywhere, a gusher…and a whole lotta mess.

Aryna impassively placed the tip of the Glock 30S barrel against Gauci's forehead and pulled the trigger.

The .45 ACP round left its chamber and blew the back of his skull off.

***

Bell had been away for a short while. However, he had observed everything at a distance, while on the line.

Having returned to assimilate the gory scene at close quarters, he comfortingly put his arm around Aryna's waist. She was clearly emotional.

'I murdered a man.'

There was often an acute sense of pointless nihility after taking a human life, even with justifiable reason.

Especially the first time.

'Think of it as my kill, best not to dwell on it. I do it for a living, remember? He had it coming to him,' reassured Bell.

'Your kill?'

Bell had the feeling that he'd picked up on the wrong vibe.

'Our little shared secret, if you like.'

'I have found my vocation, initiated by you, a master of his craft.'

He could see that his random intervention had triggered a new sense of purpose in her. Other unfortunate girls would never get the opportunity to blow the head off their pimp. The battalions of men who used them like sex toys and wank mags had better watch out; he'd unwittingly spawned their nemesis.

She had become cool and determined as he continued to hold her close, certainly not some piece of easy tail to trifle with down a dark back-alley as she slit your throat.

'You mean admitted into the sacred order of assassins,' said Bell.

'Lucky you dropped by to ordain me, Mr Hitman!'

Better run over the travel plans.

'I've made all the arrangements including an examination by a doctor, if you feel that you need it. Here's a wad of US dollars.'

'Thanks for what you're doing for me.'

'Present yourself to the British Consulate in central Hong Kong. Just catch the bus over the bridge. They will provide you with travel documentation so you can board the next flight to Europe.'

The workable gameplan elicited an excited response.

'Germany or Poland?' said Aryna.

'Whatever they've got. You have to hurry; I've reason to believe that all flights may be grounded soon.'

'I'll eventually head back to Kyiv to find my mother who will have assumed long ago that I was dead. No one will have known that I was trafficked after naively going for a high-flying job in Western Europe. Mum has an ancient Nokia and I lost her number. I'll just have to turn up on her doorstep, I guess.'

'Keep a low profile and stay vigilant. Someone might want to get after you. Here's a London phone number and a memorable, three-word code-ID so that you can leave messages for me. I need to know that you made it!'

'I'm dying to visit London.'

'If you do, I promise that I'll take you out for an evening on the town. Are you all set?'

Time was creeping on; he still had high-explosive charges to set. She needed to be heading off.

'Not all men are evil bastard vampires. Oh, by the way, his answers were Myanmar or Tokyo, and they were given one chance but missed their target. Mean anything to you?'

'Sort of.'

'May I keep the knife? It has sentimental value.'

Bell smiled and gave her a tender kiss on the cheek.

'Take it, it's airport scanner friendly. You'll stumble across some of my handiwork as you descend the stairwell. Now get going and travel well.'

'I'm a big girl now.'

'Yes, I was definitely able to see that.'

Her baby blue eyes drilled into his.

'Did you think that you were getting away with just a peck on the cheek?'

Her lips were at once impressed upon his, her passionate embrace enveloping him in what was left of her sweet, musky scent.

Was this a perverse form of speed dating?

After breaking off, her fist punched the air, accompanied by a defiant war cry.

'Slava Ukraini!'

And she was gone.

16 Beta Blanco

The lift from the ground floor was on its way up.

What?!

He had another fifty minutes, surely?

Bell had almost finished laying the charges when the main lift dinged. He ducked for cover just before the elevator doors opened. Three plain-clothes detectives and two uniformed officers appeared, shepherding an older man under arrest at gunpoint.

***

A little earlier…

Gu Chang got up from the roulette table and headed for the cashier's cage.

'Yes, Sir?'

'I'd like to cash in some chips, please.'

Gu presented his Ruby membership card in the name of 'Ji Yinan', glancing around furtively while the ID verification was carried out.

The cashier's eyes widened at the sight of rare high-denomination, lavender-hue tokens which were worth one-hundred-thousand US dollars apiece.

Four hundred and ninety-nine of them plus a random selection of lower value chips which equated to a redemption total of just shy of fifty million dollars.

Commissioner Qian and his team from the Shenzhen police department, many of whom had taken part in the Yitian Plaza Tower assault, happened to be standing within earshot.

'You do realise that any pay-out exceeding twenty-five million US dollars requires the authorisation of the Blue Dragon boss-man?' said the cashier.

Commissioner Qian's ears pricked up.

'Er…no, but that's simply a formality, isn't it?' replied Gu.

'Not quite. Mr Gauci is in the building but he won't be available for at least another hour.'

'What is this?! I can't wait. I want all my money now. Could you get him down here to authorise an urgent case?'

Qian noted the frustrated outburst and drew closer.

'It doesn't work like that, Sir, I'm afraid.'

'B…but I can exchange twenty-five million dollars in the meantime, can't I?'

'Yes, with supervisor approval.'

Although Commissioner Qian was a chancer and a fornicator, he was an intelligent police officer who knew when he had his man. His arrest of the billionaire fugitive Gu Chang would make his career, however the prospect of getting his hands on even a fraction of twenty-five million dollars in cash was exhilarating.

The possibilities were limitless.

Qian cleverly waited for the transaction to be completed before surrounding Gu and placing him under criminal detention. Qian, as senior officer, had enough police and extra-legal powers at his disposal to take full control of the situation.

The requisition and quarantine of the Blue Dragon casino was a legitimate part of his remit.

The only fly in the ointment was the MSS meddler.

Yeah, Zheng: What had he been up to?

Anyone who interfered with police and state security matters would be shot on sight. Qian and his team waved casino staff aside as they entered the lift which would take them up to the top-floor penthouse where Gu would undergo primary questioning, fingerprinting and an iris check.

Qian ensured that he was safeguarding Gu's belongings, the contents of which held the key to a new life.

After entering the opulent surroundings of Gauci's private apartments, it was only a few minutes before one of their number stumbled across Donato Gauci's dead body.

While Gu was held at gunpoint on one of the sofas, Commissioner Qian looked on in amazement at the gruesome corpse which was bound and gagged inside some sort of torture frame.

No one else seemed to be in evidence: Gauci was on his own.

Definitely not a solo-sex-game gone wrong.

Qian knew that he had walked into a crime scene which must be reported immediately. It didn't look like suicide, there was no obvious murder weapon, but the naked body had been partly dismembered in a bizarre fashion.

It had all the hallmarks of a gangland punishment killing.

Nothing for it but to get latex gloves on and cordon the area off with CS-tape. He didn't want to spoil everything by contaminating a major crime scene.

He would at least have both Gu's arrest and the discovery of Gauci's body to his name. Two major cases to add to his service-record tally.

That reminded him, had they cuffed the fugitive, yet?

Qian was suffering from event overload. A bad decision now could see a golden opportunity slither through his fingers, especially what to do about the twenty-five million dollars.

He decided to thumb through Gu's papers first, then conduct some basic interrogation, followed by returning downstairs to meet backup teams, including forensics, who were on their way.

He still had the queasy feeling that he was getting out of his depth, of being an imposter; the feeling that the moment when your luck changes and you lose everything, was just around the corner.

Gu's bulging holdall presented a treasure trove of eye openers as its jittery, and increasingly unhinged, owner watched his most personal possessions being rifled.

- Deeds of title and lists of bank accounts
- Schedules of property and assets across the globe.
- Details of firms of international lawyers.
- Specifications of a superyacht called the Beta Blanco.
- A chart depicting a sea passage from Macau to Vancouver via Hawaii.
- Not to mention piles of cash and casino tokens.

Where the hell was Zheng?

***

Colonel Zheng had arrived too late. He'd decided not to flash his police ID until absolutely necessary.

There had been a queue to get in the Blue Dragon, exacerbated by rumours of twitchy fruit machines randomly paying out jackpots without winning lines.

Huh! Maybe he had something to do with that.

It was his own fault.

He'd eventually got in there with a freshly-issued Opal card, only to witness the moment when Qian had made the arrest.

Oh, if only he had been here sooner!

After all that intricate detective work back at HQ.

Knowing Commissioner Qian, the bastard could easily blow his brother's head off on an idle whim.

It was imperative to get up to the top floor with all haste.

Zheng had one minute to make the most momentous decision of his life. There was his existence before and his new life after this very moment.

He was in this too deep to turn back.

Zheng checked his QSZ-92 semi-automatic with suppressor which fired 9x19mm Parabellum cartridges.

Fifteen of them.

Fuck it!

In the rush, he'd left two spare magazines in the police pool car.

Now or never.

The callous, cold-bloodied task he was about to execute required a ruthless capability.

A killing machine without care or contrition.

Cybocop.

He visualised Xu waiting patiently in a hotel room for him and headed for the lift doors.

**

Colonel Zheng emerged from the elevator with a breezy smile.

Five of them, excluding his brother, greeted him.

'What took you?' leered Qian, reposing nonchalantly on the sofa.

The first six bullets took out the two uniformed guys.

By the time he turned his attention to Qian and the plain clothes detectives, fire was being returned.

Bullets shattered the onyx elevator surround as Zheng rolled away acrobatically out of the line of fire.

Qian got off several shots after abandoning Gu's document stash, rolling over the back of the sofa while Zheng finished off the detective duo who were too slow off the mark.

Gu Chang saw his chance to bolt to the open lift doors, only to be gunned down by Qian with a single bullet at the elevator threshold.

Meanwhile Qian had cannily commando-crawled his way into the maze of expensive furniture to get round the back of Zheng's current vantage point.

Zheng ducked as a near miss zinged past his head, prompting him to aim return fire at where Qian's head had bobbed up briefly.

Zheng's handgun responded with an audible click which caused a triumphant Commissioner Qian to emerge into the open.

Zheng now stood with his arms in the air, lamenting his two spare mags lying idle on a car passenger seat. Qian stood a few feet away with the barrel of his gun pointing at Zheng's forehead.

A wounded Gu groaned dolefully in a pool of blood.

Commissioner Qian was jubilant. He glanced across at Gu while carefully maintaining his aim.

'I was never sure about you, Zheng. I had a hunch that you were up to something.'

'Believe whatever you want.'

'I think that we're very alike. We're both chancers.'

'Yeah?'

'You're doing a runner, aren't you?'

'W…we could work together…the Beta Blanco.'

'Ah! All I know is that you won't be sitting in my office chair ever again,' laughed Qian.

Zheng sensed that a bullet would soon be fired and Qian could make up whatever story he liked. In a futile act of defiance, Zheng decided to commit his remaining mortal thoughts to Xu and her unborn twins.

Precious final moments.

A sudden burst of MP5 fire took Qian down in a stroke.

Thomas Bell emerged from the shadows and presented himself to Zheng, holding out his hand.

'If you're gonna shoot, shoot…don't talk.'

'Who are you?' stammered Zheng, gobsmacked.

'Everyone asks that. Let's just say that I'm running out of time, as you are. It seems to me that I can send you on your way so that I can finish what I was doing.'

'How did you know who not to shoot?'

'I couldn't fathom the Keystone Cop slapstick at first. In the end, you're the horse I decided to back.'

Zheng shuddered visibly at the revelation.

'Okay, tell me what to do,' said Zheng.

'Explain your situation to me while we treat the wounded wretch.'

Gu lay motionless, panting on his back as they dragged him away from the persistent elevator doors.

Zheng peeled away Gu's prosthetic nose… it was like looking in the mirror.

Bell threw his entire trauma kit into the mix in an effort to contain the bleeding. Not looking good – the intestines, stomach, and pancreas had probably been torn through by Qian's bullet. It was a case of haemorrhagic shock, most likely.

'He's my twin brother. Will he live?' said Zheng.

'No. You've only got a couple of minutes.'

Zheng hung on to every one of Gu's rasping, laboured responses, the apotheosis of which, uttered with fading breath, was the dying billionaire's sublime idea to swap identities.

Zheng frantically switched clothing, personal possessions and ID documentation until the identical twin substitution was complete.

Bell reappeared, having set all the C4 explosive charges.

'By the time they dig through the rubble, we'll both be long gone from Macau. There'll be traces of DNA and human tissue everywhere so they'll never work out what happened,' grinned Bell.

'I owe you more than you can imagine. It's a privilege to meet you, Englishman.'

'Go on, get out of here, and don't forget to take your sea sickness pills and put your lifejacket on!'

Bell would have loved to get away on a superyacht himself. Overall, he'd done well to cover everything despite the extensive mission creep.

Colonel Zheng, or Gu Chang as he was now, disappeared through the airlock to descend the back stairs, get out into the street and hail a cab.

Bell hoped that it would all work out for him and his girl.

At least the dead billionaire had passed on the baton of life in a most peculiar way. The tale of the brothers' separation at birth and ultimate, if short, reunion was heart-rending.

Bell got re-velcroed into his pipey overalls. He slipped out the way he had come in, melting away into the night in search of a random cab to be casually flagged down on a street corner.

As soon as his transport pulled into the kerb, the top floors of the Blue Dragon exploded in a massive fireball which shook the ground under Bell's feet.

There was a certain satisfaction to be had.

His drop-off timing at the back of the Venetian Macau was bang on. There was enough time to have a quick rinse, grab a snack from the minibar, and don some formal evening wear.

A desirable and voluptuous Jana had probably spent the earlier part of her evening fighting off unwanted male attention. She was hopefully pining for him, somewhere in the rammed Taipa suite.

It's okay, honey…your ardent inamorato is on his way.

***

Jana sat at her table alone, sipping a Long Island Iced Tea, wanting some male attention.

Anyone but the smooth-talking David Rockwell.

Couples swirled and gyrated on the dance floor, only yards away, as she casually stirred her drink with a swizzle stick. She took another swig of the zesty, spirit combo.

Every time she glanced up, groups of single men at other tables would suddenly look away, afraid to catch the medusa-like gaze of a man-eating cougar.

Nerd losers with little balls.

Then it happened.

A daringly bold NL stood before her, clutching a beer.

'Er…would you mind if I, er…joined you?'

'You got this far, why not?'

'What…'

'What would I like to drink?'

'Er…what shall we talk about?'

He hadn't expected to get to first base.

Fourth base: Tonguing a slick perineum was way off the scale.

David Rockwell's disabling neck-pinch of the brachial plexus cut the timid suitor short.

'Off you go, pal.'

Nerdy boy staggered away as Daniel Roxby – known as David Rockwell to Jana, calmly took his seat.

'So, has lover boy given you the slip?' taunted Roxby.

'Get lost! No one asked you to sit down.'

'Or, has he simply dumped you for something else?'

'What's it to you?'

'I can be a lot of fun as well.'

'Get lost, anyway.'

'You will want me, but you don't know it yet.'

**

Best to leave the Haval H6 diesel where it was, parked up in a hurry in a quiet back street.

The car had been correctly booked out to Zheng by the police vehicle superintendent. Its presence would corroborate the identity of one of the corpses found amongst the charred Blue Dragon wreckage.

Police cars and fire engines blared past his taxi at regular intervals as the sweet reunion with his new love approached.

Zheng's ride ended outside a cheap, nondescript hotel. From the street it was evident that the main room lights were on.

He rushed up the staircase, lugging the bulging bag of credentials and money with him and burst in at the front door. The lounge was bare and tidy. He tore into the bedroom with manic desperation, then finally, the ensuite.

Xu was gone.

He parked himself on the low divan, knowing full well that he only had a few minutes to squander before racing off to the port marina on his own.

She must have given up the ghost and headed back to Hong Kong.

He could hardly blame her, really.

His tall tales and flaky bullshit had spooked her.

He felt something underfoot, tucked beneath the divan hem.

It was the ultrasound scan photograph from the clinic. Zheng traced his finger over the outlines of two unborn children and fell to his knees.

He felt a label on the reverse side with his fingernail and turned the photo over.

'#8'

Not so lucky.

He howled loudly in total despair, thumping his forehead into the carpet.

'No! No! No!'

Xu pushed the door ajar, lowering her semi-automatic pistol.

'What kept you?'

'Xu!'

'You didn't really think I'd do a runner, did you?'

***

The taxi dropped the couple outside a fashionable restaurant, called 'O Castiço', in the heart of the voguish Club Nautico waterfront. The upmarket eatery looked to be overrun with wealthy patrons.

The duo walked quietly past and disappeared down a side street. Buoys, fishing nets and lobster pots cluttered the commercial thoroughfare used primarily by fishermen's lockups. The smell of diesel and chum bait arrested their nostrils, intensifying as they continued on.

Presently, they took a corner and entered a seamy harbour-bar called the 'Cabelo do Cachorro'.

Zheng selected a tiny table near the counter and ordered a couple of Tsingtao beers. The couple looked totally out of place amongst the cigarette-smoking fishermen, to a man dressed in overalls covered in oil, fish guts and layers of marine grease.

Sure, they were getting some funny looks.

Zheng got up after a few minutes and stood by the grubby food counter.

A guy in an apron appeared.

'Sim?'

'I have an apartment in Albufeira,' said Zheng.

'What is your favourite wine region?'

'Alentejo,' replied Zheng, completing the coded exchange.

The guy lifted the flap, beckoned them through, handing over a sealed wallet and a powerful torch, exactly as his dear brother had explained.

They headed out the back past beer crates into the darkness.

A rat with a fish-head in its mouth stood its ground in the bright LED beam as they passed. They only had to walk a few hundred metres, past coils of thick mooring rope, to the Beta Blanco gangplank and give the order to cast off.

Wei and Xu hugged each other as the superyacht, all one hundred and sixty-five feet of her, headed out into mid-channel, plying its passage down the Pearl River estuary to the open ocean.

'Why were you hiding?'

'You've taught me a thing or two.'

'Where?'

'In a stifling linen cupboard, down the corridor.'

Their ardent, passionate kiss was long overdue.

'Yes, only fine cotton sheets for us from now on, my love.'

***

Bell snuck up behind Jana and slipped an arm around her waist. She swivelled round on a sixpence. The long black satin dress and the scent of Chanel No.5 squeezed up and enveloped him.

Back in time for basques, bacchanalia and a jiggle on the dance floor.

'I trust that nobody's been bothering you.'

'Only a little.'

'Nothing that you couldn't handle?'

Jana sidestepped the question.

'So, what have you been up to?'

'It was bloody hard work. I still have a deal to close.'

'I'd almost forgotten how wonderful it is when you hold me tight. I need you tonight.'

Their lips met.

'I need you, too.'

'It's true, we are ill-fated lovers, aren't we,' she laughed, staring deeply into his eyes.

Bell knew that she had unwittingly hit the nail on the head in jest and decided to change the subject.

'Okay, kiddo, let's dance.'

An eyebrow arched, followed by an even more passionate kiss.

'I love it when you take control.'

'Wait till I get you back in bed.'

People were breaking off in droves to head for the adjacent TV lounge – some sort of major bomb disaster, here in Macau. CNN breaking-news fodder - graphic images and gore. 'Nothing to do with you, I hope.'

17 Philippine phantasia

E ddie Wu was wanted for murder in the United States. He featured on the FBI's most-wanted list.

Following a tip-off, over one hundred bodies had been found buried in the Nevada desert.

More specifically in a barren location one hundred and five kilometres north-west of Las Vegas.

Not that you would feel inclined to visit, spade in hand.

The Nevada test site was the most important nuclear weapons proving-ground in the USA.

From 1951 until 1992, a total of 1,021 nuclear tests were carried out. These tests released an estimated 222,000 Peta-Becquerels of radioactive material into the atmosphere, enough to contaminate every living organism on the planet's surface at cellular level. From the polar bear to deep-ocean, bioluminescent plankton.

The disused site remains tainted with an estimated 11,100 PBq of radioactive material in the soil and 4,440 PBq in the groundwater. Signs warn: 'Radiation area – digging prohibited'.

Creosote and sagebrush cover much of the arid, gravelly terrain, punctuated by soaring mountains and crusty lake beds.

So, a clever choice in many ways for Murder Inc..

One hundred and thirty-seven bodies…and counting. Rotting corpses stacked in mass graves like canned oysters.

'Sloppy, Eddie, doncha think? Wouldn't sealed oil drums dumped in Lake Mead have been a better idea? I trust that you were wearing a hazmat suit and a respirator,' joked CIA officer Alex Gallen, sitting across the table from Wu.

The naturalized American citizen, chased down in foreign parts, stared at the interrogation room floor, disconsolate.

'ADX Florence for you, my friend.'

'Uh?'

'Colorado Supermax. You'll be in fine company there. A life sentence in solitary. I'm told that Fremont County is very nice at this time of year. Will be good to be on American soil, eh?'

Wu declined to comment.

Typed interview transcripts lay on the desk.

'I've read your testimony. Elaborate on your time at the Emperor Nero casino in Laos, if you don't mind,' said Gallen.

'What about it?'

The prisoner looked to be itching for a cigarette.

Tell-tale yellowed fingers clawed at three-day stubble.

Eddie Wu had been arrested in Bangkok and was now being extradited back to the United States via the Philippines.

He was currently languishing in a holding facility at Subic Bay naval base awaiting a military transporter. A seventeen-hour flight back to Peterson AFB, rather than Denver International where a brazen escape attempt could be staged by his associates.

'You like to play games. How about Russian roulette?'

Wu perked up, suddenly.

'Poker, mainly.'

'Tell me about Tucker Cole.'

'I watched him blow his own brains out. After five spins of the cylinder he gave us all the finger.'

'How did you feel about that?'

'I lost quite a bit of money.'

'Is that all?'

Several seconds of stony silence preceded Wu's answer.

'Seven isn't my lucky number. The seven chambers of a Russian-made M1895 service revolver saw to that.'

'Cole was one of the Company's finest. He was a legend…one of ours. Gao Zi Xin will remain on our hit-list until we find him.'

'I can understand that,' replied Wu.

'You've almost earned yourself a cigarette.'

'What can I offer you?'

'The current whereabouts of Gao Zi Xin.'

'Hah!'

'For that you get two hundred Chesterfields.'

A sealed carton of Chesterfield Blue Kingsize – 10 packs of 20 cigarettes - a blend of Turkish and Virginia tobacco.

'The value of that piece of information has to be measured in ten-carat, blood-red rubies, I'm afraid.'

'Like the ones which were hidden in your lower gastrointestinal tract?'

'Well, there is that,' replied Wu, coyly.

'A gift for services rendered, perhaps?'

'What?!'

'I'm not questioning your sexuality, you understand. However, it would appear that you have a colonic polyp.'

'What the hell is that?'

'Lucky we spotted it. I think it's one of those bulbous protrusions that grows somewhere up your asshole that hurt like fuck when you take a shit. As I'm not a medical man, don't quote me on that!'

Wu thought back to all the shits he'd taken recently.

'Will it kill me?'

'Probably', smiled Gallen.

'Oh, right.'

'So, you're not a squealer, then?'

'That depends.'

'On?'

'How I feel about a long sentence.'

'You mean serving a number of consecutive life terms?'

'Yes…for crimes that I didn't commit.'

'You are guilty by association.'

'Which means?'

'Who you associate with counts. You're being fitted up.'

'By the Nevada District Attorney?'

'Of course, any head on a stick will do.'

'But…'

'If that sounds like a candid revelation, it is.'

'What are you saying?

Gallen casually stripped the cellophane off a pack of Marlboros, and teasingly placed it on the table top.

'This isn't an interrogation, it's a little chat.'

Gallen noted Wu's escalating desperation for a ciggy, driven by the need and concern for continuous nicotine consumption. Common FAQs regarding US penitentiaries and smoking:-

- Can a licence to smoke be granted for good behaviour?

- Are chewing tobacco or e-cigarettes permitted?

- Is smoking allowed in the outside exercise yard?

Answer: All federal correctional facilities are 100% smoke-free.

While Gallen took time to thumb through the transcripts again, Wu carefully studied the box of Marlboros positioned next to a plastic lighter.

A black-bordered health warning in Filipino stated: '*nakamamatay ang paninigarilyo*', which could indicate anything from the risk of cancer of the oesophagus to loss of libido.

Smoking kills.

Gallen caught his detainee eyeing up the crush-proof pack. He suspected that Wu wanted him to light up and fill the unventilated room with the delicious aroma of Virginia tobacco.

Secondary smoke was better than no smoke at all.

It could easily be Wu's last whiff.

Armed with a small bargaining chip, Gallen asked a burning question.

'What about Cole's mortal remains?'

As Wu sat back to ponder the query, Gallen unilaterally offered his charge a Marlboro.

It had to be the deepest inhale Gallen had ever witnessed. Toxic chemicals in the smoke, such as benzene, arsenic and formaldehyde, being sucked down to the deepest level of delicate, alveolar lung-tissue.

The insider intel was puffed out in short order.

'It wouldn't surprise me if Gao had fired up a Russian mobile crematorium truck which I saw parked near the fence of his Laos compound. The proximity to the Mekong riverbank could also have some bearing on the matter…as in plump, well-fed catfish. In a word, nothing will remain of him.'

'Hmm, okay…useful, makes sense. Just a long shot.'

Gallen placed an unopened, casket-style pack of Camels right next to the Marlboros and a smaller box.

Camel Filters. King-size. Cork acetate filter.

A dilemma for Wu.

A Marlboro or a Camel?

American or Oriental blend? Smoke density and nicotine levels to consider.

Temporarily satiated, Wu had his own question.

'What's in the fun-size box?'

'Menthol infusion cards, manufactured by a company called Riz La Croix. Fancy the tang of cool fresh-mint now, do we? A bit girlie, if you ask me,' smirked Gallen.

That reminded him.

Better get out on the town this evening as it was his last night at Subic Bay. Tomorrow, the F-35C fighter fuselage, retrieved from the seabed, which forensic teams had pored over for three days, would be on display in a secure hangar on the base. It was hoped that they had something interesting to report.

After that he would be stationed on Okinawa for the foreseeable future while the Japanese tested their Type 12 air-to-ship missile systems which were dotted around the island.

A bit girlie?

What he required was a lot of girlie.

Seeing double and fucking two at once.

Happy hour - two girls for the price of one and plenty of cheap drinks.

Shower first, empty both tanks and take a piss immediately afterwards.

A rasping bark interrupted Gallen's bordello reverie.

Someone's cough reflex had been triggered by toxic particulates and other irritants.

'I tell you what, Eddie.'

'Yeah?'

'I may be able to cut you some slack.'

'Can I have another cigarette?'

'Looks like you're spoilt for choice, this time.'

'What do you want?'

'Intel. I think that you know of something valuable to us, but you don't know that you know it. I can't promise anything but how does FPC Pensacola in Florida sound?'

'What? You mean the minimum-security facility which is reputed to be the cushiest prison in America?!'

'Yup, basically a holiday camp.'

'…where inmates play racquetball and volleyball and have their own cinema?'

'That's the one, you got it. It's sort of in the name – you get to drink Pepsi-Cola all day long and it has a lousy inmate absconder record. Remember, you have to earn this.'

Wu already had his head cupped in his palms with his elbows on the table.

'I'm on it.'

'Have something ready for me when I return. You have fifteen minutes.'

***

'Come on, surprise me…what have you got?'

The room was full of smoke now.

Time to switch on the extractor fan.

With a Camel smouldering between his fingers, Wu was looking more than relaxed.

'Cyber security.'

'Like, CISA – the US cyber-defence unit?'

The Cybersecurity and Infrastructure Security Agency is part of the Department of Homeland Security. As you might expect, it works to understand, manage and mitigate the intrusion risk to America's cyber infrastructure.

Wu smiled in agreement.

First, a pre-disclosure proviso.

'Before we continue, I need to be sure that there is a cast iron agreement in place. I can't have you making off with what I have to tell you only to discover that I'm now seated in the electric chair.'

'What do you have in mind?'

'A deal sweetener - I release a million dollars to you only when I'm sipping Pepsi from a paper cup in Florida.'

Gallen guessed that a player like Wu had tens of millions stashed away in every dark corner of the world. Not much use to someone with an electrode strapped to his shaven head.

'Got it, but that's bribery, isn't it?'

'…and corruption. I welcome the opportunity to buy my freedom. I just hope that FPC Pensacola doesn't suddenly switch from volleyball to the chain-gang, that's all.'

Gallen visualised fit girls in tight shorts competing at the net and a venomous pit viper with its fangs dug into his thigh. Yeah, chain-gang road-strip trimming, along with exhaustion and sunburn, came with its dangers.

'Agreed. Let's hear it.'

'A recent email server breach at the US State Department, which resulted in the theft of over a quarter of a million emails, has never been fully explained.'

'Hmm, I remember,' said Gallen, pensively.

'Software suppliers put it down to a crash-dump on an engineer's laptop. The system data dump unfortunately included digital signing keys.'

Gallen paraphrased a section of text he'd remembered from an internal CIA report.

'The main hypothesis for the breach being attributed to operational errors which led to key material leaving the secure token-signing environment, if I'm not mistaken.'

'Exactly, allowing a Chinese government-sanctioned hacking group called Cyclone-39 to cut a hole through US government cyber-defences.'

'This was all a while back, though, wasn't it?'

'The point is that the matter was hurriedly signed off with the most plausible explanation. Doubt still lingers in Washington that Western encryption methodologies are at risk and that this was just a proof-of-concept test assault.'

'Surely the core-dump defect has been fixed?'

'Maybe, but that was the cover, don't you see?'

'For what?'

'A quantum computer actually unlocked the key. It eats binary encryption algorithms in minutes,' smiled Wu.

'A large-scale device?'

'Yes. The genius who developed the specialised hardware which manipulates quantum states is building a 10000-qubit machine. It will be exponentially faster. We're talking quintillions of floating-point operations per second.'

'Kept under wraps in deepest China?'

'It will amuse you to know that its creator has been rewarded with a trip to Macau with a group of other top scientists!'

'This guy is actually in Macau now?'

'Yes, staying at the Wynn Palace casino.'

'Do you have a name?'

'Codename: Yīshí.'

'How do you know all this?'

'I have deep-rooted connections from the top to the bottom in China, especially within the security services and the military. The taste of honey is hard to resist, if you understand my meaning.'

Gallen was more than blown away.

All he had expected to hear was low-level, trivial chaff that the CIA already knew about. This revelation blew everything out of the water.

Gallen sat there, open-mouthed.

Wow!

'Anything else, while we're at it?'

'Your earlier question – for a carton of Chesterfields.'

'The current whereabouts of Gao Zi Xin?'

'I don't know, but I do know of a man who probably does.'

Gallen was struggling to keep up.

'Are you real on this?'

'It'll mean a trip to Tokyo,' laughed Wu.

***

Sixty nightclubs once graced the highway through Barrio Barretto along Subic Bay at the height of the US Navy's tenure. In 1992 the Philippines government ordered the base closed following half a century of American control.

The dockyards and surrounding areas were about the size of Singapore and acted as a major ship-repair, supply and rest and recreation facility which was established originally by the Spanish Navy in the mid-1880s.

Now, after decades of absence, the US Navy was back in a big way. The USS Atlantis supercarrier and its support ships lay at anchor just offshore. Olongapo city was buzzing again, overrun with naval personnel and US Marines.

New high-end beachfront hotels were being built, other buildings renovated and the whole area revitalised as the Philippines welcomed the American presence back in force, not only in Subic Bay but the whole of the country. The reason being the rise in tension in the South China Sea and the fact that the Philippines constituted the southern linear section of the First Island Chain.

American servicemen could get themselves into trouble again with droves of attractive Filipina women who haunted the barrio, touting for business.

A couple of them were heading this way.

Some fresh meat that he hadn't seen before.

Painted talons gripped Gallen's thigh.

Double up babe, it's Happy Hour.

Any port in a storm.

'Me sucky-sucky?'

'Huh?'

'We fucky-fucky?'

The girls took seats and looked to be thirsty.

The first of many bottles of Red Horse beer stood in the centre of the table. Fancy cocktails would be next.

Gallen slipped into local patois with a smile to clarify that he wasn't a dumb tourist.

'Ano? Hindi ako turista!'

***

A little earlier...

Jalen Mack was Gallen's wingman for the evening. The naval ranks had drawn straws to see who would be the lucky guy to accompany the CIA agent for his last night out on the town.

Only party animals with a sense of adventure need apply.

Mack had the physique and menacing presence of an NFL cornerback, used to hard tackles and interceptions. As a USN Master-at-arms, specialising in security and hand-to-hand combat training, Gallen knew that someone reliable was watching his back.

You could never be too careful down the ill-lit side streets.

There was always a Beretta M9 if it came to it.

Before jumping in a cab with Mack at the base security gates, Gallen had filed an urgent report to CIA Headquarters in Langley, Virginia. The whole thing could be a pile of bullshit, carefully constructed by Wu to save his precious skin, but it had to be done.

If it was true, there were still compelling questions.

Did the US know about the Chinese science symposium in Macau - military-grade eggheads lined up like ducks in a shooting gallery? Was a golden opportunity being missed because the CIA was behind the curve?

Was it too late to kidnap the quantum guy codenamed Yīshí from under the nose of the PLA?

Worse still…were all binary encryption codes now the equivalent of toast?

Bright neon and loud music signalled their arrival at the top end of the infamous pedestrianised Angel Street, their cab drop-off point.

The two revellers put their heads around the door at a few of the regular haunts: Wet Spot, Cat Walk and The Office but it was decided to try elsewhere. In the end, the ambience and loud, pulsating music of the Kokomo lounge bar, along with a series of shots, got their vote. After some fun in there, especially with the risqué pole dancers, it was only a short dash across the road to Gallen's favourite, the Fantasia Club, which offered additional delights.

***

Expensive cocktails and more Red Horse bottles arrived.

'You speak Filipino?' asked one of the girls.

'Not really. Only the language of love,' joked Gallen.

'We love fucky-fucky. Credit card or cash?' asked the other girl.

It always boiled down to the money.

The sordid topic of coin.

Selling your body to all takers for small change.

A hard-boiled transaction without emotion which maybe came with remorse and regret. Medical roulette: The spin of the STI transmission wheel – do you feel lucky?

If you don't, stay safe and play on your own.

Stick to renting a sunbed on the Subic Bay beach or singing karaoke solo in a sad KTV lounge.

The sealed deal of their sweet, alluring flesh in exchange for crisp banknotes.

The Philippine peso or the US dollar, both of which were more than acceptable. Unlike a credit card which left an immutable and immortal digital audit-trail in the cloud somewhere.

'Cash,' said Gallen.

'Yankee dollar,' said the first girl.

'Just one thing, we want deluxe rooms.'

***

The USN fighter-jet fuselage continued to drip seawater on to the pristine, painted floor of the aircraft hangar, which was located in a secluded spot on the Subic Bay base.

An F-35C Lightning II Joint Strike Fighter draped in seaweed at the end of its unusual mission at the bottom of the South China Sea. Certain modular parts of it had been removed in their entirety, especially from the cockpit, and all inspection covers opened.

Three technicians, including one from the manufacturer Lockheed Martin, stood together in white coats, holding clipboards.

Alex Gallen and some senior naval officers stood around nearby waiting for the big reveal, hoping for some good news.

Gallen felt like shit.

What was the girl's name again?

He'd drunk a little too much last night.

Extra strong beer with a kick – 6.9% ABV and overexertion in the bedroom.

Maybe I'll feel better if this F-35C ruse has worked.

Come on, hurry up and break it to us.

***

It had been over a week since the F-35C had accidentally-on-purpose fallen off the USS Atlantis supercarrier at a specially selected coral-shelf location, in relatively shallow water.

The target drop-site in the Taiwan Strait was close enough for the Chinese to slip across and take a look.

The US Navy gaffe had been reported widely in international news bulletins, so there was no excuse.

After a suitable interval, a multi-purpose subsea diving support and construction vessel had been commissioned from a commercial salvage company based in Okinawa. USN personnel were on board the DSCV *Matisse* to assist in recovery operations to pluck the fighter from the depths of the SCS.

A remotely operated vehicle initially descended to the seafloor to attach specialised rigging and lift lines. The recovery ship then lowered its hydraulic lifting hook and raised the entire fuselage to the surface, finally swinging it up and on to the *Matisse's* vast deck space for primary inspection.

After hauling tarpaulins into place, it was full-steam-ahead to Subic Bay.

***

A huge whiteboard stood mounted on a sturdy tripod with a comprehensive inventory grid pinned at its centre. It detailed all of the sunken fighter's decoy avionics components that the Chinese might have wished to purloin.

It was assumed that the PLAN would have sent a UAV and then specialist divers to remove specific items.

Well, at least it was blatantly obvious that they hadn't made off with the entire plane and secreted it back to Fujian province. Constant US satellite surveillance of the Chang-Yuen Ridge area would have immediately registered that.

Shame. That could have been interesting.

Bright arc lights on stands continued to illuminate the seawater-infused aircraft from all angles as the prospective audience started to get fidgety and restless.

Can't stand around here all day.

Spit it out will you, for fuck's sake!

What are we waiting for?

A microphone was switched on, along with a couple of light taps.

'Good morning, Gentlemen. We have spent three days going over this aircraft with a toothcomb. Nothing is missing.'

Everyone gasped.

Gallen crushed the empty, plastic coffee-cup clenched inside his fist. He'd been with this hulk of metal every inch of the way right out of the trap. From Lockheed Martin Corporation's site in north Texas to this fucking, dripping-wet hangar in the Philippines. There had to be something.

The PLAAF had surely been responsible for the recent disappearance of an X-47B tailless strike fighter and an XQ-58 loyal wingman craft while on active service, both unmanned combat aerial vehicles. They would reverse engineer anything they could get their hands on…unless they had already obtained the F-35C's technology in its entirety, indicating a catastrophic data leak somewhere in the supply chain.

It was Gallen's turn to speak, now that the usual dumb questions asked by the others had dried up. This matter of United States national security rested upon his shoulders.

The hangover and antics from the night before were long forgotten.

A question.

'Alright, ladies, you've had your fun. Serious up. You technical motherfuckers haven't told us everything. Let me ask you a closed question. Has anything been added to that fucking plane?'

'Er, well…'

'Speak up or I'll take a baseball bat to you…'

'Yes.'

'What?!'

Gallen was handed a photograph. It was a small strip of stencilled titanium plate which had been discreetly riveted to one of the plane's bulkheads.

'We weren't exactly sure what it was. There are some gibberish-type characters cold-punched into it, that's all.'

Gallen lowered the photograph to his side.

不错的尝试!

'It does mean something, you dumb asshole.'

At least it proved that the Chinese had a clever sense of humour – even while on a war-preparation footing.

'What is it?'

A visiting card.

'In Mandarin, it says: Nice try!'

18 Falling with style

It was the morning of Friday the 7th of October.

Bell awoke with a jolt as Jana remained in a deep sleep on the pillow next to him.

A blister-pack of Doxygra and a half-drunk glass of water stood next to Jana's Gucci specs on her bedside table. A bow tie and a wad of notes kept each other company on his.

What he yearned for was the sight of a loaded semi-automatic. In recompense, a commando knife lay underneath his pillow; a purple vibrator and a tube of lubricant nestling under hers.

Can't be too careful.

He noticed scratches on his hands which caught the morning sunshine filtering through a crack in the curtains. He chuckled to himself that he could furtively wipe his cock on them while Jana was blissfully comatose.

The anterior fornix position was undeniably a load of fun. Empty both tanks and finish with a nightcap. Bell slid out of bed and headed for the minibar. He dug out all the water and soft drinks, lined them up on the low table and commenced a resolute rehydration initiative.

Jana had been in her element on the dance floor in the Taipa suite where she had looked like a million dollars.

Gotta bop, just can't stop.

Roxby represented himself as a malign presence, up to no good, cruising the packed function room like a bull shark.

Bell now knew all about him, exactly who he was.

He'd read the intelligence files. A man on the run operating under an alias and actively hunted in seven countries.

Many pseudonyms and wanted for murder, theft and dozens of other felonies, including impersonating a police officer.

Roxby, Roxborough, Rockwell.

An arrest in China could be initiated and followed up with an extradition request from the United Kingdom.

It would involve time, red tape and delay to bring him to justice.

Why not ditch the paperwork and simply cut to the chase?

Deal with the blockage by flushing an annoying glob of shit around the U-bend.

Bell rooted about and located a handful of crappy snacks in cellophane wrappers. Just something to line his stomach until room service brought up a hearty cooked breakfast.

He studied the in-room dining menu.

Yeah, it had to be the full English.

Something that would provide him with the strength to keep his finger on the trigger.

He was going to need all the calories he could get for the terrible things that he had to do later.

What about plucky Aryna, the fallen maiden from Kyiv with a heart of gold? He could check with the British embassy in Hong Kong that she had paid them a visit. Hmm…forget it - she had made it clear to him that she was a big girl and could look after herself.

If Aryna had turned up, there was no way of telling where she had gone after that.

A flight back to somewhere in Europe, hopefully. He looked forward to the moment when his assassin protégé rang in and left a message, especially if she happened to be in London.

What about Zheng and his girl?

They should be in Hawaii by now, docked in harbour after a superyacht cruise and safe within United States jurisdiction.

It was ironic that civilian shipping was heading east across the Pacific while warships were crossing in the opposite direction towards theatre-of-war operations in the SCS.

Bell dived into the ensuite and stared into the landscape mirror. He smiled at Jana's extensive collection of exfoliants and creams which lay strewn around haphazardly on the marble sink-surround.

On the mirror top corner there was a heart drawn in lipstick with the simple message – 'I love you' and underneath it, after dotted ellipses, 'I love the way you love' and a string of 'xxx' kisses.

Bell laughed inwardly.

Yeah, I've loved my time with you, Jana! Shame that she would be exposed to the unwanted attentions of the likes of Roxby, and other predators, when he was gone.

It was tempting to add to her lipstick message.

'I love the way you die, boy.'

But he settled for a cheesy riposte which should make her more than happy.

'Love you too, Jana. Xx.'

Time to dive into the power shower and let the jets of water breathe some vim and vigour back into him while his body was busy ridding itself of night-before toxins.

***

CNN was switched off as room service knocked at the door. Jana was nursing a mineral water into which she had dropped some sort of effervescent tablet.

Reports of the Blue Dragon explosion were all over the news, not just local coverage in Macau, but internationally.

Incident hacks gabbled into TV cameras in front of the stricken casino. A senior police spokesman talked in terms of a suspected gangland feud of some kind. The mugshot of a smiling Donato Gauci, spliced in next to an official statement, featured at regular intervals as part of the newsflash updates.

Nice to see his handiwork up there in lights.

But there was more to come.

The Blue Dragon was just the hors d'oeuvre.

The building shown in the background was still smouldering from the roof. Bell was pleased to see that at least a dozen police vehicles and forensic teams were at the scene. No quantity of corpses listed; however, a round-up of known arsonists and crime syndicate members was apparently underway.

Jana never said a word but Bell sensed that she had an inkling that it was something to do with him.

If she did, she wasn't saying anything.

Neither had she mentioned the note on the mirror, but he knew that she had taken a shot of it on her smartphone.

One for the archive.

Keepsakes and mementos of a squad of previous liaisons.

They were perfectly dressed as tourists.

Showered, fed and standing in fresh clothing, they were a couple ready to take in the sights of Macau old town.

Jana looked him up and down by the door.

'You do scrub up well. Come here!'

She drew him towards her and gave him a long, fruity kiss.

Bell tasted the fresh lipstick.

'Let's go and have some fun, shall we?'

As they passed Roxby's door, Bell could sense his presence simmering behind the woodwork.

While they continued to the lifts Bell knew that the door had been opened a fraction and that Roxby was peering out after them.

Their taxi was waiting for them outside the casino lobby. Soon they were squeezed together on the back seat watching Macau's sights whistle past.

Jana was pressed in to him, holding his hand.

The plan was to be dropped off in a side street, close to St Paul's Cathedral - the Calçada de São Paulo, as the starting point for a guided tour of the old town.

All they had to do was to stand in the right place where a guy with a muster stick would assemble his flock for an eleven o'clock walking departure.

It was useful to gauge the official reaction to the Blue Dragon aftermath as well as get his physical bearings during the daytime in preparation for his crucial night-time sortie.

There was no doubt that the police were on the lookout for a lone wolf who had been responsible. What better than to be seen being mollycoddled by a sugar mummy, arm in arm, taking in the sights and stopping for a coffee and a piece of cake?

The group traipsed on to the A-Ma Temple, the Senado Square and the Fortaleza do Monte.

Jana had agreed with him that they could break off whenever they'd had enough, find a sleepy bar down a side street and get some lunch at a place which did traditional Portuguese cuisine.

The mutual nod came sooner than expected.

They found themselves at a comfortable table in a picturesque, restaurante Portuguesa called 'O Santos'. It was a family-run business located near the ruins of Saint Paul's, in the Rua do Monte.

Basically, back where they had started.

There was no rush.

Bell could always use some pussy after lunch.

No tedious seduction to worry about.

Soon would come the moment when he had snuggled up to her naked body for the last time.

A lazy lunch with aperitifs and a fine wine.

After her second glass Jana was in full verbal flood again.

'It's quite strange, some of my Chinese suppliers in Hong Kong, who I thought I might drop in on, aren't taking my calls.'

'Oh, yeah?'

'People think I'm confident and opinionated, even mouthy, but I'll always be a sucker for baby-blue eyes and a cheeky grin!'

'Principally mine?'

'Especially yours, Tom. You're great fun to be with. For me, age is only a number.'

Bell understood what she was getting at: She wasn't a younger woman who wanted to trap her mate into marriage, children or an exclusive relationship. All she wanted was a good time.

No drama or games that would interfere with the pleasure she was enjoying. Basically declaring: Stick with me and your love life will be wonderful.

'Are you saying that you're a chick who's got her shit together?'

'You diplomatically omitted the word 'older', didn't you?'

'Er...'

'Sure, testosterone medication energises my libido. I'm not waiting for the menopause to be on that. It helps with my energy and strength too.'

'What about other therapies?'

'Collagen-boosting treatments and botox are fine but I have no urge to go under the knife. Obviously it's the business I'm in, for God's sake, and I do very well out of it.'

'It's said that sex itself is a form of therapy,' smirked Bell.

'Yeah, crawling with health benefits. That's why I need you to give me raunchy workouts in the bedroom.'

'Crawling on all fours naked while you whip my ass?'

'Hah! I prattle on too much, don't I?'

***

Food, alcohol and sex.

They were sat up in bed after a carnal session which Bell knew was their last. Another licentious afternoon snoozing in bed together with nothing left to explore of each other's bodies. Both of them knew which buttons to press; it was getting to be routine.

'You're sexy cute, you know that.'

Bell's sugary compliment triggered a wide grin.

Telling her that he was about to disappear without saying goodbye would have caused a diametrically opposite reaction.

Comments like that convinced her that it was safe to share her deepest secrets with him and fantasise about the exciting future that they could have together.

Jana glanced at her watch.

'I've booked the hotel health spa for five o'clock. Maybe you fancy a swim while I'm having my nails done?'

Yeah, and a raft of other treatments as well.

Bell surmised that she was limbering up for a full-on evening with him. First the extravagant Gala buffet and then the Disco Inferno retro-club-night.

She was so excited.

It was not to be.

Any swimming to be done might have to be restricted to thrashing frantically in the Pearl River estuary in total darkness.

What was the best way to end this liaison without giving the game away?

Jana's involvement had been invaluable.

A fortuitous legend enrichment enabling him to hide in plain sight with impunity… and quite a lot of fun, as well.

'I have a deal to close.'

Jana looked to have a foreboding sense of what was coming.

'You mean that you're going to abandon me again?'

'With regret, yes.'

'And this time it's for keeps?'

Bell sidestepped her supposition with a smile.

'Remember all that bullshit I told you about when you asked me what I did really?'

'Mergers and acquisitions?'

'Consolidation of corporate ownerships, assets and operations. Synergy and economies of scale.'

'So, why are you here on a gambling resort city break?'

'It's all about secrecy. I have to be on a plane at a moment's notice as new takeover bids bubble up.'

A vision of the Roze Ballon's pink neon sign photobombed Bell's mind's eye.

'Mixing business with pleasure, eh?'

'Company financials, tax law, accounting standards, and regulatory issues is what it's all about. Not that exciting, really, but it does pay well.'

Best not to overdo the bullshit.

'Just bean-counting, then. Not running around with a machine gun blowing the lids off casinos!'

Murders and executions, more like.

Manipulation and tactical disinformation.

All in a day's work for an MIX agent.

Things to do, people to kill.

Bell did his best to mitigate her disappointment.

'It doesn't mean that we can't meet up again, if you want to. Also, providing that you've remembered everything I've taught you!'

Jana moved forward to hug him tightly. She was sobbing uncontrollably now, as Bell gently wiped away her tears.

'I really appreciate it, dear Tommo. It's better than coming back from the wellness centre to find a scribbled note on my pillow.'

Alas, this is the end embrace
No more to look upon your face
My lips on yours do impress
For it is the last caress

***

Something to be done which was long overdue.

Bell had identified that Roxby was back in his room.

It necessitated a tap on his door to ask some kind of dumb question about card counting. The excuse being that he'd caught sight of Roxby at one of the poker tables and that he was an innocent greenhorn, at the mercy of the gambling floor, seeking a bit of expert advice.

Bell strode along the corridor, ready to knock. How Bell knew which room Roxby was in would have to be skated over for now. Just as Bell got to be within a stride or so…the door opened suddenly. David Roxby held it wide open with a broad, reptilian smile.

His spiel shot straight out of the gate.

'I know that we've not actually met, as such…but I have a tempting idea which may interest you.'

'Oh, yeah?' said Bell, trying to look suitably surprised and pliable.

'Easy money.'

Bell guessed that accepting an offer to step inside to hear more gave a clear signal that an illegal scheme of some kind was of interest. That he could easily be bent, corrupted and compromised with the promise of illicit riches.

'Okay.'

'Grab a seat. Drink?'

Bell declined both offers as smooth operator Roxby fixed himself a scotch from the minibar and prepared to give his pitch.

'Take this, it's yours…just a sample.'

Roxby handed across a crisp, new hundred US dollar bill. Its hologram glinted in the glare of the spotlights, the blue tint of Benjamin Franklin's portrait staring up at him.

'Why?' quizzed Bell.

'It's a North Korean counterfeit, the best in the world. I've several bundles of them to exchange and I need some assistance. I'm exhausted. The deal is you get keep half of whatever you can unload.'

Bell suspected that there was an ulterior motive.

Time to find out.

'I'm sorry, but it's not for me,' said Bell, lamely, gesturing a move to go.

Bell attempted to hand the C-Note back.

'There is something else.'

'What might that be?'

'Jana Cazenove.'

Time to demonstrate a little resistance.

'I'm sorry, I don't have time for this shit.'

'Hand her over to me and you can go.'

Bell registered the overt threat of false imprisonment and violence.

'She's not mine to hand over.'

'Not from what I've seen.'

'You mean, I can't leave this room till I do?'

'You're now privy and an accessory to my US dollar scam, even your prints are on it. What were you thinking of, pretty boy?'

Roxby had a thick-set physique and probably had some skills which he believed he could rely on. Whatever happened next had to look like an accident or suicide.

Bell noted that the balcony doors were half open.

***

Once he'd punched shit out of this insolent young puppy and had him pleading for mercy, it would be game-plan on again.

Jana Cazenove and all her money.

The unsettling thing at the back of his mind was that Jana's toy boy hadn't reacted with the fear and alarm that he might have expected.

He could sense something disquieting in Bell's eyes…also the way he coolly maintained space and distance during the stand-off. A kind of resolute capability to handle himself in sticky situations which he was used to dealing with.

Nah, he was just imagining things.

It was too late to deliver a sucker punch, the sort of cowardly, cheap shot that he'd often used to subjugate a defiant female.

Time to reveal his operational credentials.

'I work for the British Secret Service,' said Roxby.

The portentous declaration didn't seem to cut any ice with puppy-boy. Roxby produced a fake ID card to back up his false assertion, which elicited a second indifferent smirk.

Nothing for it but give puppy-boy a good slap.

Roxby went to grab Bell's throat but his unwilling stooge was too fast for him and was out of range in an instant. Bell stepped back in with a punch that smashed Roxby's nose with a sickening crunch. A palm-heel blow to the chin and an elbow strike to the side of the head followed.

Bell's next move was on its way.

In a blur of agile motion, Roxby's easy prey had come forward yet again and delivered a kick to the groin of such ferocious intensity that he felt lightning bolts shoot up both sides of his abdomen. He was sure that both his testicles had been ruptured with acute trauma, sending what was left of them back up their respective inguinal canals.

Now buckled over and incapacitated, puppy-boy was suddenly behind him, steering involuntary leg movements in a gruesome frogmarch towards the open balcony doors.

In the next moment he was staring over the balcony railing, fifteen storeys down, at the insects milling around in the hotel concourse below. Roxby had a few seconds left to ponder how his life would end.

Who was this guy? Come on Danny boy, you're slipping.

But, it didn't look like his nemesis was going to do him any favours – he'd already been levered half-way up over the balcony rail.

Bell's mouth came close to Roxby's left ear and whispered something.

'People like you give us a bad name. I actually do work for the British Secret Service.'

A final shove and Roxby was heading for terminal velocity.

No swimming pools or store canopies to break his fall just a sickening splat on to the pristine, cream-marble slabs.

Another stiff for the police and the city morgue to deal with. This time with a fat wad of Pyongyang US dollars on its person which should give the authorities something to think about.

Roxby's executioner wasted no time slipping back out into an empty hotel corridor.

19 Fatal recognition

Bell cruised effortlessly on a Benelli 752S motorbike, heading north on the Amizade flyover, ready to take a left at the Terminal Maritimo junction. Quite sweetly, police cars with their sirens blaring were all heading south.

Next stop: The Wynn Palace Casino.

This time he was travelling light. MIX field logistics would sanitise his vacated hotel room to a standard that it had never been subjected to before.

No heavy armament this time, just a back pack.

He parked the Benelli in an off-street underground car park right next to a sharply-styled all-black Kawasaki Ninja.

A concrete staircase led up to a rear hotel entrance used predominantly by workers and staff.

He was now in his room, six floors above where the delegates attending the conference rooms below would congregate for a cigarette.

Gaggles of nicotine-starved boffins lighting up a well-earned Furongwang or Huanghelo brand-named smoke. Chaining it madly before they were herded back in again.

Standing outside in groups was what he didn't want.

He needed all his ducks lined up in a row.

Nice and crispy, meat falling off the bone.

First thing to do: Get into Wynn Casino livery and proceed down to the four major conference rooms allocated for exclusive use by the Chinese scientific delegation. Function room names: Peony, Lotus, Camellia and Hibiscus.

They were using them in rotation and simultaneously for multiple seminar events. All had been mined with tightly-packed C4 high-explosive, the detonation mechanisms left dozing in an inert sleeper state.

Each device was located directly beneath the lectern mounted centrally upon a wide lecture-platform.

According to the intelligence, all conference rooms were swept twice a day at 08:00 and 18:00. The intel detailed full-house chiming points when every one of the delegates would be in their seats.

Next one: In fifty-nine minutes. Time now: 19:01.

The primary task was to awaken each bomb ensemble in turn. That meant zapping a transponder signal well within range. The finale was to press one single button at the right moment…Kawboom!… and escape on the bus back to Hong Kong, one of several exfiltration options.

Easy peasy.

MIX field logistics, as usual, had lent a hand.

***

Bell pushed his laden trolley along the hallway towards two loitering security guards who had spent their day scratching their nuts.

State Security grunts, most probably.

They moved forward menacingly to intercept him as he arrived at the Peony function-room side entrance.

Bell stamped on the footbrake.

'Can we help you?' asked the wiry one.

'With the compliments of the management,' said Bell.

'What is this? This area is restricted,' said the other.

'Bottles of drink and traditional Macau chocolates for the top tables,' said Bell.

The guards turned their attention away from Bell's name badge and the stores-requisition paperwork to the appetising display of alcoholic goodies and cocoa bombocas.

Moscatel, VSOP brandies, Bushmills whisky and liqueur-filled, dark-chocolate bonbons.

'We weren't briefed about this,' said wiry-one, sourly.

Bell daren't glance at his watch, this could end badly.

He leaned round into the trolley cupboard and extracted multiple trays of contraband – 50ml miniatures of brandy, whisky, rum and vodka which could be swigged down in seconds.

'How about some free giveaways?' grinned Bell, jovially.

They even held the doors open for him.

***

Back in his room, it was just a waiting.game.

Time now: 19:37.

Witching hour: 20:00.

Hide in the gloom while monitoring events below.

Radio trigger-device ready, finger hovering over the button.

Fully prepped for a discreet exit back to a warm Benelli bike and a deliciously pleasurable ride to the HZM Bridge bus station.

The throng of blazers continued to grow along with a cloud of cigarette smoke rising up to the atrium ceiling. Fission, fusion, rocketry, cyberwarfare, and quantum computing – a royal flush. All his chickens in the coop.

Nothing to do for a short while.

Bell relegated the impending carnage to the back of his mind.

What else to see from his high vantage point?

Steiner binoculars scanned the accommodation structure opposite.

Most of the balconies were shut up tight with curtains drawn.

But wait…halfway along the fifth floor.

A narrow gap in sliding doors and something unmistakeable.

Sharpened bino focus held the tip of a suppressor in its crosshairs.

An SVD Dragunov sniper rifle?

What the hell?!

Bell visualised the Russian-made 7.62 calibre weapon mounted on a tripod behind the net curtains.

More to the point, who the hell?!

***

A SWAT team had been despatched to the Wynn Palace Casino. A police tactical unit deployed to handle high-risk situations like shoot-outs, standoffs and terrorism; but this time the brief was to arrest of a foreign agent operating on Chinese soil.

Facial Recognition, using not only domestic data but that which was easily obtained from across the globe, had performed the identification. Specifically, activity in the locale of a casino in the city of Vladivostok in Far Eastern Russia, called the Tigre de Crystal. CCTV footage supplied on a mutual exchange basis between Russia and China.

Fatal recognition.

Target acquisition: The fifth floor.

***

Bell got there first.

Armed with a hacked swipe-card, which could open any room in the hotel without a validation beep, he silently let himself into room 0574.

His eyes had little time to acclimatise to the dark as he pressed himself tightly against the wall. The loud hubbub of over one hundred scientists, jabbering at atrium ground-floor level, was clearly audible through the open balcony doors. The noise had cloaked his ninjutsu-style entrance.

Doof!

A suppressed round leaving the chamber of a rifle.

Damn! Too late to save the mission!

The hubbub was instantly replaced by the clamour of screaming and shouting as wholesale panic took a grip.

A lithe figure casually got up from behind a gun tripod and disengaged a sniper rifle from its mountings. Bell got the impression that the marksman had hit something and had satisfactorily completed their mission.

A similar assignment to his own?

Nothing for it but to reveal his credentials.

As Bell launched himself across the room, the figure, who was dressed all in black, turned suddenly and side-stepped Bell's assault. He was on the receiving end of several balletic blows which he countered with kicks to the lower abdomen and a bear hug bulldoze into the wall.

'I'm a British MI6 agent on a mission!' screamed Bell, tightening a subjugating, shoulder-claw grip of his unknown adversary.

'I Japanese operative working for PSIA!' gasped a woman's voice.

'We need to work together to get out of Macau,' replied Bell, relaxing his grasp in order to convey operational goodwill.

'Hai, hai. I have escape plan.' came the answer.

'Who did you hit?'

'Director of Rocket Force division.'

'I want them all!' said Bell, brandishing his remote control device.

His mission might not be totally toast.

Looking down to the atrium concourse, Bell could see that the diligent security guards had just about finished hurrying all the delegates into the conference rooms, which was paradoxically what he was trying to achieve all along. A lone body lay on its back with a dark blood-spill spreading out over the white marble.

'I leave gun, we go now. My name Miku.'

'My name Tom. We blow building as we run, yes?'

Bell opened the door a little to see a Special Weapons and Tactics squad forming up at the far end of the corridor.

'Motorbike and fast RHIB to Hong Kong, hai? Why we wait?'

'We've got company. Friends of yours?'

Miku took a look for herself.

'Kuso jigoku!' she gasped.

Bell reached into his backpack and retrieved a couple of white phosphorous grenades. He lobbed them through a widened door gap as far as he could; best not to let the SWAT guys get a glimpse of them sprinting in the opposite direction.

'Now we run!' said Bell.

They burst out to the left as the grenades spewed out dense volumes of phosphorous pentoxide smoke to their right. The duo needed to run like buggery to keep ahead of the billowing toxic cloud which was chasing them down the corridor. They just needed to get to the fire door and the external stairwell.

Bell pressed the remote detonation button.

The shock wave of multiple explosions ripped through the entire hotel structure, almost knocking them over.

Now safely at the exit, Bell couldn't resist attaching a high-explosive booby trap to the back of the fire door.

Have a nice day guys…suck on that.

The SWAT team was way behind, at a standstill, disorientated and unsure, trying to understand what the hell was happening. Was that a missile, a bomb or a meteorite? Had their mission priority changed all of a sudden?

Meanwhile, Miku and Bell were flying down the outside stairwell at a lick.

Bell could feel the body blows he'd sustained from Japanese agent Miku. They hurt like fuck but he'd live…preferable to contracting Japanese encephalitis, though.

The alarms had gone off, and even the sprinkler system had kicked in for some reason. Great! The more mayhem and confusion the better.

Phew, safely at ground level and out into the open.

A lone police officer stepped out and shouted 'Halt!'.

Miku's balaclava may have prompted him.

She produced a Glock 19 from somewhere and shot him dead without hesitation.

Hmm…nice work.

Miku led him down into a familiar underground car park.

Time to hotfoot it out of mainland China.

They stood next to what must be her motorbike which, by some fluke of serendipity, was parked right next to his.

Miku peeled her balaclava off in slow motion to reveal a staggeringly attractive girl.

Wow!

She adjusted her Glock 19 in its handgun-holster as she spoke. The escape info came with a big smile and the offer of a crash helmet which matched hers.

'I have motorbike and RHIB at marina do forty knots. Bike is Kawasaki Ninja 650.'

As they were taking a moment to see who had the biggest dick, Bell retrieved a Glock 21 from his waistband.

Miku's eyes widened a little.

Yeah, a bit like penis girth, it was all about calibre – nine millimetre versus .45 ACP rounds.

'Sunappu!' yelped Miku.

Exactly – snap!

'Mine's this Benelli,' grinned Bell, donning the helmet and switching on its integrated wireless intercom. He surmised that having his arms around her slender waist could have been more fun. Maybe some other time.

'Follow me,' barked Miku, revving her engine.

Okay, cock-sucking banter over.

Better ride carefully without incident down to the Club Maritimo and hope that the triple-engine RHIB she had lined up had a full tank with the keys in the ignition.

The intercom squawked on the overpass.

Now in the groove for a slick maritime exit, Miku's spoken English had gone up a couple of gears.

'We can cross the river delta over to Lamma island, just south of Hong Kong and hide there till things cool off. It's due east sixty kilometres under cover of darkness. We can be there in two hours.'

They didn't even get close.

A road block - military vehicles, police cars and even a tank.

Access forcefully denied.

Okay, then - Plan C.

'Turn around, we'll take the HZM bus!' screamed Bell.

Their illegal U-turn over to the other carriageway had been noticed. A couple of police clever-dicks decided to lay chase.

'What you mean?'

'We'll ditch the bikes.'

'Bridge is closed!' bleated Miku.

'So?'

20 Take the bus

They got to the HZM bus station alright.

There was a police cordon. All traffic and Taipa ferry terminal sailings to Hong Kong were suspended until further notice.

Best to seek out a discreet side entrance and slip past the guards.

They were forced to ditch some expensive bikeware.

Keys left in the ignition, low mileage – a lucky find for someone.

Both of them had Glocks and commando knives, but that was it. Limited armament set against squads of special forces toting machine guns.

Cunning, stealth and ninjutsu were their friends.

They staked out an entry-point in the darkness.

Bell killed the careless guard who had left the barbed-wire gate open so that his colleague could go off and buy some cigarettes. Miku clinically silenced the guy returning from the convenience store. Both bodies were hidden crudely in the undergrowth.

They were in.

A minute later they traversed the vast booking hall which was totally deserted.

The bus depot garage and maintenance shop was next door.

Lines of luxury double-deckers parked beautifully within their pristine-white guide-markers.

Bell picked the first one and slumped into the driver seat. The key, attached to various fobs and vehicle IDs, was in the ignition, not unlike their desirable motorbikes, and even the RHIB which was regrettably still moored up in the marina.

He fired up the diesel engine briefly and checked that the 79-seater shuttle-bus was ready for action.

Half a tank…more than enough.

Meanwhile, there was some loading to do and hydraulic garage doors to check out.

Once they got going, they weren't stopping.

They headed for the parts and equipment storage zone which was located immediately adjacent to the rows of bus rolling stock.

Bell navigated to a particular stretch of metal cabinets and unlocked them with a universal key. He'd nabbed a pallet truck which would suffice.

'Better start loading up; I don't think we've got long before those bodies are discovered,' said Bell.

They piled up multiple bags of military ordnance on the lower deck of the bus and got on board.

M72 LAW rockets, M16s, AR15s, ammo, and grenades.

'How did you know about all of this?' quizzed Miku.

'British Military Intelligence is a whizz at logistics,' laughed Bell.

The 360 BHP engine powered up nicely again. He logged into the MAN ND363F onboard computer system via his military tablet, skipped over the exhaust treatment options and disabled the speed delimiter.

His finger on his touchpad allowed him to turn the steering wheel. They would mainly be going in a straight line anyway. Where to sit required a little thought.

Therefore, he was safely seated amidships avoiding any bullets which might be aimed at the driver's compartment, but with full control of this shuttle leviathan which boasted three axles.

The bus inched towards the tall concertina doors. Miku jumped out to press the green 'OPEN' button and a panoramic view of the Pearl River estuary spread out in front of them.

Shouting could now be heard echoing somewhere in the vast space behind them as Bell swung a left on to the HZM bridge in the direction of HK, his foot hard on the gas.

'Smash the rear window out and roast the depot,' screamed Bell.

Miku, who knew her way around an armoury, fired two LAW rockets in quick succession turning the bus depot into a shake-n-bake glowing inferno, complete with skyward fireball.

That was what rear view mirrors were invented for!

The bus rapidly accelerated up the incline, heading toward their destination, the dead median-point of the Pearl River channel and the bridge's central apex.

'Good girl, keep it coming. Give 'em hell.'

Several military and police vehicles were now on their tail and gaining on them quickly despite Bell reaching over eighty-five miles per hour.

Miku, God bless her, was spewing purgatory out of the back window with a cocktail of heavy machine gun fire and well-aimed rockets.

According to his calculations they would arrive at their destination point in about nine minutes.

The first salvo of air-to-ground fifty-cal rounds sprayed the side of the bus. As expected, a pair of Chinese Z-10 ground attack helicopters had been scrambled. The first one shot overhead and was now making a banking turn to port. Even if the bus console was blown away, he still had his HDMI

Ethernet connection directly connected to the vehicle's CPU. Other than that, the poor engine block couldn't last forever.

Six minutes and counting.

Can't this fucker go any faster?

Ninety-eight mph seemed to be its limit.

'Down to the last two rockets!' hollered Miku.

A missile hit the top deck, shaking the German-built chassis off course for a moment.

The bus kept going despite the roof being on fire.

Sixty seconds now, nearly there.

Bell already had the exit doors open as he swerved the vehicle sharply to a halt against the way-station wall.

He knew that the entrance led to an internal staircase which went all the way down one hundred and eighty feet to the mini-island supporting the massive, bridge pylon.

As Bell and Miku jumped out, blazing bullets into the sky, both Z-10s came to a predatory hover.

Miku rocket-blasted the furthest one as Bell cruelly raked the Chinese special forces trying to abseil on to the tarmac.

'Kuso kurae!' yelled Miku, valiantly.

Nothing for it but to obliterate the rear rotor, which exploded spontaneously. As the Z-10 lost height and control, Miku and Bell took cover from the imminent impact inside the concrete way-station.

A third Z-10 helicopter appeared from nowhere.

Miku, full of despair, screamed into Bell's face.

'We're both going to die!'

Bell gripped her hard by the arm and looked venomously into her eyes.

'Do I look beat? We're not done yet!' he said, coolly.

'Aren't we?'

Sure, they could run down the stairs but there was a much quicker way.

MIX field logistics to thank, yet again.

'Are you afraid of heights?'

Bell glanced at her footwear.

'A little,' smiled Miku, nervously.

'But you know how to abseil?'

'Hai! Hai!'

'Quick! Get this kit on. We'll be on the ground before you know it. Wear these gloves, don't look down, don't think about it; I go first…follow me!'

With a two-hundred-foot length of rope dangling down the side of the pylon in a strong estuary breeze, Bell launched himself off into the perilous void.

Mantra: Look up, not down!

He felt Miku's tremor on the rope as she followed him.

He had to keep ahead of her, as they descended at speed.

The instant he hit the deck he pulled out an inflatable raft which had been carefully hidden by MIX logistics behind some rocks. The CO_2 canisters inflated it in under ten seconds.

Bell steadied the raft as Miku landed, unfortunately with a bit of a tumble, and tore off her harness. She had taken an impact against one of the jagged granite chunks which lay randomly around the base of the pylon.

Unlucky.

No time to dwell on it.

The explosive charge booby trap, which Bell had laid at the head of the internal pylon staircase, blew and rendered it totally impassable. A radio signal to their carabiner rope-shackle released the nylon abseil-rope which crashed to Bell's feet like reels of spaghetti. Bell lobbed it into the raft.

'Jump in!' screamed Bell, as he helped her on board and they pushed off into the swirling river current.

The Z-10s had no doubt managed to disembark some Marines, but he dared to think that he had nailed quite a few of them with a trademark MIX calling card.

All ancient history now.

They had got away…but there were new life-threatening challenges to face.

The fast flow of tidal water took them away at speed into the night, heading out towards the perils of the open ocean.

Out of the frying pan into the fire.

But they were still alive…

21 Sub tropical

They had drifted further out in the Pearl River Delta. Bell felt the turbulence of the ocean as the watershed of the entire Guandong region finally met the South China Sea.

Helicopter searchlights relentlessly strafed the river's surface in the darkness, tracer beams circling over and over, but the fleeing pair seemed to have escaped the designated pursuit-grid. The wreckage of two Z-10 ground-attack helicopters still burned vividly at the apex of the HZM bridge.

Miku was looking more than worried – what was the clever plan now?

Lost at sea after all that?

Drown somewhere amongst the hundred or so uninhabited islands of the Wanshan archipelago? Or get washed up on one...if they were lucky?

The wind was blowing harder now; a typhoon harbinger, maybe.

The urban lights of Hong Kong and Macau, respectively to port and starboard of their tiny craft, continued to penetrate the pitch black. They acted as a beacon of comfort by proving the ongoing existence of civilisation and a slim chance of survival.

Bell checked the GPS coordinates.

The rising and falling in the powerful, languorous swell was resulting in random soakings.

'Do we die out here, together, just the two of us?'

Bell ignored the question.

'Just hang on, honey. We can do this.'

The flow was taking them further out to sea.

Now what? Catching the coastal current and heading south into the wider Pacific which might just get to claim their scalps?

If they beached anywhere they would surely be picked up by a PLA maritime patrol.

Bell felt a vibrating tremor beneath the water, like a sperm whale ready to break the surface. A dense body of briny unnaturally penetrated by a large, baleful object.

Maybe that was how the powers-that-be in Beijing were feeling right now about their precious bridge and the loss of a swathe of their top scientists.

The armed conning tower of a submarine suddenly rose up in front of them, dead ahead. The abrupt swell rocked their flimsy rubber life-raft precariously.

Bell hoped desperately that it was not a Chinese coastal-sub out on surveillance. Even the ageing PLAN fleet of diesel-electric tin-cans could pack a serious punch.

Bell guessed that it could easily be a conventional Chinese submarine, simply skulking around inshore waters – maybe a type 041 yuan-class. A coating of anechoic polymer tiles and an asymmetric propeller were all part of its noise-reduction and stealth armoury.

There was no discernible five-pointed star visible in the poor light.

Bell had to take a chance on it.

He braced himself for a burst of machine gun fire.

However, he suspected that he and his accomplice were wanted alive, not as mincemeat - to be subjected to torture, interrogation, a slow death, lingchi or even worse.

But, there it was, the signal he'd been waiting for.

A bright wink of light pointing in their direction.

A message sequence of light flashes in Morse code
followed…

Dit dah dit, dit dah, dah, dit dah dah,…

R-A-T-W-…

R-A-T-W-O-R-M.

Call-sign status: Awaiting response.

Bell flashlit T-O-A-S-T in acknowledgement.

Dah, dah dah dah, dit dah, dit dit dit, dah…

They started paddling like mad towards the hulking metal
beast, utilising the fading estuary current to help them glide up
against its hull. Anywhere forward of the conning tower, where
the sub hatches were located, would do.

Soon, they were alongside a British Astute class submarine
clambering up hemp netting, assisted by Royal Navy ratings.
The haul included their flimsy raft and its contents, removing
all crucial traces of the fugitive duo.

Minutes later the submarine slid back into the depths and was
gone.

***

They were immediately wrapped in thermal blankets and taken
to the sub's infirmary.

The Medical Officer checked them over.

Presently, the Captain appeared and lay his cap down on the
bed.

'A close shave, eh?'

Bell attempted to get up.

'Welcome aboard. I'll see you in the mess in an hour's time, if
you don't mind.'

'Oh, and get some sustenance and kip in the meantime. You
look beat…but you're in the safe hands now. Well, sort of.'

Bell guessed that their ultimate destination wouldn't be mainland Japan or the Philippines, as this sub was out on a long-duration assignment. A sea rendezvous with a British surface vessel was more likely. Whatever happened, it was important to get a signal off to MIX as quickly as possible.

The Captain had read Bell's thoughts.

'We need to avoid surfacing unnecessarily, but we can drop you off on the island of Ishigaki. From there it's an easy hop up the First Island Chain to Okinawa.'

Time to grab a bite to eat and indulge in some debrief chatter.

***

Bell composed a detailed chronology of recent events. He ended his MIX report with the submarine Captain's plan to disembark him and a PSIA agent on Ishigaki. It included a pragmatic suggestion.

His proposal was to request assistance from the US forces stationed on Okinawa. An aircraft to pick them up which would turn around and head straight back to the Kadena Air Force base. After a brief stopover, a second USAF flight could transport them all the way back to Yokota AFB in Tokyo. It was especially workable if there was space on a routine shuttle service.

That was probably enough contrived bullshit to sell an idea which suited his purpose.

A couple of in-flight drinks and some R&R in one of Tokyo's rave-up districts wouldn't go amiss after a tough mission.

Bell had explained Miku's awkward fall at the foot of one of the HZM bridge's pylons which seemed to necessitate medical treatment.

The MO's diagnosis indicated light concussion and cracked ribs. The prescription was strong painkillers and an MRI scan or X-Ray to check for other fractures and internal bleeding. Hopefully, it was simply a case of some healing and getting quality rest time.

***

The three of them met up in the senior rates' mess. Submariner space was always at a premium. Nevertheless, there was enough room for a framed colour photograph of the reigning monarch of the United Kingdom, gracing the wall at the far end.

Bell and Miku had both been issued tropical naval uniforms sporting two medium gold-braid-striped epaulettes. A couple of new lieutenants sitting to attention at the long table with the sub's Captain.

An orderly brought in the drinks.

Captain Charles Stanley relaxed back in his seat and glanced at his watch.

'Welcome aboard HMS Auray, which, as you probably know, is a nuclear-powered fleet submarine of the Astute class. Here's to a successful evac, by the way. Textbook stuff, eh?'

Glasses chimed together.

'All down to you guys,' said Bell.

'You put on quite a show back there!'

Pennant number: S126, the Auray was eighth in line of the Astute class submarine series. At ninety-seven metres in length and capable of a submerged speed of thirty knots, its armament included Tomahawk cruise missiles and Spearfish heavyweight torpedoes.

Diluted Admiralty rum was guzzled down in short order.

The Captain shook his head with a grin.

Thumb twiddling time.

'Well, it looks like everyone's anticipating further instructions from their superiors. All in the same boat, as it were.'

Yeah, snug as sardines in a tin.

The Captain's forced jollity seemed oddly inappropriate. Some sort of gallows-humour safety valve that commanders in his position relied upon to keep a grip.

'We could play a game of 'I spy' whilst we're waiting,' laughed Bell.

'Quite so,' said the Captain, drumming his fingers on the mahogany table-top.

Having filed an urgent report to London, Bell expected an immediate response.

A secure cable was delivered before long to the wardroom, but not from the First Sea Lord at the Admiralty.

For your eyes only.

Bell stripped it open: New orders.

He was to keep working with the PSIA agent and thrash out common ground with a senior CIA officer who was on secondment in Okinawa.

After that there was a liaison visit scheduled with the Japanese secret service in Tokyo.

So, he'd pulled it off.

Happy days!

The Captain channelled his disappointment into a morose and sombre assessment of the current situation in the South China Sea.

'It's not a matter of if, it's a matter of when. The new American president is determined to lance the boil.'

'Well, it's a breath of fresh air to have someone in the White House who's not suffering from cognitive impairment,' replied Bell, cheerily.

'You mean geriatric dementia?'

'Yeah, bidin' their time while Rome burns.'

The Captain echoed the positive spin.

'James Donald Smith was the same age as JFK when he was inaugurated in January 1961, did you know that?'

'Different political tribe, though,' said Bell.

'Eh?' quizzed the Captain.

'He means the elephant and the donkey. Don't you know your bumper stickers, Captain?' laughed Miku.

'…And the republican hawks are in the driving seat. JDS may be forty-six years old and at the top of his game, but open-top motorcades in Dallas should be ruled out,' added Bell, wryly.

The Captain was enjoying the lively exchange.

'Hawks, doves, elephants and donkeys…so why don't the British people answer to a similar menagerie of constitutional ideologies, I wonder?'

'On the contrary, apart from the lion…we have hyenas and pit vipers to a man in parliament,' said Bell.

'…and women, to be sure,' chipped in Miku.

So, a clandestine drop-off on the island Ishigaki?

Bell's comprehensive MIX briefing back in London had provided detailed info on all the Japanese island groups.

Ishigaki is a subtropical paradise and gateway to the Yaeyama Islands. With an area of over two hundred square kilometres, it is way more than a barren coral shoal with a busted up airstrip and a few corrugated-iron huts. Its idyllic subtropical setting offers the usual array of leisure activities, ocean views and traditional island culture with an emphasis on premier-class hotels and resorts.

Its beaches were reputedly up there for clear shallow water, snorkelling, diving, sailing and secluded, sheltered coves. The only thing to be aware of was the micro-mesh netted areas to protect swimmers from the habu-kurage, box jellyfish.

A neurotoxin sting which causes cardiac arrest and respiratory failure could be a serious downer.

Overall assessment: Cool...and they sell beer.

After a short spell there, it was an hour's flight north to the heavily US-garrisoned island of Okinawa.

Miku's and the Captain's communications arrived at the same time.

More orders to pore over.

Bell suspected that there had been direct liaison between MIX and the Admiralty.

Things had changed quickly.

The Captain brought up a nautical chart on the plasma screen and waved a laser pointer.

'You'll see that the Auray will navigate past the northern tip of Taiwan, past the islands of Yonaguni and Taketomi. We'll end up surfacing in the warm, pristine waters of Kabira Bay where we'll lob you back in the water with your trusty inflatable.'

Bell felt that he had detected a pang of envy in the Captain's words and delivery. Blockades was the business that HMS Auray and its crew were into right now. Hush, hush and all that - heavy shit which could result in twisted metal lying in pieces on the seabed. Cat and mouse in the deep instead of enjoying snorkelling over coral reefs, drinking cocktails and frolicking in the surf with an attractive female companion.

The Captain raised his eyebrows with a resigned, knowing grin.

More solemn recollections of time served in the Senior Service, to be listened to reverently.

'When I joined the Royal Navy as a junior officer I guess that I never dreamt that World War Three would break out on my watch.'

'You were wrong,' said Bell.

'The beached wreck of the BRP Sierra Madre was blown to oblivion this morning in an unprovoked attack. Fifteen Filipino Marines were killed.'

The Philippine military, in an attempt to reinforce its maritime claim, had deliberately run a decommissioned warship aground on Second Thomas Shoal, in the contested Spratly Islands. The Chinese-occupied island of Mischief Reef is located only thirty kilometres away. Under international law, a country's naval ship is considered part of its territory. If anyone were to touch or step on any part of the vessel, it would be an act of war.

'Unilateral escalation,' said Bell, grimly.

'Interestingly, the Chinese Ministry of State Security are saying that they have recovered the body of a British agent working undercover in Macau,' smiled the Captain.

'What?!'

'An MI6 agent running amok in the former Portuguese colony is the news item which has dominated the tabloids over the last six hours. The dead man has been identified as a key member of a sizeable terrorist force which was attempting to blow up the HZM bridge, apparently.'

Daniel Roxby would have been pleased to know that.

A second discreet glance at an Omega Seamaster.

Captain Stanley stood up and offered a handshake.

'The affairs of state summon. Singapore and the Malacca Strait for us, I'm afraid.'

***

It was better than they could ever have expected.

They were escorted ashore in their modest inflatable, lashed to the side of a powerful Gemini RIB. The Royal Navy craft discarded them close in, turning tail to head back to HMS Auray, lurking further out in a deep channel.

They jumped into warm, gin-clear water lapping up to mid-thigh, their bare feet treading fine sand all the way up the beach.

A deserted cove on Japanese sovereign territory.

Miku fell to her knees and gave the ground a thankful, Nippon-venerating kiss.

It was still an hour or two before sun-up.

A cab flagged down on the quiet coast road took them to their five-star beach resort hotel.

They soon found themselves in a luxurious, multi-roomed suite, located a short distance from the water's edge. Bell slipped down to his Calvin Kleins and placed an order with room service. His Royal Navy uniform was now folded on a hanger, stashed in one of the cavernous wardrobes. He had felt like an imposter, artificially given the notional rank of lieutenant. It seemed to be cocking a snook at generations of valiant British sailors, all the way back to the Spanish Armada, who had genuinely earned their stripes.

Medical status update.

'How are the ribs?' said Bell

'Painful!' came the grizzled reply.

It was evident that they had been provided with a king-sized bed. Miku was already in it, turned away, nearest the door, seemingly fast asleep in seconds – she was best left alone in a comatose state.

It had been an exhausting day for her.

Bell headed outside with a double scotch and water and stood on the ground-level balcony which commanded an entire strip of private beach. He looked up at the heavens to marvel at the light-pollution-free display of constellations.

A shooting star, not a North Korean missile, whistled across the firmament as he took a moment to be thankful for his good fortune.

Somewhere out there to the south, naval vessels of all types were maintaining their positions to blockade the island of Taiwan. Although possessing a thriving economy, ninety-eight percent of its energy was imported – never mind food stuffs. How long could it hold out? Sooner or later, a 'running-the-blockade' incident could trigger World War Three.

The recent Chinese dumping of Western bond and currency reserves at the same time as the bulk buying of gold, was causing an existential threat to the US dollar.

Someone in Beijing was rolling the dice and going for it.

It was now or never for the CCP.

Bell turned to re-enter the bedroom, not Miku unfortunately.

Maybe some of that later…with a fair wind, divine even.

Like the typhoons that dispersed Mongol-Koryo fleets which were attempting to invade Japan in the thirteenth century.

Miku was still struggling with the impact from her fall and was on potent analgesics. She would be provided with a full medical evaluation when they got to Okinawa.

More female hair spread out on an adjacent pillow.

This was a moment to savour, alive and safe in a subtropical paradise. The way things were going, it might be a considerable length of time before anyone could do this type of thing again.

Make the most of it, buddy.

Bell was suddenly overcome with intense fatigue.

The cool, fresh cotton sheets engulfed his tired limbs as he became aware of Miku's exquisite form, warm and luscious, lying next to him. As the first stage of non-REM sleep took control of his brain-wave patterns, the gentle chortle of the aircon lulled him into a deep, delicious slumber.

***

Bell jolted awake. Morning light filtered through the translucent Shoji screen, gradually acclimatising his eyes to its intensity.

Miku was no longer by his side.

The rising sun burst through as he soundlessly pulled the traditional paper and wood screen across and headed outdoors.

Miku surfaced in the distance and strode out of the water.

'Come on in, the water is…sutekina.'

'Not as lovely as you, though.'

'Hah! You my lover-boy now, eh?'

'How about your rib cage?'

'My training includes pain management.'

Bell returned with trunks, a snorkel, mask and flippers - all provided complementary by the hotel in a range of styles and sizes for their super-wealthy guests.

A six-star hotel rating, really…if you include the helipad and vast wine cellar.

Bell took a dive with Miku who gave the thumbs up as she submerged alongside him into the pristine depths.

They saw coral polyps, manta rays, sea turtles, clown fish and damsel fish in the dazzling, clear water. The only thing to keep an eye out for was the tricky habu jellyfish and its stinging tendrils. Truly a wonderful, semitropic idyll.

They collapsed back on to the sand, laughing.

'These islands are Japan's Hawaii, you know!'

***

The power-shower tortured their bodies with needle-like jets as shikuwasa-fruit cleansing-gel rinsed their bodies fresh and clean.

Miku knew that the moment was fast approaching.

'Don't get the notion that I'm turning into a geisha girl!'

Her wet thong had disappeared somewhere. His own sodden attire was also long gone.

They lay naked on the bed together.

'I think you saved us,' said Miku, affectionately tracing her forefinger over his bottom lip.

'Well…'

'But you knew all along, didn't you?'

'Uh?'

'The submarine.'

'Proper preparation and all that...'

'You even had a plan D?'

'Maybe,' glinted Bell.

A broad smile and big eyes accepted his evasive answer.

Bell inched closer on his side, with a hard-on.

'I have a beautiful girlfriend called Saya. I think that we are in love, and we certainly know how to get it on between the sheets.'

Bell backed off a couple of millimetres.

'Ah!'

'Lying with you is like lying with my brother. I hope that I didn't string you along?'

Miku's hand reached out to touch Bell's erection.

'My, my. This is truly a wonder of mother nature's bio-hydraulics and valve control.'

Yeah, circumference matters.

Attaboy! And not a bluey in sight.

Each of her fingers was firmly wrapped around his girth as she looked him in the eye. The same trigger finger which had unleashed a dozen or so M72 LAW rockets at Chinese assault helicopters was now expertly rubbing his frenulum.

'We can't let this go to waste, though.'

'You know that I'm about to explode!'

'Yes.'

'Maybe it's better this way, if I think about it,' gasped Bell.

'I made porn films when I was young and naïve. I was a waif and stray in the big city needing quick money. I found that I could swing both ways – also useful as a PSIA agent on a mission. I'm no stranger to muscular contractions and lubrication, whoever is on the receiving end. Girl-on-girl and boy-on-girl action. Sex and spying - subterfuge and knowing your way around a guy's dick.'

'Non-gay for pay?'

'Yes, hetero for dough…or simply for what you know. We girls have our own special way of expressing love for each other.'

Likewise, all men make love in different ways provided that they are lying next to a partner whose libido is driven by a compatible sexual orientation.

Squeeze together…and bang.

Whatever we can get our hands on, really.

Talking of hands, Miku cupped most of Bell's fresh ejaculate in the palm of her spare. It had been like a cold-blooded, reptilian nurse in a starched, clinic uniform taking a fluid sample…but he wasn't complaining.

'Is this what they mean by the fruit of your loins?'

'Well, that's all you're gonna get, lady.'

Luckily, the tissue box was within arm's reach.

'Anyway, Saya is in a J-Pop girl-band called 'Sakura Go'. In English it means 'Cherry Blossom Five'. They are massive in Japan and South-East Asia. They have a new single out this month called 'Cruel Candy'. I will introduce you. I'm invited to the launch as a special guest and you can come along. What's the world of love like for you?'

'I get by. I'm friends with quite a few women.'

'Hmm…surprise, surprise. A lot of my girlfriends want to know what it would be like to date a Western boy…or at least try being in bed with one.'

'They might not find me attractive!' laughed Bell.

'I'll have them queuing up for you. Ever heard of a 'Tri-dive'?'

Bell surmised that something may have been lost in translation. She was probably referring to a kooky genre of speed-dating that was all the rage in Japan.

'You go down for ten minutes and then come up for air?'

Miku was back with her forefinger on Bell's lips, sporting a wicked smile.

'Your tubes are cut if you fail to deliver.'

'Ouch!'

'Don't worry, I'll see to it that you get your leg over.'

22 Ok in Okinawa

It had been an hour's flight from Ishigaki to Okinawa. Their plane touched down at the Kadena USAF base located on the island's west coast.

Okinawa sits midway in the Ryukyu arc of islands which stretch from the southern tip of mainland Japan, continuing southwest down towards the northern coastline of Taiwan.

Miku and Bell were gradually working their way up the First Island Chain, all the way back to Kyushu.

The base is dubbed the 'Keystone of the Pacific' because of its highly strategic location.

The USAF 18th Combat Wing is the primary unit at Kadena, hosting associate units from five other Air Force major commands, the United States Navy and other Department of Defense agencies.

Alex Gallen, CIA, was on the tarmac to meet them.

The new arrivals were still dressed in Royal Navy tropical-whites and cap, not looking at all out of place.

They descended the steps of the USAF eight-passenger, turboprop C-12A, which had refuelled to make the four hundred kilometre return trip. The flight crew had also taken the opportunity to carry out valuable surveillance work en route.

'Welcome to Kadena AFB, Lieutenant,' said Gallen, saluting with a broad grin.

'Allow me to introduce Miku Kenji, PSIA,' said Bell.

After a few handshakes, the group headed for the main building.

Gallen had been briefed and knew very well who Kenji was. She was an ex-glamour model and exotic dancer turned spy and high-class courtesan.

An undercover agent who wasn't afraid of the firing squad.

If it turned out like that, all she could do was refuse the blindfold and blow the twelve shooters a smackeroo.

Too late to invite them to kiss her ring by then.

She used her feminine guile and mastery of a whole range of armaments, to provide valuable intelligence for her masters in Tokyo. In the flesh, she was every inch a mysterious and beautiful young woman whose seductive charms were used to ensnare her lovers. Physically slender, her feline figure exhibited the flexible grace of a feral animal with sharp teeth.

Kenji's main remit of subterfuge had been the Russian threat to Japan in the northern Kuril Islands. Latterly, carrying out successful espionage operations in the locale of Vladivostok which involved a double assassination.

She had evaded detection and capture on multiple occasions.

If anyone could escape through a small toilet window, it was Kenji. Be that as it may, when your luck ran out, that was it.

Thomas Bell's background was somewhat baffling. The intel didn't even indicate exactly which British secret service agency he worked for.

The only thing to go on was the way he'd held off all comers, virtually single-handed, at the apex of the Hong Kong-Zhuhai-Macau bridge, including a couple of Chinese Z-10 choppers. Most of the onboard Special Forces had been roasted out of existence before they could set foot on the blacktop.

But that wasn't all.

Various bombings and homicides that had occurred in the last few days in Macau were probably something to do with him as well.

Dead right to keep it to a 'need-to-know' basis.

Everyone had more than enough security clearance to discuss matters en clair. Gallen was aware that his illustrious visitors were only passing through and he was looking forward to discussing some crucial points.

One issue of special interest may require his direct involvement.

'Glad you made it. I'll show you to your day quarters. Get settled in and we'll go and grab some lunch,' said Gallen.

Gallen was aware that the duo were scheduled to be on tonight's flight to the joint Japan-USA Yokota air base, located to the west of Tokyo.

At least, there would be enough time to breathe in some Okinawan air, get some chow and have a chat before they flew off again.

With the threat of escalating conflict in the South China Sea, they'd better get a move-on brainstorming serious stuff.

US-UK-Japan intelligence liaison firing on all cylinders.

***

Gallen led the way to the base swimming pool complex.

'Let me show you something.'

Brash ice is an accumulation of floating ice made up of fragments not more than two metres across. It is the wreckage of other forms of ice. Brash ice is common between colliding floes or in regions where pressure ridges have collapsed.

A fifty-metre swimming pool, complete with diving boards.

'Do we need to get into our bathing gear?' asked Bell.

'No, but put these on.'

'Crampons?'

'This classified demonstration demands it,' grinned Gallen.

Thermal transfer at molecular level.

Sucking energy out of atoms in the land of polar bears and retreating glacial shelves.

'What you are about to see was originally developed as a method to re-freeze the polar ice caps and create sea ice, while simultaneously harvesting energy. The scientific development team eventually realised that there was a military application to be had.'

An arms race is the genesis of technical innovation.

Underwater, flexible pipes with nodes attached at regular intervals lined the base of the pool. The pipework converged on a substantial piece of apparatus pressed up against one wall.

'Stand well back,' ordered Gallen.

He switched the machine on, along with a wave generator.

A skin started to form on the surface of the water as jagged ice shapes forced their way upwards.

The soccer ball that Gallen had kicked into the pool was now firmly trapped in the ice.

The initial layer of crunchy rice-pudding was soon laminated a foot deep and getting thicker.

'The machine draws off all the energy in a molecular chain reaction, turning choppy water into solid blocks of impassable brash ice,' said Gallen.

Gallen beckoned them to join him out on the frozen crust.

The three of them exhaled misty clouds of breath; it was suddenly very cold in here.

Bell now understood about the crampons.

'Don't laugh, but the plan was to freeze the Taiwan Strait and halt a Chinese invasion,' said Gallen.

'Really?' said Bell.

Anyone could see that it was an issue of scalability.

'It was a nice idea, but you could say that it's still on the drawing board. We've had to park it indefinitely. In the meantime, if world peace prevails, the leopard seals and penguins may just get to benefit from what this crazy device has to offer.'

Bell thought for a moment.

A siege or a blockade which morphs seamlessly into a full-scale assault.

'Better stick to pouring boiling oil from the parapets,' said Bell.

'You jest, but what you are suggesting is not far from the truth.'

'Boiling oil?'

'Better than that.'

***

The trio took a table in the congenial AFB canteen.

'What's it to be, burgers, hot dogs and fries or traditional Okinawan cuisine?'

'Didn't I see Dunkin' Donuts and Metro Burger outlets on the way over?' said Bell.

'If that is your desire,' smirked Gallen.

'Only joking!'

Miku was straight in there, caressing Gallen's hand and pressing up against him. Gallen wasn't protesting.

'Alex, shin'ainaru dear, I have a suggestion. Rafute and chanpurū washed down with a Monsutā premium beer, although I won't be joining you, I'm afraid.'

A naval medic and a nurse stood at the end of their table ready to escort Miku to the diagnostics centre.

An empty stomach was preferable for an MRI scan.

Miku could eat later after receiving a hopeful green-light.

Gallen set the kitchen buzzing with their order.

Four 350ml cans of Monsutā beer arrived while the dishes, which represented the best in Okinawan cuisine, were being cooked to perfection.

- Rafute: Skin-on pork belly stewed in soy sauce and brown sugar, considered to engender longevity.

- Goya chanpurū: A stir fry dish consisting of tofu with some kind of vegetable, meat, or fish.

Conversation commenced with prosaic small talk as the two men sized each other up.

'The US naval base on Guam is twelve hundred nautical miles away, far out there in the North Pacific Ocean,' said Gallen, lazily.

Bell nodded as his host continued.

'Type 22 rocket systems is what I'm at, along with cruise missiles installed on every island in the First Island Chain. Mageshima Island was the last one to be enabled, an uninhabited outcrop twenty-one miles from the southernmost Japanese main island of Kyushu.'

'Of course, a little prank in the Taiwan Strait where an F-35C fell, accidentally-on-purpose, off the USS Atlantis didn't quite pay off. You could say that we was had.'

'Duped?' said Bell.

'Sorely fucked over. The Chinese had been all over it but left us with a titanium post-it note attached to the fuselage.'

'Saying?'

''Nice try'.'

'Sounds like they already had everything.'

'Do bears crap in the woods?'

It was time to get down to the real business.

'Okay, let's cut to the chase, what's up?' said Bell.

'Gao Zi Xin.'

'Ah, yes. My Antwerp flitter.'

'You attended his abortive arrest at Schiphol airport.'

'He escaped in his private jet from Deurne Airport. He's still at large.'

'I know. We want him just as much as you do. However, there is one thing.'

'What?'

'A certain person is reputed to be aware of his current whereabouts. I have it on unimpeachable authority.'

Gallen pushed an index card across the table. Bell glanced at it.

'The head of the Yakuza?'

Bell knew that the kumichō was only known as 'Toratako'.

虎蛸

It meant tiger octopus in English - lucky number eight.

'Yes, he's currently on death row in Tokyo's Fuchū Prison.'

'Who told you this?'

'A former associate of Gao's.'

It seemed that the authorities had at least some major players in custody.

'Your impeccable source?'

'Give or take the spin of a roulette wheel.'

'A gambler and a chancer saving his skin?'

'Yes, but we have reason to believe him. The electric chair if he's wrong.'

'How long have we got?'

'The execution is scheduled for a week's time but the inmate wants to cut a deal to spend the rest of his days under house arrest in exchange for information.'

'And?'

'The Japanese government is considering the idea. Your input would be to augment the deal with the disclosure of Gao's exact location. A face-to-face meeting in his prison cell to get it over the line. We've lobbied the Japanese Ministry of Justice through the channel of their secret service, the PSIA, to accept the proposal.'

'Is that it?'

'Er…there is also the question of some missing fissionable nuclear material which would form part of the package. Your task is, with Miss Kenji as interpreter, to pay a visit to Fuchū and obtain the answers we need. You'll have full executive authority to act.'

Mission creep.

'Okay, we're on.'

'Lastly, the CIA wants to be in on any reprisal mission to nail Gao.'

'Yeah?'

'That means me as your wingman.'

Hmm…being lumbered with a desk-bound intelligence officer could be a problem in a firefight.

At that moment the food arrived.

It grieved Bell that Miku wasn't sitting next to him, tucking into this veritable feast.

What was the turnaround time in the diagnostics suite?

Maybe she would appear at any moment and squeeze up next to him.

***

The conversation was running freely now - tongues and vocal chords lubricated by 5% ABV sauce and great food.

Gallen was first out of the trap.

'I know what you're thinking – who is this arsehole who is going to be my wingman?'

Bell laughed spontaneously.

Gallen proceeded to explain his background.

- Covert CIA operations and Navy Seal training.

- Combat parachute drops and close-quarter fighting in the dense and unforgiving jungles of South America.

- Explosives, limpet mines and bunker buster bombs.

- Hand-to-hand combat, reconnaissance and intelligence.

- Interrogation, torture and assassinations.

- Mangrove swamps, leeches and mosquitoes.

'…And apart from all that, there's always the cartridge out there which may have your name etched into its casing. Just shit, blood and bullets, eh?'

The sentiment struck a chord with Bell.

A kindred spirit he could work with.

Not an unfit box-ticker amassing visceral fat.

Before he could respond, Gallen had a little more to say.

'So, like, my boss sitting at his desk in Langley, Virginia is dead impressed with what you pulled off on the Hong Kong-Zhuhai-Macau bridge. They all loved it.'

Bell picked his moment to set the record straight.

'Don't forget Miku – it was a joint effort. Her finger was on the trigger the entire time, blowing those PLA mothers away. Without her I'd have been yet another rotting stiff floating down the Zhujiang river.'

'Has her trigger finger been anywhere else?'

Touché…a conversational curveball.

'Well, as a matter of fact, it has.'

'You bastard! There I am paying top rates at the local cat house,' grinned Gallen.

'It was love at first sight.'

'What is this?! I never stumble into a naked blonde in the mangrove swamps of Honduras and El Salvador! That's fucking unfair!'

'Life is unfair and things are not always what they seem.'

'Eh?'

'The truth is that she has a girlfriend called Saya.'

'AC/DC?'

'You could say that.'

'Looks like you're in the cat house with me then.'

'Maybe next time, after we've busted some balls and taken a shit down someone's neck.'

'That's fighting talk mister, I like it.'

'Hopefully, you'll get your chance to avenge Tucker Cole.'

'Yeah, there is that. Alex Gallen, the Ace Avenger – super hero. When I was a kid I never wanted to be Batman…I always dreamed of being the Joker.'

'Sounds like you need a shrink.'

'Well, as long we both know how to fire a gun - two monsters emerging from the crypt, blowing everyone away.'

'That's the beer talking. I missed my chance, goddamn.'

'Uh?'

'In Antwerp, I could have put a bullet into the back of Gao's head but the idea was that he be extradited to face a life sentence in an Australian supermax. Opportunity missed.'

'Say, why do we call you guys, limeys?'

Surely, Gallen knew the answer.

This was a wind-up.

'Scurvy causes bleeding and gum disease from ascorbic acid deficiency.'

'Yeah?'

'Yeah, so squeeze lime juice into your grog to avoid it on long sea voyages.'

'Grog?'

'What is this? – Twenty questions?'

'I'm learning, okay? Bear with me for fuck's sake!'

'It's British Admiralty rum: Royal Navy strength.'

'Hell?! You British swabbies were guzzling rum forty-five years before the Declaration of Independence in 1776?'

'The brand is called Pusser's Blue. I'll send you a bottle.'

'Sounds like if we come out of this alive, we can drink each other under the table!

'Enough of rum and Gao Zi Xin. Are we done?'

'No. The Taiwan blockade. The island is shaped a bit like a lung. At this very moment the Chinese blockade is squeezing the air out of it. Something is about to happen.'

Bell knew that a response to the Sierra Madre incident in the Spratly Islands was still being considered by the Western Allies.'

Today's date was the seventh of October.

***

Bell's alert tone dinged.

Miku was on her way back.

Gallen immediately signalled the head chef and ordered three more tinnies of Monsutā.

Word had got out.

The HZM-Bridge debacle was on everyone's lips.

The girl who had helped give the Chinese a bloody nose and had suffered injury in the process was surely owed the best chow that the USAF catering staff could muster.

They exited the kitchens en masse and lined up as a guard of honour by the table. Bell and Gallen joined the salute line as Miku entered the dining room to a standing ovation.

'I have a thing for women in uniform,' said Gallen.

'Is that a cross-dressing fetish that you're into?' smirked Bell.

'That's kinda funny, I guess, jerking off on my own in women's panties.'

Rafute and chanpurū dishes par excellence were laid out ready.

But, there was more.

A special dessert for a Medal-of-Honour-grade warrior.

Heavenly haupia pie.

Crunchy shortbread crust, layered with sweet potatoes and topped off with coconut pudding which had been laced liberally with rum-based coco spirit.

Gallen and Bell gave her a big hug.

Miku whispered discreetly into Bell's ear.

'I'll live, but I have other news.'

Gallen also whispered something into Bell's ear.

'You limey bastards have all the luck! Next time, save some for me, will ya?'

Whatever Gallen desired.

In uniform or out of it.

When it came to covering his back in mortal combat, Bell guessed that this guy would unflinchingly step up to the plate with all guns blazing.

Yep, I can work with this person.

Rest and recreation might be shortlived.

Time for some binge therapy.

Am I in bed with two chicks or am I suffering from diplopia?

Their plane to Tokyo took off within the hour.

23 Five Eyes Plus

'So, other news?' said Bell, as the plane levelled out at cruising altitude.

Bell and Miku were seated together in an almost empty cabin. The drinks trolley was already heading their way.

Miku turned and smiled.

'I've been grounded.'

'What?'

'No more field operations for me.'

'Why not?'

'Nande? Because my cover has been blown.'

Bell's stark expression of incredulity prompted an explanation.

'Vladivostok, the Tigre de Cristal casino, a couple of months back. I took down my intended targets easily enough but I made a couple of mistakes leaving the building. It turned into a bloodbath and I was lucky to get the hell out of there. Escaping over the North Korean border wasn't really an option. In the rush I must have been picked up by the security cameras.'

'No KIA for you, then.'

'Our informant revealed that the Russians had shared their intel with the Chinese.'

'Which would explain what happened in Macau.'

'Exactly. If you hadn't burst in when you did I would be…'

'…Toast!'

'But it's not all bad. Saya, my girlfriend, has had enough of being a pop idol and wants to quit after several years of daily dance practice and sleep deprivation. She's exhausted. We've decided to run away together, leaving our past lives behind. We're going to travel, chill out, and make up for lost time in each other's arms.'

'I guess that the manager of Sakura Go won't be happy.'

'Unhappy? He'll detonate when he finds out. There's a huge investment teetering on the edge of the abyss.'

'The new single - 'Cruel Candy'?'

'I'm scared for her because they won't let them out without an armed guard. She's only able to keep in contact with me because she has a secret cell phone. He's been known to beat girls to within an inch of their lives.'

'Like life-changing and disfiguring injuries?'

'Yes, and he can get away with it. No one dares to say or do anything. The worst thing is that I think he enjoys it. There's no shortage of fresh, vulnerable meat out there. It's an open secret. Welcome to the dark world of J-Pop.'

Ueda Kage was a high-profile band manager, music producer and lyricist with a predilection for sexually abusing young girls.

'Has he ever hurt your Saya?'

A bottom lip trembled.

'Unfortunately, yes.'

Bell's mental note was filed away for an opportune moment.

He was a ruthless gaijin, a brigand kaizoku, unconstrained by fear and submissive acquiescence. Trained to kill clinically without remorse, it would be no more trouble than wringing a rooster's neck.

***

Roughly three miles northeast of the bright neon lights of the Shibuya district stands a non-descript grey office building.

Shibuya is a special ward in the Tokyo Metropolis.

As a major commercial and finance centre, it houses two of the busiest railway stations in Japan, Shibuya and Shinjuku. Shibuya station is world-famous for its scramble crossing located in front of its Hachikō street exit. When vehicles come to a halt at the radial junction, up to three thousand pedestrians at a time swarm the entire intersection in all directions.

The intel unit is known as 'C1' and is located inside a high-security compound that houses Japan's Ministry of Defence.

This is not an ordinary military facility – it is the secret spy agency headquarters for the Directorate for Signals Intelligence, Japan's version of the US National Security Agency.

Four subterranean floors, eight above ground.

Its role is to eavesdrop on communications, but the operations that its electromagnetic-wave sections carry out are highly classified.

In addition, at their southern operational base of Tachiarai, experts spend time analysing digital traffic between orbiting satellites:

- Emails, online chats and encrypted file transfers.

- Harvesting exabytes of data.

Miku's boss entered the windowless room. Air conditioning units bathed the three of them in a cool, soothing breeze.

No cheery introductions or pleasantries, just a series of bows and straight down to business.

The whole building was a hive of frantic activity.

This wasn't going to take long.

Congratulations regarding assignments in Macau were short-lived. The blockade of Taiwan and the imminent prospect of global hostilities occupied centre stage.

In the red corner sat China, North Korea, Russia, and Iran; Western allies were limbering up in the blue corner.

The boss-guy cut to the chase with a candid assessment.

'The Taiwanese are our blood brothers and we will stand by them no matter what. We are already at war.'

Taiwan: There was reason to believe that there were sleeper cells, sympathisers and agents, secreted like maggots inside an apple, ready to pupate and burst forth into the light of day.

The Chinese were providing the North Koreans with expertise, in an act of proxy aggression, to send ICBMs into orbit over Japan which, for now, landed harmlessly out in the Pacific.

The dispute over the island chain known as the Kurils, which stretch north across the Pacific Ocean from the Japanese island of Hokkaido to Russia's Kamchatka Peninsula, remained a festering sore. To this day, the two nations had never signed a peace treaty, going all the way back to the end of World War Two.

Japan's military posture had changed from defensive to offensive, combined with a dramatic increase in percentage of GDP spend.

Japan was now fully integrated into the Five Eyes fold - the Anglosphere intelligence alliance comprising Australia, Canada, New Zealand, the United Kingdom, and the United States. It operates a robust global surveillance mechanism called ECHELON which straddles the entire planet.

Five Eyes Plus.

The 35th Fighter Wing at Misawa air base in northern Japan had mushroomed in size with an influx of Lockheed Martin F-35 stealth and Boeing F-15EX fighters - the most advanced US planes with air-to-air combat and anti-ship strike capability.

They were armed with AGM-88 anti-radiation missiles, stowed in their internal weapons bays, for the Destruction of Enemy Air Defences.

Kawboom…you're DEAD.

Long range, hard-to-defend-against precision strike weapons were a vital part of the DEAD toolkit.

Hypersonic land-attack, Tomahawks, and other types of missiles had been installed all the way down to the southernmost Japanese island of Yokoguni. Aegis Ashore, a land-based version of Aegis BMD, can engage MRBMs and IRBMs with SM-3 guided missiles.

Japan was a ready as it could be…for now.

For all the bluster about the augmented ability to meet the first wave of Chinese forces, it would only buy valuable time needed to allow for reinforcement squadrons to arrive from North America.

'All our military efforts will be wasted if there is a successful internal uprising in Taiwan which paves the way for a land invasion.'

Back to sleeper cells, sympathisers and Chinese agents.

The boss-guy seamlessly switched away from Japan's blanket role in the Indo-Pacific region to the topic of Gao Zi Xin and Toratako.

'The teams here have decrypted messages transmitted from somewhere in northern Taiwan to the Emperor Nero casino in Laos – sender still to be conclusively identified. We have long suspected that Gao is working for the PLA.'

Bell broke his long silence.

'He's our maggot?'

The boss-guy smiled for the first time.

'Maybe. Do the deal with Toratako and find out.'

The whereabouts of a consignment of Plutonium-239, which Toratako had been trying to sell on the black market before his arrest, was unknown. Pu-239, of course, is the primary fissile isotope used for the production of nuclear weapons and has a half-life of 24,100 years.

Toratako's cache was reputed to be 99.96% pure, in the form of actinide metal rings of a silvery-grey appearance which tarnish if exposed to air.

You could try bombarding the stuff with a stream of slow thermal neutrons to initiate a nuclear chain reaction, but take care to wash your hands afterwards.

Yeah, you'll need to be wearing more than oven mitts.

Toratako could easily instruct his henchmen from his prison cell, to detonate a simple dirty bomb in central Tokyo. This was a big worry for government ministers when they already had enough on their plates - not sushi or sashimi, unfortunately.

Recovery of the stash of Pu-239 and Gao Zi Xin's exact location equated to a get-out-of-jail card for Toratako, but only for him to spend the rest of his life under house arrest.

Like Gallen's Eddie Wu, a condemned man due to hang at the end of the week will agree to anything to save his skin.

Irezumi – skin expertly tattooed in the style and tradition of the Japanese Yakuza. Exquisite designs in the forms of koi, dragons, snakes, samurai, onis and, of course…tigers.

Bell doubted anything like that would be on display.

A strict inmate dress-code and other harsh rules were rigorously enforced inside the toughest penal institution in Japan.

Final confirmation of the meeting in the Fuchū prison would come through once the Japanese government had ratified the decision at the highest level – sometime within the next twenty-four hours.

***

Miku and Bell emerged into daylight, back on the street, and stood there dazed from the stream of classified revelations. Miku hailed a cab and posed a gnawing question.

'Are you hungry?'

'Er…yeah, I guess.'

'Traditional Japanese food?'

'Anything, just put a plate in front of me.'

'I know a good place for a late lunch.'

Just what Bell had wanted – a period of time where he didn't have to think and he could relax where someone else was calling the shots. One of the Tokyo locals who knew the drill, with him trotting along behind lapping it up.

It was even more wonderful that the person in charge happened to be the beautiful Miku, even on a platonic basis. He was getting used to the idea. There was no harm being celibate for a while – half a day, at least.

Retirement from operational danger seemed to have breathed new zest into her. She had been offered promotion to an administrative role which he knew she was going to turn down. The prospect of a new life with Saya filled her with radiant joy.

What of his own prospects?

'Friends with quite a few women', had been his answer to Miku's leading question.

The latest batch:-

Lovely Jenna and her feisty side-kick Stacey.

Yeah, that was one hell of a night with them in that crusty hotel. A musical-bedrooms romp where his combat pants finally ended up lying on top of a warm thong.

A breathless message from Aryna had been forwarded on by MIX administration. She had made it back to Kyiv via Germany and Poland and had given her dear mother a big surprise on the doorstep of her tiny apartment.

Aryna was all for a meet-up in London at the earliest opportunity. No other info updates – they could do all that while dining well in a fine West End restaurant.

He guessed that Jana Cazenove was presently on a premier cruise ship somewhere, enjoying the ocean wave. Only a deluxe suite stateroom would be good enough for her – but she could easily afford it. Unless she had digested and implemented everything that he had taught her, there would be a new scam-artist lothario in tow.

Was he truly friends with them?

Not really.

Sure, he'd known quite a few in the biblical sense. A series of short, often ill-fated, liaisons which led nowhere.

There was only one constant in his life.

The delectable Miss Madden.

Were they anything more than just fuck buddies?

Kinda.

Oh, to be lying next to Judy right now!

Her beguiling, green eyes and a tongue like a buggy whip.

And, of course, not forgetting Miku herself, just like ships passing in the night.

Loving her in vain.

She was already spoken for.

A port navigation light disappearing into the darkness.

The imperative was simple to comprehend.

Enjoy the moment – live each day as if it was your last…or as if the next bullet heading in your direction had your name on it.

***

Back in mid-metropolis, their cab had dropped them off at the mouth of a long, yokocho alleyway.

After a short walk they found themselves seated in a snug and comfortable izakaya bar. In no time they were supping Kirin Ichiban beer and toasting their good fortune. It was marvellous to be able to sit back and enjoy the sublime ambience.

Decorated lanterns danced in the light breeze as Miku rattled off their food order and attention returned to the events of the day.

If the Fuchū visit decision was a 'No', then he would be on the first flight back to London.

A 'Yes' probably meant jumping on the first flight to somewhere else.

In the meantime, a dish of takoyaki with rice and some veggie side dishes arrived.

Chopsticks at the ready.

Best to line his stomach for alcohol consumption later on.

Imbibe intoxicating liquor, by all means, but stay sharp.

Miku outlined the rest of their day as they ate.

- A cab back to her apartment in Roppongi Hills.
- Shower, fresh clothes, catwalk inspection and a cocktail.
- Limousine pick-up to the Yamato TV Studios.
- Audience participation as Sakura Go performed on stage, showcasing their new release 'Cruel Candy'.
- Decamp for an after-launch party at the amazing Mizubukure nightclub to frolic the rest of the night away.

Mizubukure - 'Blister' in English, was a wild venue located in the Akihabara district. Its rabbit warren of lounges, bars and state-of-the-art laser dance-floor were legendary. The record company had booked the place in its entirety.

Bell thought about it for a moment.

Well, he had wanted some R&R, hadn't he?

Careful what you wish for.

El Cartero and his crew, on fire below the waistline, would have loved it. Tanked up on tequila and testosterone, they could have run amok like street urchins in a candy store.

Alex Gallen would simply want to know how that jammy bastard limey had pulled it off again.

Hmm…blister - a lump under your skin filled with clear fluid, blood or pus. As long as that didn't reflect upon the content of their beer and cocktails, it was game on.

***

The iris scanner granted them access to the building's marble-lined entrance hall. After ascending several floors in the elevator, Miku unlocked the supersize solid teak door to her apartment. Bell admired his new surroundings, a spacious entryway stretching off into the far distance. With footwear safely stowed, they donned slippers from the getabako shoe-cupboard and headed for the lounge.

'Another beer?' said Miku, as he slumped into one of the sofas.

'How about tea?'

It was going to be a long evening – plenty of time for booze later. She shot him a gleaming smile and headed off to the kitchen. The place was massive: Polished steel, expensive fittings and chic minimalism – it must have cost a bomb.

Miku reappeared, placing the tea on a low, glass table.

'No tea ceremony today, I'm afraid. I'll whisk up the matcha powder next time.'

As host, Miku was following the Japanese tradition of entertaining her guest in the correct manner. She had made both green and black tea as well as laying out a tray of appetizing wagashi bites.

'The sweets are made from mochi, anko, and fruit.'

'Shall I be mother?' grinned Bell.

'Nani?'

'I'll pour?'

'No! Little Japanese girl do this!' replied Miku, in mock indignation.

'Englishman know not to mess with you!'

His answer triggered an amiable glare which always happened when he'd overstepped the mark.

He revelled in the good-natured banter - being with her was so much fun. Maybe he'd explore this platonic celibacy thing a bit more, at some time in the future.

A finger shook in admonishment.

'Englishman drink tea! I show you bedroom next!'

***

Miku left him at the threshold of one of the guest bedrooms.

'I know what you're thinking. How can she afford all this?'

'Er...'

'The answer is: Don't ask.'

She was dead right. It was none of his business how she'd managed to trawl in the amount of serious wonga you needed to buy a place like this.

But he couldn't talk.

He had laid his sticky fingers on rubies, diamonds, crypto, hard currency, and even a small Caribbean island in his travels.

Silence is golden.

Part of a secret agent's toolkit.

Mum's the word, omertà, chinmoku.

Call it whatever you like.

But you had to live long enough to enjoy it.

Bell drifted past the king-size bed into the ensuite bathroom.

For use before and after sex, and for personal hygiene:-

The ensemble included a smart toilet which came rigged up to a touchpad bolted to the wall. If you produced a stool or urine which its sensors didn't like, it would call an ambulance. The array of buttons on display was more complex than the shutdown console for Chernobyl's No.4 reactor.

The bonus feature was the variety of lubricated probes connected by flexible hoses. The one which tested your sperm count was still in its clear, plastic packet, tossed randomly next to the soap dispensers. Its artificial, vulva-vagina business-end was alluringly visible.

Now showered and shaved, Bell surveyed the evening wear which Miku had laid out for him – in a range of sizes.

He was soon suited, booted and ready to get out on the town. Well, he couldn't leave the house looking like a junkie scrounging for his next fix, could he?

The long mirror told no lies.

Not bad for a killer kaizoku.

Miku entered the room wearing a little black dress, high heels and some exquisite gold earrings. She had her hair up and her facial skin was as pure and smooth as porcelain.

'My, my, you do scrub up well,' said Miku, eyes sparkling with delight.

'So, I guess that I'm your escort for tonight?'
Her index finger was back on his lips again.
'No, baby…you're more to me than that.'

24 Sakura Go

The chauffeur-driven BMW 7 Series cruised on past the frontage of the Yamato TV studios in the Minato district of Tokyo, and sped to the back of the building.

The driver knew the score.

Bell and Miku, travelling comfortably in the rear seats, craned their necks to witness the pandemonium taking place behind lines of crowd-control barriers.

Hundreds of Sakura Go fans carrying placards, chanting, pushing and shoving, were testing the mettle of the overstretched security guards.

Ground zero, a swathe of plush, red carpet, was kept ruthlessly clear of demonic crazed acolytes as the imminent arrival of the band counted down.

Minutes later, a pink stretch-limousine coasted to a halt on its spike marks, as the frenzied mob surged forward to get a glimpse of their pop idols. Camera crews and photographers, some balanced precariously on stepladders, burst into action as Akari, Yui, Kokoro, Satomi…and Saya emerged into the dazzling limelight.

***

Bell and Miku vacated their ride and headed for an unmarked external door which opened spontaneously. After a stringent guest list check, they were presented with laminated ID badges on glittery lanyards.

Their guest escort soon had them ensconced in a sumptuous lounge with other VIP invitees. Apart from the cohorts of young women, Bell guessed that they were rubbing shoulders with big-cheese luminaries from the worlds of music, media and entertainment.

Before they could catch a breath, waiting staff were all over them with champagne and mini-bites.

Sakura Go were on in twenty minutes; a bell would ring to call them all to their pre-allocated seats in the TV stage auditorium.

Better hurry up and get quaffing this Premier Cru.

Miku had something to say.

'You do realise that the band's arrival was all staged?'

'Yeah?'

He was showing his ignorance.

'The Fab Five have already spent half a day doing sound checks and dance practice. Only synchronised perfection will be good enough. When you're on an enforced diet, doing late nights and carrying muscle injuries, it's hard to keep smiling. I'll be glad when Saya is well out of it.'

'What about all the money they're earning?'

Miku's nostrils flared.

His sweet innocence was touching.

'You should see the contract that they signed!'

The penny was beginning to drop.

Miku moved closer and lowered her voice.

'If you negotiate with Ueda Kage, he'll end up owning your house.'

Raped financially and physically.

When this TV showcase caper was over, the real let-your-hair-down moment would come when they got inside the wicked Mizubukure nightclub.

What limey luck...keep it coming!

At least he wouldn't be spending the evening as a lonely, single male, timidly entering a kyabakura cabaret-club on his own. A saddo loser crying into his Asahi beer while buying overpriced cocktails for the sexually-inaccessible young hostesses dressed as maids.

A few snatches of flirtatious conversation and some sterile karaoke was no substitute for authentic carnal union with a woman.

Bell had taken the trouble to study Mizubukure's internal layout from the publicly available blueprints and the extensive catalogue of images on the club's website.

It was simply a matter of waiting for a fortuitous moment when a wrong could be righted and someone got what was coming to them.

***

The compère, dressed in a gold lounge suit and matching bow tie, came on first to get the audience warmed up and used to putting their hands together. He also outlined the potential viewing figures and where in the world the Yamato TV transmissions would be syndicated.

The band strode on to an explosive round of applause and a standing ovation – exactly as the audience had been instructed. After answering a few staged questions, instrumental music kicked in, as a teaser, before a secret signal was given whereby the singing and dancing proper began.

The first part of their set: Four songs from their chart-busting back-catalogue of hits:-

- Lovesick Loser
- Float Me Away

- Crazy For You
- Honey, Honey

Starting with their iconic track – Lovesick Loser, the girls segued seamlessly from song to song.

The audience's excitement was palpable - Sakura Go delivering a thrilling spectacle of harmonic vocals and choreography which was both mind-blowing and uplifting.

Rapturous applause erupted and a short interval followed.

The cut-down medley of their previous smash hits was just the appetiser.

The entrée was yet to come.

The premiere of their latest single - Cruel Candy.

Because the assembled throng was bursting with anticipation and clearly impatient, the compère guy sensibly cut his banal patter short.

Silence fell as the five band idols took their start positions for this auspicious moment.

A deadly hush, then the first few bars.

Miku was beside herself with excitement as her girlfriend Saya glanced fixedly in her direction.

A beat-drop wall of sound erupted and the high-energy performance began.

Verse-chorus-verse-chorus-bridge-chorus:

Love me, love me
Please say it's true
Taste your sweetness
O, candy you

Love me, love me
Say we are one
Eat each other
Sweet union

***

Mizubukure surpassed its hype, a multi-level pleasure palace swarming with everyone who had attended the Sakura Go launch event.

The alcohol was flowing in abundance and the dance floor was rammed. Shoals of beautiful young girls roamed the place, having a ball, pop idol wannabes vastly outmanning the hook-up advantaged males.

Miku had left Bell to do as he wished, without guidance or supervision.

Where was his wingman, Alex Gallen, when he needed him?

A deep-drilling expert from Texas!

A night-joy, smooth operator who knew the local lingo much better than he did.

The inability to utter the crucial phrase 'I love you' in colloquial Japanese was a severe impediment. Simply saying hello - kon'nichiwa, one of the few expressions he knew, with a fixed glare, was too creepy and unlikely to lead anywhere.

Ah, never mind!

Maybe it would just have to be a quiet night.

He'd please himself with another beer and soak it all up – he might just catch someone's eye. The language of love was meant to be universal, wasn't it?

The truth was that without Miku, he was lost.

Bell could see her in the distance, seated in a passionate embrace with her dear love, Saya, who was committing the ultimate taboo-transgression for a J-Pop idol – having a romantic partner and flaunting it in public.

But, it didn't matter now because Saya had given notice to quit with immediate effect. Ueda Kage had to be restrained when she had informed him an hour ago, nearly bursting a main blood vessel.

Bell knew from his research that other performers who had played the same trick on Kage had died in mysterious circumstances.

Saya's and Miku's ecstatic jubilation might be shortlived.

***

It was no accident.

Bell had been waiting for this moment. He wasn't unused to hand-to-hand combat in the latrines. The last time it had occurred was in the Ladies at a deluxe hotel in central Berlin.

He would have to work quickly and clinically.

Ueda Kage had slipped into the Gents' toilets alone, most probably to line up a snort.

Bell followed after a suitable interval and fixed a door jammer in place.

Trap number three was slightly ajar - sloppy.

Bell burst the cubicle door open.

'Get out of here!' screamed Kage, in total surprise.

Pop world flunkies might obey but not the angel of death.

A line of coke was already chopped out on the toilet cistern lid, sitting next to two twisty-bags of a white substance, and a syringe. All the forensics-team evidence had been nicely laid out.

In the flesh, Kage resembled a bloated glob of gristle that you were forced to spit into your napkin.

Bell softened him up with a pistol-whip across the face which seemed to disturb some expensive dental work.

'Call that a syringe?' mocked Bell.

'Who…who are you?'

'Shi no tenshi.'

Kage's eyes widened in horror.

Yeah, buddy, I'll be guiding you to the afterlife.

Bell forced the barrel of his Glock semi-automatic into Kage's mouth and produced his own loaded hypodermic - a fatal heroin, xylazine and fentanyl overdose.

The shot would augment the surfeit of cocaine and alcohol already coursing through Kage's veins – a toxic cocktail of…cruel candy.

Sheer terror was exhibited as the plunger rammed home.

'Sayōnara, beibī,' cooed Bell.

Polysubstance abuse is chic and de rigueur until the spectre of death stands before you.

The corpse might not be found for several hours, hopefully not until the morning.

Luckily, the tiled restroom floor wasn't awash in a sea of stagnant piss, as in the obligation to slip the boatman a few yen to punt you across to the sinks. It was a pristine surface - you could safely eat sushi or sashimi off of it.

Bell locked the cubicle door and slipped out underneath.

After a quick hand-rinse and a pat-down for stray rooster feathers, he was back to the party as if nothing had happened.

***

Time to burst the blister with one last try.

Fly a kite with the emperor penguin routine.

Stand alone, out in the open - I'm easy and available.

321

Let's see what plankton drifts past.

Give it ten minutes, then call it a day.

Without warning, he was taken by both arms from behind.

Had the bouncers rumbled him for the blatant offering of sexual services which was against the rules? Or had the police already found the body and were arresting him as the prime suspect?

Nothing of it.

Two beautiful girls, introducing themselves as Emi and Keiko, led him off to some comfortable lounge seating and held on tight.

Drinks arrived in short order while they fought for his undivided attention.

Presently, Miku and Saya appeared.

'Time to go, we can all go back to mine,' smiled Miku.

'What about...?' said Bell.

'They can come, too. There's a cab waiting outside.'

'But...'

Miku rattled off some high-speed, local patois.

Emi and Keiko both laughed and held out a closed fist each.

The game of chance began, chanting in unison:

'Saisho wa guu!'

'Janken pon!'

Rock, paper, scissors – guu, paa, choki.

Everyone in Japan plays janken to settle disputes.

Paper!

'Aiko desho!' - It's a tie!

Again...

Rock!

Tied again.

Paper!

Tied yet again.

Three attempts were enough for Bell who held up his hands. He was itching for a fun cab ride back to Miku's apartment with all four of them. He produced a five-hundred-yen coin and got ready to flip.

'Let's toss for it instead, shall we? Paulownia or bamboo?'

Eyes blazed as the coin spun.

Bamboo landed face up.

'I win!' screamed Keiko.

'What are you playing for, anyway?' quizzed Bell.

'You, of course,' grinned a joyful Emi.

Bell felt slightly confused. He also had the sneaking suspicion that his undoubted magnetic presence might not have been entirely responsible for all of this.

'You're not a sore loser, Emi?' said Bell.

'No…I get to watch!'

***

The sperm count attachment and its flexible hose lay unused and unopened in its packaging in Bell's ensuite bathroom.

No call for it, now.

The king-size bed was fully occupied with naked flesh.

Bell entered Keiko, lying on her back, for the second phase of face-to-face intercourse.

More variations and permutations to come.

All men make love in different ways.

Western boy beds Eastern girl.

Emi, as official spectator and observer, pressed herself closer to the delicious, thrusting union. She could contain herself no longer and reached down to encircle the base of Bell's slithery penis with a petite finger and thumb.

Hopefully, his erect girth measured up!

Having flipped Keiko over, raised up over several pillows, Emi lay her head on her friend's lower spine as Bell lined himself up for some augmented doggy-style. Emi glanced up at him and pursed her moist lips open, while spreading Keiko's labia tantalisingly apart for him.

Bell eyed up the tube of lubricant.

So much choice…where do we start?

All that mattered was that everyone got to finish with a happy ending.

***

Bell's bedroom door opened slightly.

Miku and Saya peeked through the crack, giggling.

The aperture had to be widened a little more to fully enjoy the spectacle of tri-coital antics.

Bell managed to glance in Miku's direction.

Miku gasped.

'I promised you that you'd get your leg over.'

25 Yakuza

Fuchū Prison, the largest prison in Japan.

The penitentiary is located to the west of Tokyo Metropolis central, in a city of the same name.

The thing that hits you is the smell.

A pungent odour unique to penal institutions.

A combination of cleaning and bodily fluids, slop buckets, stale air, and fear.

Death row cell: #893.

The guard looked through the peephole at Toratako and unlocked the steel cell-door in one seamless movement.

The accommodation was designed to house up to six inmates but as head of the Yakuza, he had it all to himself.

Not only that, the cell had been knocked through to the one next door, therefore turning all the available space almost into a comfortable studio apartment.

Bell and Miku stepped inside gingerly.

The sight which presented itself was not what Bell had expected.

Toratako lay on his side, on a comfortable floor mat.

The buzzing hum of a tattoo pen filled the air, as a tattooist focused on his work of touching up the image of a koi carp on his customer's shoulder.

Toratako glanced up at the duo as they stood deferentially in the centre of the cell. Their host appeared to be completely immersed in a manga comic which Bell guessed to be Slam Dunk by the artist Takehiko Inoue.

Toratako didn't appear to be in any rush to greet them.

He continued to turn the pages of the manga while taking regular drags from a cigarette, even though Bell was sure that smoking was prohibited.

The buzzing stopped suddenly.

The tattooist wiped the area he had been working on with an anti-bacterial wipe and stood up.

After thanks and goodbyes Toratako got up.

Greetings, bows, acknowledgements and invitations to be seated followed. Miku was the translator-in-chief.

Time to get down to business.

A knock on the door preceded the guard entering the cell with a tray of sake glasses, accompanied by a fresh bottle of Reikyo Absolute Zero.

Drinks and smiles all round.

Toratako cut to the chase.

'We have a deal, then?'

'Yes,' replied Bell.

Toratako handed over a folded sheet of A4.

Bell glanced at its contents and locked it away in his slim attaché case.

What now?

Bell's inquisitive thought was answered in the next breath.

'I rarely get to see foreign visitors; another drink?'

The head of the Yakuza refilled the glasses.

Bell detected a great sense of release from the elderly man sitting opposite him. A man whose lifetime career had brought him to within a whisker of execution.

In short, this guy fancied a chat after clinching a reduction in his sentence – the death penalty commuted to lifetime house arrest.

Who was he to deny him that?

Bell chimed his glass with Toratako, with a smile.

A pack of Seven Stars cigarettes appeared and Bell was offered one, which he declined.

Toratako grinned back and started off.

'House arrest will not be so bad, you know. It will allow me to reconnect with my Japanese roots, listen to chattering garden waterfalls and see Mount Fuji in the far distance. I need a source of ikigai – a reason for living. This land mothered me and, by the same token, everyone whose life I terminated while I held the role of kumichō. Maybe I'll find some lasting peace.'

Torataku's candid admission reminded Bell that he was dealing with the convicted murderer of dozens of people.

'Japan may be at war very soon,' replied Bell, soberly.

'I read the papers and I see the news. Warrior blood runs in our veins. The spirit of the Samurai lives on.'

'Eddie Wu sends his greetings via the CIA and the United States prison service, by the way.'

Toratako laughed out aloud and slammed his glass down.

Back to more prosaic matters.

'I understand that you are an agent of the British Secret Service and that you have accomplished certain things recently. You are a warrior of distinction, in your own way. You will receive whatever assistance you may require from my men in Taipei when you arrive there. We stand shoulder to shoulder with our Taiwanese brothers.'

The last bit definitely echoed the sentiment of Miku's boss. The feeling of unconditional solidarity ran deep.

'We must leave you now – things to do, people to kill,' smiled Bell, rising from his seat.

'Smoking also kills, and it may kill me…but I love it!'

26 Ten Ten

9th of October.

Gao Zi Xin found a desk in one of the offices.

It came with a chair.

At least the abandoned low-rise commercial building, acting as a hideout in a rundown quarter of Taipei, had its plus points.

Anonymity and seclusion.

Storage and warehousing out the back.

Dark alleyways heading off in all directions.

The sounds and smells of the narrow street, two storeys below, flooded in through a couple of shattered windows.

Motorbikes, diesel fumes and car horns.

The eco-hotel next door was itself flanked by a love hotel. The dental clinic on the other side incorporated an illegal pharmacy and a plastic surgery production line.

It was the ideal place to organise insurrection while PLA forces landed on the beaches.

Gao switched on a tablet and logged in.

A 256-bit encryption key unlocked a text file which was digested in seconds.

He was shocked – it was only three pages, not hundreds.

Relief washed over him.

Just do what Beijing have requested and everything will be fine – it was the price he had to pay. Someone in the Zhongnanhai compound had a caustic sense of humour.

Meanwhile, he had his own affairs to straighten out.

Shunting illicit billions around the globe in a sinuous, labyrinthine manner under the skilled guidance of a criminal firm of lawyers called: Lambert, Truelove & Bolte.

The meeting was set for 09:00 tomorrow morning at their offices, situated on the eighty-first floor of the Taipei 101 Tower.

Waiwai, Gao's personal bodyguard, who had been leaning against the wall, stepped forward to receive detailed instructions.

Legal paperwork wasn't all that was required.

'We'll need guns and explosives,' said Gao.

'Transport?' growled Waiwai.

Gao explained the elaborate precautions he had in mind. Waiwai didn't turn a hair.

'Can't be too careful, eh? I want to live long enough to bet everything on red in my own casino again, and keep doing it for as many times as I like,' said Gao.

***

9th of October.

Bell arrived at Taoyuan International Airport, to the west of central Taipei, on the next available flight.

Alex Gallen was waiting for him in arrivals.

Saying goodbye to Miku, Saya, Emi and Keiko had been a tough one. It wasn't every day that a quartet of beautiful, young Japanese girls fought with each other to smother you with farewell kisses. Best not to divulge anything to Gallen who might easily suffer a FOMO meltdown.

Anyway, he'd come away with plenty of phone numbers.

Ueda Kage's corpse had been removed from the Mizubukure nightclub the following morning after police forensics had examined the potential crime scene.

Initial speculation in the media was that the cause of death was an accidental overdose or suicide. A pathologist might form a different view, however, determined by Kage's broken jaw and the analysis of his blood.

Whatever. In the meantime, the stratospheric sales of Sakura Go's latest track, Cruel Candy, Kage's sad swan song, was making the headlines.

***

Gallen drove, cruising along National Highway One towards central Taipei.

'Where are we headed?' asked Bell.

'The Lin Sen Bei Lu district, more specifically the Minzu Road. It's the red light district, of course,' laughed Gallen.

Bell guessed that it was a well-disguised CIA safe house.

'What about Gao's place?'

'There's a list.'

'Uh?'

'A bit like the US Government who owns any number of buildings in Taipei. The intel we have reveals a carousel of hide-and-seek deception - Gao and his associates constantly flitting from place to place.'

'So, what's the drill?'

'We get prepped and tooled up ready to move in at a moment's notice. Tomorrow morning onwards according to our mole.'

'I'll brief the local Yakuza guys who'll be acting as our backup, leaving the two of us to get on with the real dirty work.'

'How many men is Toratako providing?'

'Ten of his best…well-disciplined in urban firefights.'

'Let's hope that they can shoot straight. I guess that Toratako's neck is kinda on the line with this caper?'

'Yeah, along with couple of barrels of Plutonium.'

The car pulled up outside a shithole, what may have been a shopfront once, a repository for garbage and dumpsters which half-concealed a comatose junkie lying face down on the sidewalk.

'We're here!' announced Gallen, brightly.

'What is this, the Beverly Wilshire Hotel?'

'All you need, buddy, is a place to put on your body armour and take a shit…but I get it.'

'Hey, Alex, tell me that you got hold of all that ordnance I requested?'

'Yeah, babe, we had most of it in stock already. It's like fucking Macy's inside! Tell me what we haven't got. Show me your pussy and I'll get something out from below the counter that you can paste lube all over!'

Bell circumvented the playful banter.

'It goes without saying that it's Taiwan National Day tomorrow.'

'Ten Ten, the ROC's big day…who could forget.'

There was a gnawing feeling at the back of Bell's mind.

They wouldn't would they?

The day celebrating the Wuchang Uprising of 1911, marking the beginning of a revolution which would overthrow China's last imperial dynasty.

The Sierra Madre incident.

The lost province.

Payback for a century of humiliation dating all the way back to the First Opium War in 1839.

Surely not?

***

10th of October – 07:45.

They had the building surrounded.

Yakuza foot-soldiers held strategic positions, ready to muscle their way in with Bell and Gallen when the signal was given.

Get in there quickly and corner their quarry.

Bounty hunter scalps: Gao Zi Xin and his associates – dead or alive.

Gallen lowered his Steiner binoculars.

'Say, buddy, the place next door has a butt-lift and a tummy tuck on special all this week – what a great deal!'

'Yeah, best to save the sepsis, blood loss and tissue trauma for some unwelcome bullet holes.'

***

Five guys were shackled to steel pipework in an empty warehouse, one was lashed to a chair, taking centre stage. A dozen bloody corpses of their comrades, overwhelmed by firepower, littered the area.

No Gao; woeful misinformation.

The guy screaming in the chair was a tough devil.

Two fingers lay on the concrete floor but no answers.

Gallen had seen this sort of thing before.

The five hoodlums strapped to the pipes glowered back at him defiantly.

'Which one of you has the prettiest face?'

'He likes a pretty one,' added Bell.

'Yeah, I get a hard-on for a nice piece of meat.'

Gallen turned suddenly and snapped his fingers.

The interrogator holding the bolt cutters drew a semi-automatic from his waistband and blew the silent canary's brains out.

His colleague, wielding a blowfish filleting knife, slit the fresh stiff's bindings and dragged the body away.

Gallen stood in front of a pretty boy, fourth in the line.

'Unlucky número four, eh? You poor bastard.' laughed Gallen.

Number four was rapidly strapped into place.

The seat was still warm, awash with blood and urine.

A galvanised cage was fitted around the hollering unfortunate's head as he gazed in horror at a starving rat pacing up and down in a similar cage on the ground.

Gallen peered into number four's eyes.

'Death by a thousand bites, eh?'

It didn't take long.

Gao and Waiwai: 09:00 at the offices of Lambert, Truelove & Bolte, international lawyers, floor #81, Taipei 101 Tower, Xinyi district...and a getaway rendezvous in the Philippine Sea?

Was it all over?

***

Two guys in peaked caps and overalls pushed a cleaning cart across the mall concourse of the Taipei 101 Tower building.

At over half a kilometre in height, the Taipei 101 is one of the world's tallest buildings. Its iconic postmodernist style, evoking

Asian aesthetics, produces a silhouette shape which is instantly recognisable as the mascot of Taiwan itself.

One hundred and one floors, the top one being the Sky-Top open-air observation deck, complete with helipad.

Bell and Gallen hurried to the high-speed elevator doors to leave the excited Taiwan National Day melee behind.

This primary elevator shaft delivered them to the sixtieth floor where they could briefly admire the amazing view of Taipei city from the enclosed sky lobby corridor.

A second elevator dinged. It would take them up another twenty-one floors into the ethereal heights of the high-office zone.

Gallen tapped his concealed semi-automatic holster and glanced at the cleaners' cart.

A grin overwhelmed him.

'Say, did you really need to bring all that stuff?'

'Expect trouble,' smiled Bell.

Firing hot in fifteen seconds.

Gao and Waiwai to be blown away in a law partner's office.

The elevator doors drew open.

A tract of lavish carpet, expensive oil paintings and a large reception console welcomed them to the Far East office of LTB.

The first thing Bell noticed was two feet sticking out of one of the storage cupboards.

'What's going on here?' said Bell, flashing his fake police ID.

The lone receptionist, sitting bolt upright, whimpered plaintively through her nose.

'It's a dead security guard,' said Gallen.

'I know you can't speak…and can't move. Have these two men been and gone?' said Bell, holding up a pair of mugshots to the girl.

The mewing was in the affirmative.

Bell understood immediately.

Gao knew that he had been followed and the girl was wearing a bomb vest.

So, where were the staff and partners?

Bell lifted a stern, instructive finger.

'Stay as you are, lady. Help is on its way.'

Bell knew that it was a lie as he beckoned Gallen to race down the office corridor to flush out a law-practice partner.

The first door they burst open revealed a gagged lawyer seated behind his desk with his back to a vast plate-glass window.

'He's wired, too!' hissed Gallen.

'Where are they now?!' screamed Bell.

The man's eyes rolled up repeatedly without moving any other muscle.

Bell pointed skywards.

'On the fucking roof?!'

The lawyer nodded violently as Bell and Gallen hit the deck together.

The explosion blew the guy and his chair clean through the shattered expanse of argon-infused triple-ply.

**

No time to lose.

The helipad – of course!

A trip out eastwards into the emptiness of the western Pacific meant that you either had your own aircraft carrier or…you ditched the chopper after making a superyacht rendezvous, and settled in for a long pleasure cruise.

Clever bastard.

Clever enough to have flown away by now?

They jumped back in the elevator and hit the ninety-nine button. It would whistle up past the restaurant floors and mechanical ops levels in seconds.

Bell had wheeled the cleaning trolley in with them.

Best to be tooled-up with AT4s - a recoilless anti-tank weapon, M72 LAW rockets, sub-machine guns, and of course, grenades.

They would have to drag several bags of kit up the last two flights of stairs to the Sky-Top open parapet.

Expect trouble.

Some desperate fugitives might be lying in wait.

***

Gao Zi Xin had made it to the hundred-and-first floor with his personal bodyguard, Waiwai.

Now out through a hatch, they had only antenna arrays and lightning-earthing rods for company.

The blast from the eighty-first floor vindicated Gao's meticulous exit preparations.

The Aerospace H135 chopper was nowhere to be seen.

What the fuck!

A vision of Candy, Kara and Tiffany, lying around the pool on the third deck of the superyacht Caligula, burst into his mind. It had slipped its moorings at the Macau marina a few days earlier.

Waiwai peered over the precipitous edge, Heckler and Koch MP5 machine pistol at the ready.

Half a kilometre was a long way to fall.

***

As the chopper approached, Bell and Gallen popped their heads up.

Gallen got some shots away as Waiwai returned fire while covering his boss as he clambered aboard.

Bell kept low, tearing the canvas bags open.

An M72 or an AT4?

He decided to go with the 66mm M72.

Waiwai had taken a hit but his sheer brute strength saw his intimidating bulk disappearing behind a slammed door. Although a commercial helicopter, designed for executive use, it had been fitted with machine guns in the nose cone.

The intense rotor-wash and typhoon-strength wind, combined with fifty-calibre shells coming their way, had inhibited their ability to make a couple of kills.

Bell could only wait until the H135 made a rising turn to starboard to pull the trigger.

No more than a few seconds.

A one-shot deal.

As the chopper rose up and dipped, Bell fired at the back rotor which was encased in a protective cowling.

The projectile bounced off the tail with an explosion, but debris had been sucked in which had damaged enough of the rotor vanes to reduce lateral control.

With the sideways thrust produced by the tail rotor compromised, the torque generated by the main rotor would spin the helicopter's body in the opposite direction.

It was enough - the helicopter wasn't going anywhere.

A rapid descent down the side of the tower loomed.

An inelegant splat on the ground…at best.

How to get down to ground level quickly and check out the wreckage?

If Gao and Waiwai got roasted in a high temperature blaze it would mean ID with dental records and maybe a fingerprint obtained from a scorched, crusty digit salvaged from the debris.

But, if the pilot was skilled enough to land the son-of-a-bitch with a controlled crunch, two internationally-wanted felons could feasibly get to disappear down a maze of dark alleyways, never to be seen again.

Option one.

He and Gallen could retrace their steps down the stairs to the elevator where they had left the doors jammed open.

Simply type in the override code for a maximum negative-G free fall down two elevator shafts back to the mall concourse.

'HALO *jump to hell, baby!*' and '*Can't this motherfucker drop any faster?* ' – would, without doubt, be Gallen's cage-hollering accompaniment ringing in his ears.

Running fully armed for what could be quite a distance to the chopper crash site, held limited appeal.

Option two.

Bell had a better idea which was momentarily stalled in its tracks.

The City of Taipei suddenly filled with the cacophony of invasion alarms, howling out across the entire conurbation.

The first missiles were hitting their targets with dozens more flying through the air.

Taiwan National Day.

All the parades and citizens on the streets rushed to take shelter in deep bunkers as Chinese missiles continued to fall.

The Taipei 101 took several impacts, one after the other, and the entire building shuddered.

The elevator was a lousy idea anyway.

His hunch had been right; the blockade had been a feint for a full-blown invasion.

He and Gallen had to move quickly.

Why not glide to earth and land softly with a ram-air parachute?

The second bag lay open.

Gallen, no stranger to making practice drops out of a C-130 at Fort Bragg, North Carolina, had his chute on in short order.

Bell joined his comrade-in-arms on the edge of the parapet.

They watched the chopper crash-land in an open park area.

Their PLA – Parachute Landing Area awaited them.

'Let's go,' screamed Bell.

'Aren't we meant to be holding hands?' laughed Gallen.

'You can suck your own cock!'

Airborne: Nine elliptical canopy-cells fully engorged as the directional toggles steered their chutes down towards their target.

Descend quickly; land sweetly.

But Gao and Waiwai had emerged from the wreckage and had a head start…

When it came to running, Waiwai was at a definite disadvantage. His lumbering form was still capable of a burst of speed despite the tell-tale indications of a limp, probably sustained in the crash. He'd also taken a bullet.

They landed near the burning wreckage in time to see the fugitive duo disappearing into the urban sprawl.

The pilot and any crew had been burned to a cinder in a roasting fireball which seemed insignificant amongst the blanket bombardment of rockets now flattening the city.

Waiwai turned and took a speculative shot at Bell, then scurried off on his own.

Gallen had split off, sprinting after a solitary Gao, with an impressive display of Navy Seal fitness.

Bell pressed on into the narrow streets, his MilLoc, buddy-finder device showing that his CIA wingman was tracking Gao on a parallel course.

Waiwai had the advantage of an H&K MP5. For Bell it was simply a Beretta 92F and a commando knife.

As Bell turned a corner into a deserted commercial area, every inch of it adorned with gaudy signage advertising foodie-bar joints, a burst of fire took chunks of masonry out of the wall.

Yeah, skewers of meat still cooking on grills as the bombs continued to fall.

Bell instinctively hit the deck as more machine gun shells exploded just above his head.

**

Gallen took cover in a small cobbled square.

An oasis of tables, chairs, ornamental fountains and artificial foliage, an urban refuge normally alive with joy and merriment.

There were no diners now.

Gallen knew that Gao Zi Xin would have to run this way. The confluence of alleyways terminated at this junction.

Chinese jets were intermittently flying overhead at low altitude, but several of them had been shot down. There was every chance that Taipei City could get consumed by a firestorm conflagration.

Gallen knew that he was vulnerable out in the open but he would have to live with it for now.

He also knew that on his watch, the drug kingpin with his own private fiefdom in northern Laos, wouldn't be spending the rest of his life in an Australian supermax.

Bullets from his Sig-Sauer semi-automatic had the drug kingpin's name on them.

Gao Zi Xin suddenly burst into the square, heaving with breath, still staying sharp and alert even though he'd survived a terrible helicopter crash only twenty minutes earlier.

Gallen jumped out and took Gao by surprise.

'So, you thought it would be that easy, eh?' taunted Gallen.

'Name your price!' shouted Gao.

Gallen inched closer.

'This is your parting gift from Tucker Cole and the CIA!'

Don't talk, shoot.

Gallen's first bullet hit its mark between Gao's eyes.

Yeah, buddy, there's your greetings card from Langley, Virginia.

Gallen walked over to the corpse and put two more bullets into Gao's cerebellum, for good measure.

'Suck it up, motherfucker, there's a couple more for ya.'

Gallen registered the GPS coordinates, took some photographs and hacked off Gao's right hand.

What the fuck is my limey pal up to?

Gallen fired up his MilLoc.

Hmm…not far away…

***

Bell wasn't having it so easy....

Waiwai was a tough and resourceful dude. He wouldn't have survived this long in narco-world if it had been any other way.

Fuck it!

The bastard was hiding in a Ramen stall and burst out on top of Bell, wielding two cooking knives.

This was going to have to be quick.

After a series of blows, Bell pressed the barrel of his 92F into the narco-enforcer's head and pulled the trigger.

The life of him drained away in an instant.

Gallen appeared all of a sudden with a plastic carrier bag.

'I'm collecting hands and fingers – let me do it.'

The raining down of missiles had intensified. Chinese jet fighters were making regular low passes.

But wait! There was another one blown away! A ground-to-air heat-seeking missile fired by Taiwanese forces.

It wasn't all a gung-ho turkey shoot for the PLAAF.

'Hey, buddy, we'd better get out of here,' said Gallen.

Both knew where they were headed.

Out on the main road, there were any number of cars with their doors hanging open, some with engines still running.

A Mercedes S-Class would do.

Now for a treacherous sixty-kilometre drive down to Hsinschu City on the west coast. Roads littered with abandoned vehicles, necessitating weaving manoeuvres in and out of blockages and chicanes along the clogged motorways. The further away they got from the burning capital, the easier it became.

With only five kilometres to go, a PLAAF helicopter swooped down on them with an initial pass.

The Z-10 gunship, armed with a Gatling minigun, banked hard to starboard to line up along three lanes of asphalt for a return visit. Bell noted the air-launched munitions attached to its underwing hardpoints as Gallen floored the gas.

They were just under a kilometre away from the entrance to a concrete underpass.

'Hell, fuck it!' screamed Gallen as the Merc accelerated to one hundred and forty miles-per-hour.

Shells pocked the road ahead as the Z-10 came at them head-on. Three thousand rounds per minute spewing from the six-barrel pivot-mounted rotary minigun.

Gallen picked his moment and made a violent swerve across the carriageway which nearly sent them into the crash barrier.

A few more seconds and they entered the illuminated safety of a long tunnel.

But the Z-10 wasn't done yet…

It had touched down at the entrance to the underpass and fired an anti-tank missile after them.

Gallen gasped as he glanced in the rear view mirror.

'Mother fuckers!'

'Clever bastards, more like,' said Bell, catching a glimpse in the wing mirror.

An articulated lorry driving in the opposite direction shot by and took the blast which caused a massive fireball explosion.

'Lucky, lucky…sucky, fucky! How about that?!' yelled Gallen.

'Yup, they think they've hit something and they can fucking well keep it!'

They dumped the car one minute away from TMFC's headquarters on the Hsinchu trading estate.

Stay alert - keep an eye on the sky.

The duo raced up to the front of the Taiwan Microchip Fabrication Company Limited building. Basic company ID cards for normal employees were swiped and they were inside. A lone security guard behind a counter nodded as they swept past.

The main elevator doors were open.

The touch-screen console accepted their special-access iris scans which re-painted its display to offer a different set of options.

Bell selected basement level minus fifteen.

The bomb tremors dissipated quickly as they descended the deep elevator shaft, stencilled numbers decrementing past.

As the doors opened, guards escorted them down the corridor to a conference room.

Taiwanese, Japanese and American officers in uniform sat around a long table.

The welcome and introductions were kept short.

The equivalent of ground-control Houston, complete with living quarters would be their new home for a little while.

The battle command centre was hidden right underneath the microchip processing plant located directly above it.

No option but to sit tight while the invasion of Taiwan played out. If necessary, long underground tunnels would lead military personnel-at-risk to clandestine evac points, then pick up chopper rides to the relative safety of a USN carrier group.

Gallen held up a bloodied plastic bag.

'Can I put something in your fridge? It won't keep otherwise,' he said, sheepishly.

***

The operations theatre was a vast cavern of space, with a massive interactive screen, which drew together all the strands of the live battle arena for Taiwan and its territorial waters. The system was, of course, fully integrated into the US war management system with support nodes spanning America.

Rows of military personnel faced the nerve centre display in a semi-circle of consoles, each one focusing on their specific sphere of control.

Bell and Gallen stood at the back as the pixelated wall zoomed out to reveal a real-time status map of the Chinese east coast.

Two thousand kilometres from Shandong province in the north, on the Yellow Sea, down past Hong Kong and Macau to Hainan island in the south.

Then, live-streaming images of Taiwan's west coast beaches and the expanse of water which was the Taiwan Strait.

An armada of troop ships heading this way.

Up to half a million PLA assault troops on conventional carriers and commercial fishing vessels aiming to set up a bridgehead and make landfall in benign sandy shallows.

They were wasting their time…and their lives.

A generation of only-child Chinese soldiers scythed like wheat on gooey mud flats.

Any clown can fire missiles from a Fujian missile silo while sitting behind a VDU terminal sipping a Diet Pepsi.

The PLAAF certainly wasn't having it all its own way – porcupine asymmetrical defence systems were downing enemy aircraft at an astonishing rate.

Even the weather was helping – a typhoon was on its way. The sea state was more than inclement for a day's perilous joyride to the home of advanced logic-chip production.

If the invasion were to gain winning traction, then the TMFC and its satellite buildings would be scorched in the mother of all explosions; charges were set ready to blow.

Nobody is getting their paws on our advanced tech…we'll destroy it first.

Semiconductor fabrication after that?

A reset from the ashes of Armageddon, most probably.

The dithering of the allies over the sinking of the Sierra Madre had emboldened the Chinese, but the West still had a chance to get in full harness and turn the tide.

Gallen turned to Bell with a sigh.

'If this caper goes seriously tits-up, maybe I'll still be able to retire on a Navy Seal pension.'

'You could always get a job as a meet-and-greeter at Disneyworld, I guess,' smiled Bell.

Doctor Ning Chan suddenly appeared and presented herself.

The digital, sterile-white lab coat had been replaced by the real uniform of a Taiwanese Army Major.

She was even more attractive than her avatar.

'I told you that you'd be back!' she grinned.

Gallen looked startled.

'Yeah, only to hear about your dirty little secret.'

27 Sierra Madre

World War Three broke out on the tenth of October, Taiwan National Day, and paused briefly a week later after a ceasefire was agreed between the US and China.

Some historians will look back and point to the obliteration of the Sierra Madre in Philippine waters, and subsequent retaliation by the US, as the spark.

Others will say that the tenth of October was simply a pre-ordained, inviolable date with destiny.

***

So, what caused the PRC to roll the dice?

For China, there are only two narrow choke-points to reach out into the Pacific: to the north of Taiwan is the Miyako Strait which lies within the territorial waters of Japan, and to the south is the Bashi Channel which sits between the waters of the Philippines and Taiwan.

Capturing Taiwan means that China is fully able to control the Western Pacific – total domination of sea lines of communication upon which US allies like Japan depend, and pushing Uncle Sam out of the region completely. The US Navy's role of guaranteeing international sea lanes gone up in smoke.

In the meantime, the South China Sea is where it's at - a hugely significant area for trade, with one-third of the world's maritime shipping passing through it.

One problem, though…

Our blockade is bigger than yours.

The Malacca Strait.

The Strait of Malacca, named after the sultanate which once ruled over it, is a narrow stretch of water approximately eight hundred kilometres in length.

It lies between the Malay Peninsula to the northeast, Singapore and Sumatra to the south, connecting the Indian Ocean and the South China Sea. The shipping channel is one of the most important shipping lanes in the world.

It is certainly of maximum significance to the PRC which, before the US Navy sealed it off, imported most of its crude oil, LNG, food and other raw materials through it.

China had got the hostilities off to a good start but the US and its allies were catching up in such a way as to force a temporary ceasefire, a truce, a deal…or even an unconditional surrender.

Maybe a key decision could clinch it?

***

Late at night.

Location: The Incident Room, West Wing, The White House, Washington DC.

'The jugular, then?' said JDS, addressing the table.

'They crisped their duck when they hit the Sierra Madre,' replied the Director of the CIA.

'What about this dam of theirs?'

'It's bigger than the Hoover, Mr President,' said the Secretary of Defense.

'Bigger?'

'Yup, like serious water. Loads of it.'

'Let's shoot it up then. What have we got?'

'They have the home-field advantage but we have what it takes to pull it out of the ground by its roots,' said the Chairman of the Joint Chiefs of Staff.

***

A ceasefire is in place after a week of intense fighting.

A fragile and tenuous armistice which will allow for some sorrowful wound licking.

Death and destruction suffered by both sides, in diverse theatres of war – air, sea, land, cyber and space, is assessed.

* US and allies military asset losses:-

- Air: 100s of fighter jets and planes
- Sea: 3 carrier groups, many ships and several submarines
- Land: Okinawa, Guam, Philippine and Japanese bases
- Cyber: Systems failures affecting US infrastructure
- Space: Satellites destroyed in orbit by PLA killer satellites

* Chinese military asset losses:-

- Air: 100s of fighter jets and planes
- Sea: 100s of ships and the entire Taiwan invasion fleet
- Land: All seaboard province bases + Three Gorges Dam
- Cyber: Systems failures affecting PRC infrastructure
- Space: Satellites destroyed in orbit by US killer satellites

* Other losses:-

Human life, world maritime trade disruption, loss of energy supplies and destruction of vital civilian infrastructures.

***

Although a long-term peaceful solution is under consideration, both sides are learning from their mistakes and preparing for a full resumption of hostilities.

It is not who is right but who is left that counts.

***

Doctor Ning Chan hyper-jumped the Baburu Jetto bubblejet to a steady height of ten thousand feet.

Bell was pressed up against her in his avatar suit as she marshalled the joystick and spatial coordinates with unparalleled expertise.

The realtime VR universe simulation would allow them to check out the damage wrought along the entire west coast of Taiwan.

'Let's go take a look, shall we?'

Bell instinctively clutched his star-buckle as the craft plummeted down to only seventy feet, the alloy skids hovering safely above the cresting waves crashing upon the sands.

The aftermath of Sea Tick's and Big Hair's dirty work was much in evidence – classified US DARPA anti-amphibious invasion systems employed in battle for the first time.

Killing and devastation on an industrial scale – piles of bodies and burned-out husks of marine vessels rolling in the fluming breakers…and a terrible, eerie absence of life.

Sea Tick - Marine drones working as an intelligent swarm find and destroy target vessels by rising up off the sea bed like a biblical pupation of lake flies, attaching themselves and then exploding.

Big Hair - Spumes of an advanced, napalm-like substance which rises to the surface from an undersea pipe network. Once exposed to air, the compound turns into a fluffy, airborne type of hair-styling-mousse which sticks to anything and burns violently at nearly three thousand degrees centigrade.

Not a salon favourite, then.

Similar scenes presented themselves all the way down to Tainan and Kaohsiung.

'Better get back now, I guess,' said Chan.

***

Bell rolled on his side and got back to reading one of his manga books, well illuminated by a flexi-arm reading light.

Peace at last.

He'd shut his eyes and allow himself to drift away in a relaxing, drowsy sleep in a minute or two.

The sleeping pod he was in was exactly what you would experience in a Japanese capsule hotel.

Soundproofed and comfortable…and bomb-proof fifteen storeys below ground.

Although the food was good and there was a gym, he was becoming stir-crazy after a week cooped up down here.

A tap on the window disturbed his quiet reverie.

Ning Chang was invited to climb in.

Army fatigues and moist lips pressed up against him.

The composite aroma of toothpaste and perfume gave him a hard-on.

Her hand slipped down to squeeze it.

'Now then, big boy, we can't have you jerking off on your own in here all the time, can we?'

'What do you suggest?' mumbled Bell.

'How about drilling an army Major in her luxury apartment?'

'Now? During the ceasefire?'

'Why not? My apartment block hasn't been hit by a missile and it overlooks the Touqian River.'

***

The senior telemetry officer stood at the front of the briefing room and poked an aerial photograph of northern Taiwan with a bamboo stick.

'What's this?'

A targeting officer stepped forward with a magnifier.

'That's the Hsinchu Lotus Mansions.'

'Still standing?'

'It was selected to assist with empirical triangulation and ranging.'

'Not any longer.'

The PLARF installation in the city of Fuzhou, Fujian province, located close to the Min River estuary, had been chosen to launch the missile which would unequivocally terminate the delicate ceasefire arrangement.

28 A chemical romance

Abandoned ebikes got them there.

Bell's fluorine floozy, Doctor Ning Chan, led the way into the marble entrance hall of her apartment block.

So, this senior-grade chemist's dirty little secret was that she doubled as a Major in the Taiwanese Army. As a secret, it didn't seem that dirty. Maybe there was other stuff to be had.

There was certainly a lot more to her than fluoropolymer compounds.

It was understood that the elevators couldn't be trusted.

'Better take the stairs,' said Ning.

Bell did what he was told, fixed himself a drink and slid the balcony doors open while she disappeared into the bedroom.

A top-floor apartment with magnificent panoramic views.

There was smouldering devastation in all directions, barely a soul out on the streets. Despite the strong breeze, the air was clogged with throat-gagging toxic fumes.

An ugly and sad sight for what had been a vibrant and bustling cityscape going about its daily business.

Bell turned and closed the glass door.

A distant voice called him from the bedroom.

'Come to bed, won't you?'

It was a bit business-like but, in the circumstances, it made pragmatic sense to get a move-on.

Time for his trouser zip to make its descent.

He had expected to find a naked body, lying ready between the sheets. Instead, Ning stood by the bed in a black latex body suit, perfecting her lipstick.

'I have a rubber and latex fetish… it makes me feel so horny. What about you?'

'I'll stick with my birthday suit, if that's okay.'

'I haven't had a man back here for some time, so I'm a little bit rusty.'

'Horny and rusty…got it,' laughed Bell.

He could see that her knickers had been neatly folded on top of her army fatigues. He carelessly lobbed his own kit on top of hers.

'I have a special request,' whispered Ning.

Ah, here we go.

'No kissing?'

'No, not exactly, but we can do tangly tongues, if you like.'

'What do you have in mind?'

She handed him a tube of pH-friendly lubricant, which was curiously classified as a medical device on the label.

'A game of chance.'

'Huh?'

'This latex suit comes fitted with two apertures.'

'Er…yeah?'

'Do you have a coin?'

Bell glanced across at his crumpled camo-pants. Sure, there was a five-hundred-yen coin zipped in there somewhere.

Paulownia or bamboo?

Something that gave a good poke was always preferable.

***

Bell awoke with a jolt.

A small detail eating away in his subconscious thoughts.

Something she had commented on in the heat of the moment.

A casual remark: '*It's strange how all the other luxury blocks have taken some kind of hit…just lucky, I guess.*'

A ruby-red warning light blinked brightly on his internal, warning dashboard.

It could be nothing.

But nothing might be something and he needed to be worried.

In all the excitement he'd taken his eye off the ball.

It was one thing to have your name etched on a bullet cartridge but another to have it embossed on the outer casing of a Chinese DF-17 Hypersonic Glide Vehicle.

A different game of chance was also being played.

Bell rolled off the bed and dressed in a hurry.

'Ning, we need to get out of here!'

'What's the problem?'

'We've cheated death, that's why.'

'But, there's a ceasefire…don't worry.'

'Are you coming or not?'

'Okay, okay…give me a minute.'

'What is this place called, anyway?'

'The Hsinchu Lotus Mansions.'

She was already half-dressed; they would be running down the staircase together in the next few minutes.

Ning stopped suddenly.

'Come on, get on with it!' screamed Bell.

'Wait! I love my bed too much, I'll catch up with you later, dear lover. We can do this again, can't we?'

Bell didn't have the time or the inclination to stand there and argue.

***

Bell was back on his ebike heading towards the TMFC building.

A pressure-wave phantom seemed to violate the airspace cocoon around him.

The explosion forcefully knocked him off his ride, with him ending up in a crumpled heap on the sidewalk.

The Hsinchu Lotus Mansions had taken a catastrophic hit: The top four floors blown apart, the bottom six floors engulfed in an out-of-control conflagration.

Bell crawled to his knees and howled a grief-stricken lament.

'No! No!'

Make love once and die.

They didn't need a place called hell.

This was it.

29 Whack-a-mole

Terracotta mosaics welcomed Bell as he entered the walk-in wetroom. Extractor fans kicked in automatically as the sensors detected his presence, salicylic-acid cleansing-serum firmly in hand.

Exfoliator meets gladiator.

Bell glanced down at the plastic bottle.

You can help me.

Whatever comes out of these showerheads, we can work together.

As the water flowed, he began to weigh up the risks.

Further escalation of hostilities in the South China Sea.

World War Three.

Multiple nuclear warheads finding their targets.

Mutually assured destruction easily beating irreversible climate change in the race to destroy the blue planet.

The premature end-of-life state of a unique jewel floating alone in the vast expanse of the cosmos.

The wonderment of biodiversity snuffed out by the alpha lifeform which had monopolised it.

The end of the human race.

Our fragile world to be inherited by cockroaches and sentient robots.

Battlebot annihilators, manufactured under licence by Cyber Dynamics in Santa Clara, California, lavishly empowered with super-advanced logic chips. Hyperalloy components providing the composition of a combat-chassis endoskeleton which is

shrouded with artificially grown human tissue in the likeness of
its extinct creators.

We had it coming.

What was the point of everyone on the planet having
smartphones when there was no signal?

Just go back to playing 'Snake' and be happy with it.

Five seconds before midnight.

Defcon 1.

A cocked pistol.

Was there a chance to step back from the edge of the abyss?

Maybe…

Bell broke off from his macabre reverie and cut the waterjets.

Dripping and fresh as a daisy.

In his line of business he knew too much.

Bell downed the bubbling summer-fruits liposuction, poured
from the screeching juicer. No intravenous sedation or
inconspicuous incisions beneath the bikini-line required.

Sunday morning.

A break from scooping protein powder and waiting for a
whey shake to emulsify.

What, no squats? A day of rest.

Aux Merveilleux de Giselle, the French bakery around the
corner, had made their delivery. The café was reputed to be one
of the best places in London for Gallic pastries.

There had been missile attacks on London.

The Internet backbone had been breached and core router
connections compromised. Satellite communications were out
while World War Three was also being waged in outer space.

The new American president and the hawks in the
Republican party had brought this one to a head.

Like lancing a boil or draining a cyst.

Slugging it out in the South China Sea.

***

Pine Gap is a satellite surveillance base and Australian Earth station located eighteen kilometres south-west of the town of Alice Springs, Northern Territory, in the centre of Australia.

It is jointly operated by Australia and the United States and is known as the gateway to the Red Centre, a vast area of ancient soils tainted by the remnants of iron oxide.

It had been hit by three Chinese DF-17 rockets and was now completely out of action.

Cyber attacks were piling in on the western hemisphere.

All the AUKUS subs were luckily out on patrol because a hyper velocity missile had hit their home base of FBE.

Fleet Base East at Port Kembla, gracing a section of Australia's eastern coastline provides support for the nation's nuclear-powered submarines which patrol the Indian and Pacific oceans. It has sufficient mooring capacity and capability for a squadron of AUKUS boats.

The Americans had lost an aircraft carrier and seven other surface ships in this Antipodean sector alone.

But, it was still non-nuclear at this stage.

Twitchy fingers hovering over red buttons.

The Americans were hitting the Chinese hard and had targeted multiple dam infrastructures following the waves of bunker-buster attacks on the Three Gorges Dam.

B-2 Spirit bombers stealthily delivering their payloads.

A billion tonnes of TGD reinforced concrete had been dislodged in the process. A trillion-gallon backlog of the untameable Yangtze river, equating to over forty cubic kilometres of water, resulting in wholesale flooding of the

Richard Gill

Yangtze basin, swamping the provinces of Nanjing, Shanghai and Wuhan.

The Russians had been told to stay out of the conflict by the US, in the same way that the North Koreans had also received a warning.

There was extensive damage in Taipei and the densely populated west coast, but not a single PLA soldier had progressed beyond the killing-ground beaches. By the same token, Chinese paratrooper airborne assaults had all been annihilated by the agile, well-armed Taiwanese forces who were waiting for them.

The iconic Taipei 101 tower had taken a direct hit and was still standing. It smouldered day and night. The Hsinchu industrial district had mainly been spared carpet-bombing, maybe because of TMFC's microchip manufacturing capacity which the Chinese wanted to seize unscathed.

The Malacca strait blockade was still intact, and Yonaguni Island fielded batteries of Aegis Ashore – a US defence system against medium and intermediate-range projectiles, while all the other islands along the First Island Chain were continually firing a variety of missiles deep into China.

Guam, Okinawa, Hawaii and a whole list of US bases on the Japanese mainland had taken heavy hits, but the US military was well in harness now that the ceasefire had been broken.

So, still a localised scrap restricted to South East Asia, sort of.

Titans testing each other's strength.

Who had the tenacity, manpower, equipment and shells to keep going?

The person who couldn't afford to lose.

***

Bell slumped back into bed.

Judy studied the sombre headlines, swiping through the news reports on her phone, sitting there with her knees up under the sheets.

A war footing.

The preliminary skirmishes were over.

It was now a full-blown exchange of high-tech ordnance.

The financial markets had reacted violently but had already factored in the conflict.

Flight to the base elements of gold, silver and platinum.

Flawless rubies, also, if you could get your hands on some.

Regime change in China possible, but Taiwan was standing firm.

Ten Ten, the tenth of October – Taiwan National Day, the day hostilities had kicked off big time.

America standing firm under the leadership of its forty-seven-year-old Republican president – James Donald Smith.

MAGA.

Unafraid to go head-to-head with the Chinese.

Unshrinking from the task of taking a hard line on fentanyl and liberal policies which were destroying cities across America.

Restoration of American values.

Saving the Western democracies from their own wanton, self-destruction.

Reassertion of the USA's position in the world.

Pain, baby, pain.

Yup, he was gonna trump the yellow-belly, cocksucking Democrats and their geriatric corpse frontman who had bequeathed him all this shit. What was found when the archaeological team opened the sarcophagus of the pharaoh Tutankhamun would have done a better job.

'JDS thinks that they're winning the war,' said Bell.

'Maybe everyone loses...in the end.'

'Or prevails...there's a presidential address this evening.'

Judy threw her phone down and sighed.

'I think we need to get out of town before the world ends.'

'Let's go to the coast.'

***

The Gatwick Express train blasted smoothly through East Croydon station, heading south. New rolling stock, to match that of Swiss Federal Railways, whispering over the points and speeding on to LGW, London's second airport, in West Sussex.

Tom and Judy sipped their coffee in their private first class compartment as the carriages hurtled over the M25 orbital motorway.

In under forty minutes they would arrive in Brighton, regretfully leaving their warm, lounge-like bubble behind.

The wind hit them as soon as they set foot on the platform.

It was blowing a hoolie out there - a sou'wester howling off the English Channel.

They hurried along the windswept pavements, down towards the seafront, taking a sharp left down Duke Street into the historic Central Lanes district.

A jink left off Ship Street heralded the start of a labyrinth of narrow alleyways lined with brick pavers. This was the epicentre of old Brighton of what, in bygone days, would have been bustling fishermen's cottages. It was now occupied by little restaurants, cosy pubs and jewellery shops.

All best explored on a windy, autumn day.

A quick browse, then a brisk leg-stretch along the promenade towards the entrance to the Palace Pier.

Arm in arm, the fresh breeze assisted their progress.

Powerful waves crashing on the pebbles, driving menacingly through the Victorian pier screw-piles, did not deter them as they took the leeward side of the boardwalk and headed for the first amusement arcade.

A simple swap from a violent wind to the shrieking cacophony of slots and fruit machines.

Further delights along the pier's length awaited them.

Oval pavilions selling fish-and-chip suppers and alcohol.

Colonnades of stalls tempting day trippers with the prospect of shooting gallery prizes, fortune-telling, candy floss, donuts, crêpes and Brighton rock.

They pressed on over the hardwood planks to get to the wide end-platform which housed the final, domed arcade. It was surrounded by multiple fairground attractions - a helter-skelter located precariously close to the edge, bumper cars, the haunted house, water slides and a pendulum ride.

Best to stay under cover.

The arcade initially enticed them with the seaside favourites of the Penny Falls, Whack-a-Mole, What-the-butler-saw peep-shows and a line of claw machines with squeezy toys piled high awaiting the descent of a mechanical grab.

The Whack-a-Mole machine still had its Mogura Taiji logo visible – Mole Buster signage which meant that it may have seen service in Japan at some time in the past.

Bell drifted on, drawn inexorably towards the line of pinball machines. A state-of-the-art offering from the likes of game manufacturers such as Bally, Gottlieb, and Stern provided much to choose from.

Rock group themes – Aerosmith, Iron Maiden and, of course, Para Noya. Other all-time greats – Deadpool, Mata Hari and Twilight Zone.

And there it was.

Total Nuclear Annihilation.

Spooky!

The graphite rods super-bonus had shut down reactor core number three. Eerie Geiger counter clicks continued as the back screen blazed in a burst of white light.

Game over!

Bell couldn't get more pound coins out of his pocket fast enough.

***

Bell and Judy emerged, giddy and dazed, back into the breezy daylight, sated and overexposed to everything that traditional, British seaside fun could throw at them.

A fifteen-minute yomp saw them sheltered again amongst the cobbled alleyways of the Brighton Lanes.

After a few final strides they found themselves enveloped by the welcoming atmosphere of a restaurante pequeño in Union Street, called Casa Don Carlos.

Red-and-white check tablecloths and wooden chairs.

San Miguel Especial lager came in 330ml bottles - Bell ordered four of them.

Bent in opposite each other at their table-for-two, they quickly got to work with lovers' chatter and beery toasts. Recollections, revelling and sentiment, recalling all the pleasure they had enjoyed together in the past.

Fuck buddies and still loving it.

Bread, aioli, mixed olives, and beer.

What was not to like?

Presently, the main tapas dishes arrived.

Meatballs, garlic mushrooms, whitebait, Spanish omelette, chickpeas with spinach and croquetas da la casa.

Yeah, that was enough to constitute basic sustenance.

Bell was a sucker for this stuff.

Their glasses chimed together for the nth time.

Judy gazed into his eyes, ruefully.

The burning, what-have-you-been-up-to question came out of the blue.

'So, Tom, overseas audit in Hong Kong and Macau?'

'A banking client with a global reach,' parried Bell.

'No money laundering then?'

'Just routine compliance and stress testing.'

'How about casinos?'

'What about them?'

'Did you get to play?'

Had he played around as well?

Yes, he had.

'I gambled everything on red,' came the cryptic reply.

Bell could see that she had picked up on it.

'Are your answers generated by AI?'

'You're the lawyer, Judy,' grinned Bell.

A legal mind changed tack.

'My dad's a happy man, all of a sudden.'

'Oh, yeah?'

'It seems that the CEO of the Blue Dragon Group met an untimely demise. He was a ruthless, fraudulent operator called Grachi who had swindled my father out of his BDG shareholding and more besides.'

Bell almost corrected her name gaffe. The sight of Donato Gauci's dead body drifted into his mind's eye.

She had come close.

He sidestepped nimbly with a transparently evasive response.

'CNN were reporting multiple explosions and gangland reprisals at the time. Small beer when you consider what's happening out there now. I'm glad to be back in England.'

Judy wasn't stupid…she may have an inkling.

Her hand crept across the table.

'You mean, glad to be back in my arms, kissing me and making love to me,' smirked Judy.

His next utterance had to be laced with a touch of humour.

'Before you get too excited, we'd better settle up.'

'Whatever you say, dear lover.'

'How about a nightcap?'

A couple of steps across the alleyway took them inside the Font pub, a converted chapel dating back to the year 1688.

The developers had retained all of its original features: A semi-circular amphitheatre layout with galleries supported on Corinthian pillars, ornate ceilings and arched stained-glass windows.

Judy had already nailed her vodka and tonic.

Bell drained the last of his pint of Stella Artois.

'Back to mine?'

***

A secluded, detached property located high up in Hove's Goldstone Valley area. It offered views out to the Isle of Wight on a clear day. One of several properties Bell owned through the legal entity vehicle of a limited company registered in the British Virgin Islands.

Three in the morning looking out to sea from the balcony.

Bell stood there in the late October chill knowing that a warm, snuggly duvet and an even warmer Judy awaited his return to deep slumber and bodily embrace.

All the more reason to treat every day as your last. No warning would be given as you took your last breath.

The bullet with your name on it.

It was just a shot away.

Murders and executions.

A body with bloody exit wounds lying on the carpet.

Viktor Bazarov, the plucky and resourceful Russian oligarch he had befriended while on a previous mission.

Before Viktor was murdered in his Surrey mansion, perhaps at the behest of someone in the Kremlin, he had undertaken to sign across a Caribbean islet to Bell, mysteriously called Mosquito Island, in the US Virgin Islands archipelago.

Bell hadn't given it a second thought until some title deeds to the island had arrived from a firm of lawyers in New York.

The clue was in the name, he had guessed – maybe to be renamed Deet island, by the sound of it.

The necessity to spray on potent insect repellent as you inspected what was nothing more than a barren, bleached, coral outcrop of little utility, was all that he had expected.

He knew that Bazarov had only acquired it on a whim – a poker game, wasn't it?

But no, he had been wrong.

He had checked out the exact GPS coordinates and zoomed in on the satellite view. It was much bigger than anticipated – there were actually buildings and palm trees on it!

Hopefully, there was an undiscovered Spanish galleon lying just beyond its outer reef.

Poor Bazarov had known that he was a doomed man, with dark forces swirling around him. It was a shame to lose him.

He had the heart of a Russian bear and the squat physique of a Japanese daruma doll. Knock him over and he got straight back up again.

The GRU never offered you a choice in the method of your passing – bullet, balcony or blob of Polonium 210 in your Caesar salad.

Bell owed it to his benefactor Bazarov, who had been true to his word, to honour him by flying out there at the earliest opportunity.

Someday his own luck would run out.

He had been in too many scrapes already.

A life-plan was beginning to form.

It boiled down to the simple pleasures in life.

Living in the moment.

A sweet kiss, a caress and the sound of laughter among friends sharing food together.

All you needed was a pair of jeans, a leather jacket and a credit card and the world was yours to enjoy.

He had been a small but significant cog amongst the mischief taking place in the South China Sea, but where would it all end?

In a few days it would be Hallowe'en. All Hallows Eve when the ghouls, vampires, banshees, and demons came out to play. They were already out there tearing the world apart.

Trick or treat?

Give us the candy or we'll open the sealed authenticator verification codes and turn the two firing keys simultaneously.

Bell felt a tremor under his feet, preceded by the night sky becoming eerily illuminated.

Measurable Richter scale peaks radiated from a distant epicentre: seismograph oscillations causing him a mild knee trembler.

A cold, clammy realisation hit him.

Serious shit going down.

Central London.

A vision of Big Ben and the Tower of London shot into his mind.

Something could be nothing but you needed to be worried.

A hypersonic glide vehicle firing a retro-rocket to de-orbit before its final approach to deliver its multiple warhead payload.

Warm arms threaded their way around his bare torso, a soft cheek pressing firmly between his shoulder blades.

His yelp of surprise pierced the stillness of the night.

'Judy!'

Also by Richard Gill…

Paloma Azul
Lebensrune

www.richardgill.uk

Graphic novels out soon

Register for email updates!

Pilot graphic novel chapter for Paloma Azul follows…

Illustrated by Alice Bloomfield
www.instagram.com/bl00mfield/

Acknowledgements

Reference on p. 325 to manga: 'Slam Dunk'
written by Takehiko Inoue.

A special thanks to L.J. Raubenheimer for
his outstanding contribution regarding matters
concerning China, Japan, Taiwan, the Korean
peninsula and further afield in the Far East.

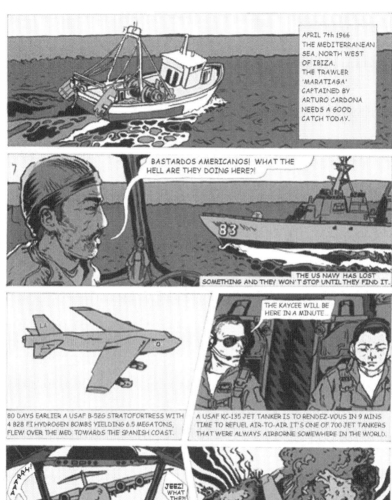

1

THE NON-NUCLEAR EXPLOSIVE CHARGES OF TWO DEVICES HAD DETONATED, COVERING A LARGE AREA IN RADIOACTIVE PLUTONIUM, CAESIUM AND BORON. PU239 HAS A HALF-LIFE OF 24,100 YEARS.

THE US NUCLEAR DISASTER TEAM LOCATES THE 3rd B28 FI BOMB ON THE DRY ALMANZORA RIVERBED. IT IS INTACT, UNLIKE THE OTHER TWO DEVICES.

...A LOT OF TOXIC TOP SOIL WILL HAVE TO BE SHIPPED BACK TO THE US IN SEALED OIL DRUMS...

CAPTAIN E. KURTZ ABOARD THE BRIDGE OF THE *USS PETREL*, AFTER TWO MONTHS OF FRUITLESS SEARCHING THE PROBABLE IMPACT AREA, THE FOURTH THERMO NUKE IS STILL AWOL...

ANOTHER GODDAM FUCK-UP! THEY'RE GONNA HAVE OUR BALLS ON A STICK. ONLY MY CLOSE FRIEND JACK DANIELS IS GONNA GET ME THROUGH THIS....

...THAT BITCH FIRECRACKER MUST BE DOWN THERE ...SOMEWHERE!...

THE PARACHUTE HAD DEPLOYED AND NOW BOMB #4 LAY ON THE SEABED AT A DEPTH OF 80 METRES.

...IT SHOULD JUMP OFF THE SCREEN LIKE A BRANDED MUSTANG! WHERE THE FUCK IS IT?

WEARY SONAR OPERATORS WITH TIRED EYES...

2

Printed in Great Britain
by Amazon